D1154451

Persuasion is an essential proficiency for leaders, to enable them to get the best out of people. Using a lens, influenced by the arts and humanities, Stephen Carroll and Patrick Flood provide us with highly original insights into the mystique of leadership. The two authors took me on a "leadership" adventure that I found extremely enjoyable. I very much recommend this book to people wanting to deepen their understanding of the vicissitudes of leadership.

Professor Manfred Kets de Vries, *Raoul de Vitry d'Avaucourt Chaired Clinical Professor of Leadership Development, Director INSEAD Global Leadership Centre*

Much of the material in this book was given in many executive development classes conducted by Syracuse University. I observed all of these classes and found that the executives rated these classes very highly.

Dennis Gillen, *Chair, Management Department and former Associate Dean of Executive Education, Whitman School of Management, Syracuse University*

Success in business and even our personal lives almost invariably comes down to good leadership – values-based, convicted, example-setting, and above all, self-less. *The Persuasive Leader* offers a much-needed dusting off of our thoughts on leadership for modern times, demanding times requiring a new style of leader ... all of us ... capable of bridging the impersonality of the information age.

Paul Jensen, *CEO, HALO Maritime Defense Systems, Andover, Massachusetts*

This is a timely and engaging book. Rich in examples and precise in definition, the authors provide an insightful approach to leadership from the arts and everyday life. The emphasis on persuasion is, in my opinion, pertinent and feels right for the times we live in.

Alexandre Ricard, *Chairman and CEO, Irish Distillers Pernod Ricard*

The social science of leadership is extensive, but not complete. This new book provides a thoughtful and comprehensive account of why persuasive leadership is important and how the arts can give added – and often unique – insight into its operation.

Rob Goffee, *Professor of Organisational Behaviour, London Business School*

Professors Carroll and Flood bring a lifetime of experience with the arts to one of the most difficult tasks of the leader's work: Persuasion. In doing so, they have managed to compellingly join the visual arts, literature, film, music, and theater to mainstream leadership theory and practice. Unlike many other books that use the phrase "art of leadership" and then never mention "art" again, this book does the opposite – the authors' treatment of both art and leadership sets a refreshingly new standard and is a fine contribution to what is an important up-and-coming field. For anyone who has wondered what the arts might genuinely contribute to leadership, this book is really a must have.

Daved Barry, *Professor of Creative Organization Studies, Copenhagen Business School*

Carroll and Flood provide a refreshing and convincing alternative to other highly empirical and less accessible works on the subject of leadership. They show that positive persuasion can be seen in examples from all walks of life and that much can be learned from history, literature, and film. They do not rely too heavily on obvious popular references and as a result the reader is much better off for the richness and depth of experience this approach provides. A recommendable book for anyone who strives to become a better leader or indeed for those who need now more than ever before to ensure that leadership skills are fostered in others.

David Finlay, *EDC Manager Inbound Operations, Inventory & Projects at Siemens Healthcare Diagnostics Products GMBH, Germany*

A key theme pervades this book – leadership is a privilege – and with privilege comes great responsibility. We must lead by example and remove the obstacles that prevent employees from going the extra mile. This book shows how leaders can do both in imaginative ways inspired by the arts.

Peter Durante, *Pirelli Car Tyre HR Director*

The Persuasive Leader sheds new light on what it takes to be an effective leader. Written in fine style and showing great erudition, the book develops a distinctive and compelling analysis of leadership. Drawing on a wide range of sources from business and particularly from the arts, this book is a major advance in thinking on leadership.

Dr Philip Stiles, *Senior Lecturer in Corporate Governance and Director, Centre for International Human Resource Management, Judge Business School, University of Cambridge*

The Persuasive Leader provides a fresh perspective on leadership with examples drawn from the rich fabric of history and the arts. The authors have articulated the importance of persuasive leadership in the modern world, providing examples of the positive and negative outcomes that can follow leadership actions, and have framed this in a moral and ethical context.

Matthew Line, *Pensions & Benefits Manager at Standard Bank and Executive Education Alumnus at Judge Business School, University of Cambridge.*

Lessons from this book have helped a lot of managers in my leadership training courses to become aware of the potential leadership they could develop not only in their job, but also in their day-to-day life whatever the setting or social entity. As for me, I find that the adoption of the positive side of persuasion, "the art of persuasion", attributed to leadership by the authors, can help to generate the successful, effective, and acknowledged leaders we need in the present time and for the future.

Francesco Fanelli, *Associate Partner, Coreconsulting, Milan*

Rich in illustration, precise in definition, holistic in approach, the authors provide us with essential leadership lessons from the arts and everyday life. This is a timely and engaging book, the emphasis on persuasion, is to me, correct in logic and emotion. I recommend it to anyone interested in improving their leadership impact.

John Purcell, *Leadership Development Manager, Irish Distillers Pernod Ricard*

The Persuasive Leader is a welcome addition to the leadership literature. It offers an insightful and practical examination of leadership today. This book provides practical wisdom for anyone who is interested in becoming a more effective leader. I highly recommend this book!

Eithne Hannan, *Chartered Organisational Psychologist and Leadership Coach, previously Senior Manager of Learning & Development, Ernst & Young, Sydney, Australia*

Leaders have much to learn from the world of arts in improving their presence and communication. This book provides many lessons on the importance of combining persuasive ability with firmly rooted ethical values to guide decision making in the public interest.

Professor Amit Gupta, *Indian Institute of Management, Bangalore*

The most successful military commanders, humanitarian directors, war lords, village elders, peace activists, politicians, and tribal chiefs that I have encountered have all had the ability to persuade those around them to follow a particular course of action. This book identifies many of the subtleties in persuasive leadership behaviour that other leadership writers have until now chosen to ignore.

Captain David Clarke, *Irish Defence Forces*

The Persuasive Leader

Lessons from the Arts

Stephen J. Carroll
and
Patrick C. Flood

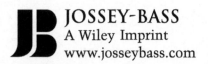

JOSSEY-BASS
A Wiley Imprint
www.josseybass.com

HM
1261
.C37
2010

This edition first published in 2010

© 2010 John Wiley & Sons Ltd

Registered office

John Wiley & Sons Ltd, The Atrium, Southern Gate, Chichester, West Sussex, PO19 8SQ, United Kingdom

Under the Jossey-Bass imprint, 989 Market Street, San Francisco CA 94103-1741, USA www.jossey-bass.com

For details of our global editorial offices, for customer services and for information about how to apply for permission to reuse the copyright material in this book please see our website at www.wiley.com

The right of the author to be identified as the author of this work has been asserted in accordance with the Copyright, Designs and Patents Act 1988.

All rights reserved. No part of this publication may be reproduced, stored in a retrieval system, or transmitted, in any form or by any means, electronic, mechanical, photocopying, recording or otherwise, except as permitted by the UK Copyright, Designs and Patents Act 1988, without the prior permission of the publisher.

Wiley also publishes its books in a variety of electronic formats. Some content that appears in print may not be available in electronic books.

Designations used by companies to distinguish their products are often claimed as trademarks. All brand names and product names used in this book are trade names, service marks, trademarks or registered trademarks of their respective owners. The publisher is not associated with any product or vendor mentioned in this book. This publication is designed to provide accurate and authoritative information in regard to the subject matter covered. It is sold on the understanding that the publisher is not engaged in rendering professional services. If professional advice or other expert assistance is required, the services of a competent professional should be sought.

ISBN 978-0-470-68828-1

A catalogue record for this book is available from the British Library

Project management by OPS Ltd, Gt Yarmouth, Norfolk, UK
Typeset in 9.5/13pt Melior
Printed in Great Britain by TJ International Ltd, Padstow, Cornwall, UK

Dedication

Stephen (Steve) Carroll dedicates this book to his wife Donna, brothers Creighton and Robert (Robbie), and to his brother-in-law Keith Sueker with gratitude for the years of intellectual stimulation through discourse they have given him. His mother, Helene Carroll, was a professional artist, dancer, and singer and his father Stephen J. Carroll inspired him to read great books.

Patrick Flood dedicates this book to his wife, Patricia, and sons, Chris and Patrick Ellis, and his mother, Catherine, for their ongoing love and support, and to his late father, Bartholomew, who gave him a life-long interest in art, poetry, and literature, and taught him to search for shapes in the sky and in wood.

We also dedicate the book to the unsung leaders in the world—in homes, classrooms, communities, hospitals and surgeries, military units—as well as those at all levels in organizations everywhere in the world.

University Libraries
Carnegie Mellon University
Pittsburgh, PA 15213-3890

Contents

Foreword

Leadership is a social force that makes common goals achievable. It's as ancient as Herodutus, Exodus, and the Bhagavad Gita. At the same time, leadership at its most powerful is fresh and utterly alive.

Looking back on how 20th century social science parsed the subject, leadership research would seem to be a mixed bag of unfulfilled promises. Diminished to supervision, "leadership" studies often left out its heart and aspirations. Set up the task. Direct the people. Reward appropriately. Repeat. Not much for the imagination.

Leadership is too critical a matter to be routinized. Science, trying to interpret the world appropriately, has moved on. In the 21st century, we see a far more compelling take on leadership's fundamentals. Contemporary leadership studies put the complexity and richness back in. Part of a larger movement, with lots of names from integrative pluralism to multidisciplinary practice, we see what biologist Edward O. Wilson referred to as consilience, a synthesis of fields.[1] Wilson notes that the sciences, humanities, and arts share a goal: to give a purpose to understanding the details, to lend to all inquirers "a conviction, far deeper than a mere working proposition." Integrating the sciences, humanities, and arts means taking their distinct ways of knowing and reading them into each other. The result recognizes the world as a different place than any single field could discover.

Stephen Carroll and Patrick Flood's *Persuasive Leadership* brings consilience to the realm of leadership as it can be known through the arts, humanities, and science. Their book encourages the reader to re-imagine, or better to re-image, a fuller representation of the ancient and enduring, fresh and visceral phenomenon that is leadership.

Denise M. Rousseau

H.J. Heinz II University Professor of Organizational Behavior and Public Policy at Carnegie Mellon University's H. John Heinz III College and the Tepper School of Business

---

[1] E.O. Wilson (1998) *Consilience: The Unity of Knowledge.* New York: Knopf.

Preface

The already extensive literature on leadership needs no repeating. This book takes a fresh look at the leadership role from a number of different perspectives. One example is in its emphasis on the persuasive requirements in leadership especially in today's new world in which so many social, economic, political, and technological changes have taken place. Another is in its emphasis on looking to the arts and humanities and to life examples for leadership persuasive principles instead of research carried out in the field of organizational psychology. This is actually a current trend in advanced executive training. The writing on leadership from the perspective of organizational psychology is already so extensive the authors have chosen not to explore it further, even though they are quite familiar with it, recognize its importance, and use many principles which are derived from psychology. Another aspect of the book is in its focus on leadership efforts carried out in everyday life in addition to leadership activities in various types of work organizations including non-profit, education, and government, medical, and military entities. In addition, the book discusses many current issues in leadership such as moral leadership, harmful leadership, learning from failures, leading through sub-leaders, the leader as a counsellor, leadership in specialized professions, and so on. Furthermore, this book explores leadership used for socially desirable ends and leadership as a life legacy activity which often remain unexplored in leadership books.

The book idea originally came out of courses in persuasive leadership lessons from the arts taught by Stephen J. Carroll to executive audiences at various teaching locales of Syracuse University. He also presented it to managers and MBA students at other locations in Australia, Italy, Poland, Ireland and programmes at the University of Maryland. It was at one of the sessions at the Syracuse Blue Mountain Facility that Patrick C. Flood was exposed to the material and incorporated it in his various executive development programmes in Ireland (at Dublin City University Business School), Italy, the United Kingdom, and The Netherlands. It was also at that session that the authors agreed in principle to write this book.

Stephen J. Carroll

Acknowledgements

We are particularly grateful to Professor Dennis Gillen, then Associate Dean for Executive Education at the Whitman School of Management at Syracuse University who gave us the opportunity to test our ideas on leadership with subsequent cohorts of the MBA Upgrade executive Programme.

The book was greatly aided by the editorial assistance, good humour, and efficiency of Rachel Kidney, PhD research scholar in leadership at Dublin City University Business School.

We also wish to acknowledge the encouragement and ideas in this project of various academic colleagues. These include Professors Daved Barry and Stefan Mesiak of the Department of Leadership, Politics and Philosophy, Copenhagen Business School; Professors Ken Smith and Henry P. Sims of the Smith School of Business, University of Maryland; Dr. Philip Stiles, University of Cambridge; Dr. Aoife McDermott, DCU Business School; Dr. Johan Coetsee, University of Northumbria; Professor Jim Guthrie, University of Kansas; Professor Paul Sparrow, University of Lancaster; Professor Nigel Nicholson, London Business School; Professor Michael West, Aston Business School; and Professor Denise Rousseau, Carnegie Mellon University. We also give our heartfelt thanks to those academic colleagues and professionals who have generously endorsed our book. They are listed inside the front cover and on the back cover of the book.

As authors we have worked with John Wiley & Sons before and it has always been a good experience.

We are also greatly indebted to our editor at Wiley, Rosemary Nixon, who recognized the distinctiveness of the book in its earliest stages and made several helpful suggestions. Other staff members at Wiley such as Louise Cheer and Michaela Fay, and Neil Shuttlewood at OPS Ltd were extremely helpful and professional and made useful contributions to the final shape of the book.

About the authors

Stephen J. Carroll is Professor Emeritus of Management and Organization at the Robert H. Smith School of Business at the University of Maryland. He holds a PhD degree from the University of Minnesota and a BA from UCLA. He is an Elected Fellow of the Academy of Management, The American Psychological Association, The Society for Industrial and Organizational Psychology, and is a Charter Fellow in the Association for Psychological Science. He was one of the founders of the Organizational Behavior and Human Resources Management Divisions of the Academy of Management and was president of the latter group at its inception. He was selected as a Distinguished-Scholar teacher at the University of Maryland and has received many other academic honors. His outside activities include being a consultant and executive teacher in more than 30 industrial and government organizations. He has been a research Fulbright Professor in Japan and an invited scholar in residence for government agencies in Japan and China. He has also been a visiting professor at various universities in Australia, China, Japan, Ireland, Italy, Poland, Taiwan, and in the USA. His more than 100 academic papers include articles in journals such as *Administrative Science Quarterly, Journal of Applied Psychology, Academy of Management Journal, Academy of Management Review, Personnel Psychology, Human Relations, Human Resource Management*, and *Public Opinion Quarterly*. He is the author or co-author of 14 books, 2 monographs, and 3 book revisions. These include *Management by Objectives, Ethical Dimensions of International Management, Managing Organizational Behavior, Management, The Management of Compensation*, and *Performance Appraisal and Review Systems*. In 2010 he received the Heneman Lifetime Scholarly Achievement Award from the Academy of Management.

Patrick C. Flood is Professor of Organizational Behaviour at Dublin City University. He is Head of the HRM-Organizational Psychology Group and a Director of the Leadership, Innovation and Knowledge Research Centre. He serves as Honorary Professor of Management at Northeastern University, China and as an Academic Fellow at the Centre for International HRM, Judge Business School, University of Cambridge. He earned his PhD  at the London School of Economics under the supervision of John Kelly and is an alumnus of the International Teachers Programme at London Business School. Patrick teaches leadership and organizational change to MBA students and executives. His new books include *Leadership in Ireland* and *Persuasive Leadership: Lessons from the Arts*. Other books include *Effective Top Management Teams*, *Managing Strategy Implementation*, and *Managing without Traditional Methods*. Patrick held faculty positions at the London Business School and University of Limerick, and various appointments at the Australian Graduate School of Management, Irish Management Institute, London School of Economics, and the R.H. Smith Business School, University of Maryland. His teaching and research has been recognized with awards for excellence. These include fellowships from the Fulbright Commission, European Human Capital and Mobility programme, British Council, and Irish Cement Ltd. His research programme on organizational effectiveness has generated significant research income. He has published over a dozen books and monographs and numerous articles in journals such as the *Journal of Organizational and Occupational Psychology*, *Human Relations*, and the *Strategic Management Journal*. Much of his research work addresses the impact of leadership and management practice on organizational performance. He is particularly interested in improving hospital effectiveness. An experienced executive educator and keynote speaker, he has taught in Ireland, the UK, Australia, Italy, China, The Netherlands, and the USA. A Consulting Editor of the *Journal of Occupational and Organizational Psychology*, he is also on the editorial board of *Business Strategy Review*. He has served as an examiner at the University of Oxford, Trinity College, Dublin, and Queens University, Belfast.

CHAPTER 1

Persuasive leadership in life and work

"Even when he attained a high position, he could hear the crying below."

—Anon.[1]

"The most unholy and savage animal is a human being without virtue."

—Aristotle [1]

"A new civilization is emerging in our lives and blind men everywhere are trying to suppress it. This new civilization brings with it new family styles, changed ways of working, loving, and living; a new economy, new political conflicts; and beyond all this an altered consciousness as well ... The dawn of this new civilization is the single most explosive fact of our lifetimes. It is the central event—the key to understanding the years immediately ahead. It is an event as profound as the First Wave of change unleashed ten thousand years ago by the invention of agriculture, or the earthshaking Second Wave of change touched off by the industrial revolution. We are children of the next transformation, the Third Wave ..."

—Alvin Toffler, The Third Wave

---

[1] Many of the quotes in this book can be found in McKenzie, E.C. (1991) *14,000 Quips and Quotes for Writers and Speakers*, Monarch, Eastbourne; or in Prochnow, H.V. and Prochnow, H.V. Jr. (1942) *5100 Quotes for Speakers and Writers*, Baker Book House, Grand Rapids, Michigan.

BEGINNING CASES

Dorothy Collins was appointed principal of a dilapidated high school in a disadvantaged area within a US city. The students were amongst the lowest performing students in the city and were producing grades well below the national average. Ms Collins was an articulate African–American female of considerable energy and optimism and showed superb ability and dexterity in her leadership skills. She devised a plan to improve the school's performance. This involved completely re-structuring the discipline level tolerated in the school and exploring various alternative teaching methods that suited the school's problematic students. To facilitate the newly implemented strategy she ensured the competence of each teacher was improved by selecting certain key teachers to study new teaching methods as they were being used at other schools. These teachers then were required to teach them to the other teachers in their school who would then employ them in the classroom. This notion of identifying and applying "best practices" is a characteristic of effective social entities of all types.

In her role as a school principal she would frequently directly encourage parents to participate in their child's education and learning processes as well as inspiring her teachers to do the same. She convinced local business professionals to donate funds, assist in the rehabilitation of the school's infrastructure and increase the supply of teaching materials. On a typical day, she would wander around the school greeting students between classes and listen attentively at doors when classes were in session. On occasion, she would ask teachers to step out in the hall and provide suggestions on how to improve their performance. In doing so, she adopted the role of helpful counselor and mentor. After several such years, her school became one of the highest ranking schools in the city producing exceptional academic results.

—From a TV documentary

As a young man, Abraham Lincoln was unsure what to do with his life. Prior to becoming a lawyer, he worked as a clerk in a general store and became popular and well respected by his local community. During this time, he also worked on a riverboat and was distressed to see slave auctions taking place at the shipping wharf. Soon after, at the time of a "frontier war", he enlisted in the military and was quickly promoted to higher ranks. It was here he made a huge personal discovery—he had leadership skills! With this came exuberating confidence and the decision to pursue a political career. Despite his limited education, he became well known for his masterful speechmaking. It is believed that he had only one year of formal education; however, through determined self-study and practice he became one of the greatest public speakers and persuaders in American history. Lincoln remains an inspirational example for others of the potential for self-education. Through his familiarity with the *Bible* and the works of Shakespeare he developed a sophisticated command of the English language. This helped him to obtain the word mastery and language skills he later demonstrated. He was especially adept in the debate format which was popular practice at the time.

His rise to presidency was catalysed by the formation of a new political party with ideals he believed in and by an extremely persuasive and influential speech he gave in New York City early in his political career which gave him considerable prominence. This speech was pivotal in his career as he evolved from being an unknown Midwestern local politician to a national figure. He was a wonderfully charismatic man who would often draw from his vast collection of stories with a quick wit and humor which instantly engaged his audience. Never did he show his anger or lose control of his temper but remained humble and poised like a true gentleman. Lincoln was one of the most persuasive presidents in US history presiding successfully over the abolition of slavery and the triumphant conclusions of the Civil War. Many addresses today echo the rhyme of Lincoln's persuasive elegance that was heard amongst the political platforms hundreds of years ago. It is right and proper that this year (2009) we are paying special honour to Lincoln's memory not only in America but around the world also; without his persuasive abilities the world today would be much different than it is.

Jack Welch, retired CEO of General Electric (GE), is considered to be amongst the most effective business leaders of all time. Perhaps this accounts for the extensive biographical material available on him. We are aware that some readers say too much has been written about him. Several bestselling books, including his recent autobiography, recount his proficient approach to leadership which has taken both practitioner and academic communities by storm. When appointed the new CEO in 1981, Welch launched an explicit vision for GE, setting bold targets to be achieved by the end of the next decade. He then set about implementing these through the force of his persuasive powers and through various procedural and policy changes.

His remarkable persuasive leadership skills are highlighted clearly by his professional accomplishments and in films of one of his periodic speeches to senior executives at GE. The authors (Carroll and Flood) observed him in action several times in such a company film. During these speeches, his hands and arms are in constant motion emphasizing the significance of each issue, whilst the cadence of his voice oscillates appropriately in direct sequence to the content of his address.

His voice varies in tone from happy and enthusiastic to sadness with tinges of regret as he speaks. He would acknowledge various managers and divisions who were performing exceptionally well and describe new company initiatives which they can be jointly proud of. He describes his visits to customers, investors, and executive training programs at GE headquarters. On one such occasion, he vividly recalls a story of an individual customer whom he met that year with complaints regarding the service he received from GE. Throughout the story, Welsh expresses genuine distress, his eyes sombre and voice tinged with an irrefutable sadness.

"We can do better than this; this is not what we are about."

Throughout such speeches, he often referred to those present as "the team", reminding them of the united vision they have for the company. As always, he attempts to persuade his senior executives to accept this vision and align their personal goals with the wider ambitions of the company. He presented logical and emotional arguments for implementing his visions and uses stories to illustrate successes and failures in the company's actual modes of operating. He often emphasized ethical issues in such stories. He at times would reiterate how this vision can be achieved through the use of problem-solving teams. These teams would include lower level management groups working together to improve operating efficiency and resolve errors and wastefulness mistakes. Welsh would address all these serious issues in a wise and intimate voice—like that of a much loved uncle advising his admiring nieces and nephews.

What is leadership?

"The function of leadership is to engage followers, not merely to activate them, to comingle needs and aspirations and goals in a common enterprise and in the process to make better citizens of both leaders and followers."

—James McGregor Burns, *Leadership* [2]

"Leadership is the heart and soul of management. It is the ability to inspire other people to work together as a team, following your lead, in order to attain a common objective, whether in business, in politics, in war, or on the football field. Leadership is learned ..."

—Howard Geneen, *Managing* [3]

Persuasive leadership in a new world

These are the best of times and the worst of times for leadership. It is a more difficult time for leaders because the challenges of today are truly enormous. In *Managing Strategy Inplementation* [4] we documented some of the more significant changes which have occurred in the past 50 years in this world we all inhabit. These changes included not only significant changes in our world-wide economic, technological, and political systems but in our social attitudes, relationships, and expectations as well. Knowledge rather than physical effort is increasingly important in today's world. Obedience to authority can no longer be assumed. In fact there is documentation of world-wide changes in reactions to authority by people everywhere. Nevertheless, in spite of all of these changes we do know a great deal more about managing some of the problems arising from such changes than we did before, which is not to say that we still face much uncertainty in this new world in which we all must live.

Over the decades, there have been countless definitions of leadership emphasizing the different elements necessary to achieve greater leadership effectiveness. We have purposely chosen the previously cited definitions to conceptualize our understanding of true persuasive leadership. We believe this type of leadership is necessary to thrust through the many difficult problems we face. These problems are old and new, certain and uncertain, solvable and unsolvable. We feel that Harold Geneen, a former executive and president of an international telephone and telegraph company, captures the most relevant components of leadership in his definition. However in reading his writings on management we are not sure he actually followed this definition when he was actually managing—it seems rhetoric and reality may not always match up. Nonetheless, we see merit in his definition even if he failed to achieve it consistently in practice. Geneen's definition suggests that leadership is ubiquitous—it is an ever-present, world-wide phenomenon which reflects our natural way of thinking. It is found wherever human beings cooperate to achieve mutually desirable goals—in the home as well as at work and on the athletics and battle field, and in the pulpit and classroom and in all friendship groups.

The definition explained by Burns is conceivably the most widely referenced book on leadership and is equally relevant for our perspective on leadership. Burns emphasizes the importance of engaging the mind and emotions of followers. Of course philosophers since Aristotle have also said the same thing. We perceive this as the first necessary step to initialize an effective leadership strategy. It is our strong belief that borrowing from the arts is the most effective means of achieving this mental and emotional engagement. Furthermore, like Burns, we believe that effective leadership should aim at creating and developing better people for long-run benefits and in the greater scheme of things rather than merely using leadership as a short-term task solution. The examples at the beginning of this chapter clearly illustrate this type of persuasive leadership, which we want to discuss. This book arose out of a chapter by Carroll in a book entitled *Managing Strategy Implementation* which we authored with others. This chapter established the increased importance of adding persuasive approaches to the older management techniques of goal setting and strategies.

A newer focus on emotions and logic

Since its inception (around 1910), the "scientific management" approach has influenced management techniques within formal organizations. This involves the application of logic and analytical skills to management decision making. This approach brought a scientific perspective and analytical methods into all types of organizations. However, Peters and Waterman strongly argue that, in today's world, newer, more intuitive, and artistic perspectives are needed by managers and leaders and claim this has already been documented in the actions and methods of higher achieving business organizations [5].

Present research in human neurobiology illustrates that emotions and logic are in fact inseparable components within the information-processing system. During the decision-making process, emotional sections of the brain tend to be active when rational processes are functioning. The great philosopher Hume seems to have been correct when he argued—"rationality is typically the slave of some passion" [6]. This is not to say that logic, science, and systematic analysis are no longer needed—rather, emotions are a central facet of effective leadership in organizations today. Thus, leaders must emphasize both the rational and the emotional in their relationships with others. This has always been one of the primary perspectives of the arts and the humanities.

Leadership as a social role in all living groups

Leadership has always existed as a social role necessary for the survival of all human groups. Early hunter-gatherer bands and early agrarian groups consisted of men and women cooperating within functional collective groups to survive and reproduce. Of course, as Jack London describes in his great book *Call of the Wild*, the animals these groups hunted would also consist of groups with a leader at the top of their social hierarchy. It appears that the evolution of human kind, from primitive socialization processes to a fantastically higher level of human functioning can be attributed to the efforts of billions of parents, teachers, and other leaders throughout human history. These individuals may consider their efforts to be meagre on the larger scale of human existence but collectively they have accomplished a truly remarkable progression in human evolution even though periodic regression to past more primitive modes of behaviour frequently occurs. We can expect that the collective teaching and persuasive efforts of leaders and teachers throughout history will certainly pay dividends to the important future achievements of mankind. Nonetheless, much remains to be achieved in terms of further advancing human behaviour and thinking.

> "When the long winter nights come on and the wolves follow their meat into the lower valleys, he may be seen running at the head of the pack through the pale moonlight or glimmering borealis, leaping gigantic above his fellows, his great throat a-bellow as he sings a song of the younger world, which is the song of the pack."
>
> —Jack London [7]

Leadership legacies

Historical biographical accounts and history in general document how the actions of an individual leader can change the whole future dynamic and identity of nations, organizations, groups, and the inter-relationships among these collectives. Like the butterfly effect in weather, the death of a leader can have significant consequences. Although Geneen discusses leadership at a group level it obviously also involves one-on-one relationships. For example, if a person had not received positive contact with a particular leader in their life whether the relationship occurred in the workplace, at college, in school or at home, their whole life would have been vastly different as reported in many autobiographies and memoirs. The exposure to effective leadership is so critical to human life it is not entirely unexpected that it has attracted attention from thousands of writers, scholars, and practitioners worldwide. Lately there have been a number of "what if" books written. What if George Washington, Abraham Lincoln, Stalin, or other leaders had died in their infancy? What would the world be like today? What if a crucial Civil War battle had gone the other way because the actions of certain military leaders and the Confederate States had won the Civil War in the US? What if Hitler's ego had been different and he had never invaded Russia? What if thousands of parents in the past had raised their children differently—what great new leaders might have emerged?

Geneen indicates that leadership is learned although certain innate human characteristics may facilitate its exercise. He believed the biggest obstacle of leadership effectiveness is a common tendency of managers to become arrogant (he was aware of the toxic power of positional leadership). This can be illustrated by looking at the paintings of Napoleon through different stages of his career. In his early years, he dressed simply, had a humble demeanour and showed compassion towards others. However, over time, he gradually became intoxicated by the admiration of others and can be seen wearing more elaborate uniforms and exuding a lofty, arrogant manner. Later in his career, paintings show him as an emperor cloaked in golden robes and draped in lavish jewels. Geneen and many others have described the enormous differences in the effectiveness of leaders that they have encountered. These variations in leadership effectiveness can obviously have significant effects on human life in both positive and negative ways, as we shall see later in this book.

Our lives are gifts. In exchange for them we have duties, obligations, and responsibilities. Almost everybody in this world of ours believes that we ought to leave behind us when we depart a positive legacy of some kind. As we will see in subsequent chapters, performing the role of the persuasive–responsible leader effectively is an important cause of success in leaving such a positive legacy. We hope to provide suggestions for doing so.

Leadership goals

The fundamental goal of organizational leadership has been to improve or, at the very least, sustain performance at an individual and organizational level. Nowadays, many organizations aim to advance their human capabilities to facilitate organizational continuity and growth. Such leaders are accountable for the selection, development, and retention of employees as well as an abundance of other responsibilities. Also, many organizations aim to promote employee happiness and satisfaction to ensure a productive working environment and the retention of star performing employees. However, ensuring employee wellbeing goes far beyond the positive outcomes for an organization's bottom line—there are much larger implications to the greater society. The concept of improving personal wellbeing can be found referred to in the original constitutions of nations all over the world. It is logical to assume that all leaders are also bound by duty to a moral responsibility which is to contribute to the accomplishment of this all-encompassing objective. This is why we have chosen to discuss being the persuasive–responsible leader in this book.

Leadership sub-roles

The leadership role often involves the performance of multiple sub-roles and behaviours which include the director, the reward giver and punisher, as well as the teacher and counsellor to name a few. Recent research suggests that leaders tend to vary considerably in carrying out these sub-roles and also in the emphasis they place on such roles [8]. Given the momentous change occurring in the world we live in today, there is an increasing demand for persuasive teaching characteristics in the leadership role. Regrettably, the counselling, teaching, and problem-solving sub-roles are often neglected in comparison to the other sub-roles previously mentioned. In these pages, it is our intention to discuss and highlight the significance of some of these more neglected sub-roles. Leadership is an important aspect of an individual's personal and professional life and the leadership role discussed in this book is applicable to both settings and social entities. For far too long, the more generalized nature of leadership has been forgotten in literature. In writing this book, it is our intention to correct this issue by illustrating the importance of leadership in all aspects of life.

Leadership in changing crcumstances

Traditionally, leadership literature focuses primarily on the use of power and authority in leader–follower relationships. However, leadership relationships are often exposed to uncertainties in the environment in which the leadership relationship is embedded. Changing cultural and social norms have led to a variety of different leadership approaches necessary to achieve effective leadership outcomes. Again, humans have changed in terms of their attitudes, values, competencies, and other characteristics. In Japan, for example, the authors encountered an unusual turn of phrase: "the new humans". This term refers to the unique characteristics of the younger generation as compared to those born in past eras. In *Managing Strategy Implementation* [4], we argued that a progression towards adopting a persuasive approach rather than relying on the traditional authoritarian effort is necessary if we are to be successful in any leadership effort. This is partly due to the recent change that has occurred on a global scale in political, economic, social, and technological environments. These changes require adaptation of our leadership practices as well as addressing deeper changes needed to function more effectively, more so than we have done in the past.

Many organizations such as schools, hospitals, law enforcement, and business firms place human resources to be of primary importance as compared to their mechanical assets. This naturally renders persuasive leadership of utmost importance to organizational outcomes. Even when the use of machinery and equipment is essential, most tasks require a high degree of human motivation and commitment to avoid costly economic and human catastrophes. Our improved understanding of the basic elements of human behaviour can facilitate change in our leadership approach and elicit the types of reactions necessary to achieve our ever-increasing performance expectations.

Leader agendas

Research by Carroll and others indicates clearly that leaders and managers at all levels operate from a mental agenda or a "to do" list that they attend to and implement when circumstances require or permit [9]. Many items in such agendas refer to future desired states of performances, behaviours, thinking patterns, knowledge levels, and so on. Some agenda items are very long term and some are short term. Many such items require for their attainability a very long series of incremental changes. Persuasion efforts directed at attaining such visions or states obviously may have to be made on a more or less constant basis.

Leadership and the arts

There is a remarkable renewed interest in drawing from the arts in leadership practice today. Hundreds of programs are now being implemented which involve coaching executives, managers, and leaders in multiple settings on lessons that can be learned from the arts. For instance, fundamental characteristics of famous artists involve the ability to see and notice what most overlook, the ability to focus on chosen ends and incorporate diverse elements into a harmonious whole, and the use of intuition as well as logical thinking processes to accomplish exceptional ends. Today, many leading universities, such as Harvard in the United States, have made the arts and humanities a foundation for educational programmes in all parts of the university including their professional business schools. Many university programmes draw from particular artistic fields such as theatre in their educational and leadership development programmes. Carroll belongs to a world-wide network of more than 300 individuals involved in creating arts-oriented programmes for use in managing organizations and groups of all types.

Parents as persuasive leaders

Parents carry out one of the most significant roles in the development of a child's social skills, cultural adaptation, and moral values. Collectively, they are responsible for the developmental activities in all human societies. It is their duty to pass onwards the legacy of their ancestors to their children in the form of customs, values, principles, knowledge, and philosophies. Children must be persuaded to not only accept these, but incorporate them into their identity. Parental teaching, whether through explicit discussion with children or discrete role model behaviour, is fundamental to the future creation of secure independent human beings. Of course, the quality of teaching received by the child is dependent on parents' morals and values. Such teachings may be beneficial or harmful not only to the individual but to larger groups in society in which the individual is contained. Barack Obama, the new president of the United States, is a suitable example of an individual who received beneficial parenting. In one of his political addresses, he spoke of the role his mother's parenting played in his own development. He mentioned that everything he is today is a product of her influence. He recounts how she would wake him every morning at 4 am to study and attend to his school work. When he complained, she would reply "this is no fun for me either Buster". She certainly adopted what we know today as the "tough love" approach to parenting and often cautioned him against the "good time Charlie" attitude towards life encouraging him to prepare to meet challenges directly. After her untimely death, her parents (Obama's grandparents) continued the development process with the future president.

Leadership and strategies

Over the past two decades, strategic management has received growing attention although it has been a topic explored for many years with respect to military operations. Strategies are of course the means by which one achieves important goals, not only for organizations such as armies and companies and governments but for individuals as well. To achieve goals one must devise an approach for doing so. Concepts drawn from economic and psychology fields have been integrated and effectively applied to such strategic programs. In *Managing Strategy Implementation* [4] the authors discussed extensively how the most difficult part of strategic planning is in the implementation stage. Here, individuals who carry out the various steps necessary to achieve the strategic objectives must be persuaded to do so as well as being taught how to do so. Hence Carroll documented the need for an effective goal-setting process to successfully implement visions and strategic meta-goals for companies, groups, and individuals [10]. Goals often start with a vision—an image of a desirable future which can be easily remembered even though the steps necessary to realize it might not be understood. He also documented the significant motivational power of goal setting in achieving such desired ends. These visions of an attainable future may require thousands of independent activities over long periods of time to realize their ultimate objectives. Many individual and group intermediate goals are a critical step in linking the desired vision to the successful attainment of that vision. Persuasion is obviously necessary throughout all these intermediate steps in order to progress and obtain our final accomplishments. We will discuss later some principles for utilizing goals.

"... and the vision implanted in my brain still remains ..."

—Paul Simon, *Sound of Silence*

Do leaders need charisma?

Charisma is a term often used in discussing leaders. It is not a new term and has often been used in describing historical leaders in biography. More recent research, however, has identified some of the typical behaviours and powers of so-called charismatic and transformational leaders. These discussions illuminate leaders who have inborn special abilities that make them powerful agents of social change within their groups or organizations. Of course, to implement change outside their own groups, these leaders need to be especially persuasive since authority cannot be utilized in these situations. A recent documentary detailing Tony Blair's leadership of Great Britain illustrated his remarkable persuasive dexterity. Blair had the amazing ability to persuade not only his nation's citizens but other leaders and groups around the world. For example, he convinced all other nations that his home city of London was an attractive location to host the forthcoming Olympic Games. He was equally successful in persuading political leaders in several European countries and the United States of the desirability of adopting his "humanitarian interventionism" proposal. However, it does appear that natural charismatic leaders are in short supply as many observers will have noticed. We argue that effective persuasion does not require an innate charisma but can be learned or improved as persuasion is based on knowledge as well as genetically inherited personality characteristics. One should use charismatic leaders when available but relying on them to fill the many leadership roles required in nations, organizations, classroom, churches, and homes is impossible. Charismatic leaders are persuasive but persuasiveness can be learned by those without such innate capacities. The roots of persuasiveness include passion, conviction, and energetic purpose—all of which can be found and cultivated in many individuals. We would also point out that many leaders with unquestioned charisma and powers of persuasion have been among the most evil persons in the history of the world creating great damage to many persons, groups, nations, and the world itself. Our concept of the persuasive leader involves the concept of ethical, responsible, and even noble leadership in terms of behaviours and goals.

Persuasion as a key to all leadership efforts

Again, today's focus on building and developing skills, knowledge, and morale emphasize the need for a wider range of leadership abilities. These abilities include clarifying performance expectations, setting or negotiating goals, training and coaching, rewarding and disciplining, delegating responsibility, and managing conflict to name a few. Of course, the various leadership responsibilities mentioned are primarily driven by persuasive efforts. Our emphasis on persuasion in this book will reflect the more subtle psychological standard practice especially in business organizations but these must be increasingly supplemented by the fine art of persuasion if individuals in leadership roles are to be truly effective.

Leaders as coherent wholes

Leaders as human beings are a complex mixture of many traits, behaviours, values, and perceptions. In spite of this, many thousands of studies have attempted to pinpoint these human elements and to measure them specifically and precisely. There is disagreement among scholars on the wisdom and desirability of doing this especially from among scholars in the arts and humanities. They, and clinical psychologists, believe that human beings should be understood as totalities and described and analysed as such. In the arts, including literature, individuals are approached as a whole and as a complex mixture of characteristics interacting with the various social forces in a particular setting.

Learning from examples

The cases described at the beginning and end of this chapter identify four very effective change-oriented leaders who worked in different settings—family, welfare, education, business, and politics. They all used a persuasive leadership approach to attain significant and favourable performance outcomes. The arts and humanities can provide many examples of effective and ineffective leaders who vary in their persuasive skills. The persuasive leadership examples provided in history, biography, literature, theatre, and film present leaders performing in various situations using a variety of persuasive techniques. We can evaluate these variations in terms of lessons and principles. We will use such models of leaders throughout this book drawing lessons from them. Humans have always learned how to behave through observations of other human beings—parents, friends, peers, leaders, celebrities, and others observed in many different ways. We have described many leaders who seem especially effective or especially noble as our examples in this book. While most of us cannot expect to reach their level of effectiveness or nobility they do convey to us what excellent behaviour looks like as a guide in our own efforts. We will provide a few stories of bad or harmful leaders as well to provide a contrast. We all must learn to cope with life's many trials and opportunities and the examples of others can serve as a useful guide in our efforts towards survival in this difficult world. Of course, when we learn from behavioural models it is obviously best to emulate the first rate rather than the second rate. We should at least know what the more ideal is even though we ourselves may not be able to achieve such performance levels ourselves.

Types of persuasion settings

Persuasive leadership can be applied to major long-term change projects or just intended for short-term action. The persuasive change effort may involve complex activities involving several elements or only a few words spoken in haste during a presentation. A long-term complicated change project requires a series of persuasive efforts by one or more individuals to many different audiences. These efforts may be designed to achieve questionable harmful outcomes or noble dignified ones. All the persuasive leaders described in this chapter had to exert their persuasive efforts to various audiences with different basic values and assumptions. For example, Jack Welch (see End case) had to persuade and teach not only key subordinates but investors, supplier groups, and the media and through this medium the general public. Also, because of the size of GE, he had to focus his efforts on a small group of top managers. These he had to persuade to influence lower levels in a cascading process to pursue corporate objectives and policies and incorporate them into their work practices throughout the organization. Our high-school principal was successful in persuading not only teachers but her students, their parents, local business professionals, and community leaders to accept her plans and agenda. Due to the future long-term survival needs of the nation, Lincoln had to perpetually convince the general public to resist premature attempts to end the Civil War. In addition, he had to constantly persuade and teach not only his own cabinet which was typically hostile and disrespectful towards him but other nations as well.

Types of Leadership

Contingency leadership theories increased in popularity several decades ago. These theories propose that leaders vary their supervisory approach in response to different circumstances the leadership relationship is exposed to. A revised version of this perspective was the life cycle approach. This theory suggests that the style of leadership will predictably change as a work group matures. For example, a new and perhaps low-performing group may require a more directive leadership approach with an emphasis on task accomplishment. As the group's performance gradually improves, a participative leadership approach may emerge with an increased emphasis on reducing turnover by building morale and satisfying subordinates' needs. When the group has reached a stage of high morale and performance, the leader can effectively withdraw leaving the subordinates in a self-leadership modus operandi. Some of these later movements emphasize the leader's ability to promote not only organizational performance but provide individual development opportunities to facilitate subordinate wellbeing and happiness. As recognized by current literature and research, individual development is obviously critical to ensure organizational continuity and growth. This is particularly relevant in today's rapidly changing economic environment. The idea that leadership approaches must change as individuals and circumstances change will be recognized as obvious to just about every person. As parents and teachers we are very aware of the changes needed as our children grow in knowledge, competence, and maturity.

Leadership skills as identified in the arts and humanities

As previously mentioned, the conceptualization of persuasive leadership in this book involves drawing primarily from the arts and humanities. For centuries, these disciplines have been an important aspect of human learning. This branch of knowledge includes the fine arts, performing arts, applied arts, literature and poetry, linguistics, philosophy, and other such disciplines. All of these offer principles and insights that show us how to achieve more effective persuasive techniques. Whilst some of these have been applied to persuasive fields such as marketing and public relations, in recent years the application of principles from these disciplines has become increasingly popular in the management field. However, their value in performing leadership roles may not appear so obvious at first glance. All persuasive efforts require some form of communication which intends to influence the audience to react in a desirable way. As is standard in all communications, the critical first step is to ensure the message is received by the audience. Engagement is the key concept here.

Second, it is imperative the message is understood and retained. To achieve this, the message must be presented in an attractive manner intended to ensure that the audience is aroused and attentive. This occurs when the presentation is engaging, vivid, and stimulating to the audience. Certainly, it is apparent that the intention of the arts is to impact the audience with their specific messages or visions. Great art has the ability to elicit such responses. For example, Barack Obama, as a US presidential candidate capitalized on the use of his preferred rhetoric and especially through his use of poetical devices such as alliteration, repetition, metaphors to engage his audience as a first step in delivering his political message. This approach is similar to that of many other successful political, social, and organizational leaders throughout history. President Ronald Reagan is another leader who effectively used principles from the arts in pursuit of various political and social objectives. His training as an actor was obviously of great value to him in becoming known as "the great communicator". Arts and literature also represent a unique expression and in many cases can create a new perspective which may have been previously overlooked. Leadership performances communicated through an artistic or literature base can obtain insights or visions in such a way to make the message clear and memorable. The artist and writer have always been said to have a special way of seeing reality and special skills in presenting their insights to the world so as to engage attention and make their insights memorable. Such skills are obviously needed today by all leaders at all levels of human society.

Do we need empirical studies of leadership?

The authors fully understand that thousands of empirical studies have been carried out examining leadership effectiveness from various specialist fields including industrial and social psychology, organizational behaviour, and political science. We ourselves have carried out a number of such studies. However, some scholars have noted that empirical and statistical approaches used in such studies have, by their very nature and limitations, failed to capture the true profound complexity of leadership. Some claim that the softer narrative approaches used in literature and history do more effectively capture the fundamentals of leadership in all its complex interactions among various personal and situational characteristics. This is a longstanding dispute in academic circles especially when dealing with issues about human behaviour. Is it better to study a very tiny aspect of behaviour in detail with great precision or study human behaviour in less precise observational ways with greater richness and understanding of the many complex interacting causal factors that are typically involved? In early psychology, the Gestalt psychological approach decried perceiving human activity as the result of small discrete elements. Humans are a total entity where many elements work together in complex ways to produce a response to a particular situation. In addition, individuals primarily learn through the observation of others directly or through legends, myths, or vicariously through stories. Unlike our previous writings we have chosen this more story-oriented, holistic, and artistic way of thinking in this book. This is not to say that behavioural science theory and research is irrelevant to the study of persuasive leadership. It should be studied and used in pragmatic ways along with the lessons provided by the arts. That is our feeling. Both contribute in different ways to a more complete understanding of the human world we live in. In fact, much of the research-based theory in the psychological sciences is quite congruent with what the arts and humanities tell us about the realities of persuasive leadership. We have inserted in Appendix D of this book a brief description of the psychological theories which we feel are most relevant to this subject of persuasive leadership. Each of these theories is supported by many specific research studies carried out in the behavioural sciences.

Leaders and ethical behaviours

Much has been written in recent years about the ethical behaviour of those in leadership positions. Leadership is a social role and adherences to ethical standards are especially expected of those who are in such positions. The general public and most subordinates expect and desire that their leaders act ethically. Ethics is highly related to trust and trust is the foundation for any social system in this world of ours. Many organizations have ethical standards and codes which their members are expected to follow. All accredited business schools are required to teach ethics in courses or their majors. Of course, what is acceptable ethical behaviour varies from one culture to another, as documented in a book on international ethics by Carroll and a colleague [11].

It is also documented in the aforementioned book that ethical issues have dominated much of the writings in religion, philosophy, and literature all over the world for the past several centuries.

Leaders as examples of persuasive and moral principles

All societies in human history have used historical leaders as exemplars of good and bad leadership. Human beings need such figures to provide comparative models for their own behaviour and assist in their judgements of others. Throughout this book, you will find descriptions of many outstanding leaders which we promote as desirable persuasive leaders. Some of them will be known to our leaders while others are unknown to most but still exemplary in terms of their persuasive abilities and nobility of character. Of course, we sometimes include their opposites, bad leaders who exhibit harmful behaviours that we should aim to avoid if we are to aspire to be noble leaders. The leaders we have chosen reflect our personal views of persuasive leadership. Unfortunately, there exist many effective leaders present in all communities who, because they lack fame, are known to few and will rest in "unvisited graves", as so eloquently said by George Elliot. We have encountered such individuals primarily through personal relationships and recent research of obituaries. This book incorporates such undiscovered individuals as exemplars of effective leaders. We write primarily for those who aim to achieve more effective leadership capabilities and strive towards a more meaningful life. This is after all the goal of most human beings, as has been revealed through literature, case studies, and experiences in the authors' lives. Persuasion is used as often for undesirable, harmful, and selfish ends as for desirable ones. Therefore we emphasize the use of persuasive skills for ethical, moral, or responsible ends. Persuasion is a tool which can be used for many different ends. Moral ends are our goals although there are often legitimate differences in opinion as to what these are.

SUMMARY

This chapter presents a brief history of some of the changing conceptions of leadership in our society. It has presented arguments promoting the need for a greater emphasis on the use of a persuasive leadership style. We have also argued the need for leaders in all types of societal and institutional organizations to promote the intellectual development of its members as well as their personal happiness. In addition, we have stressed the need to increasingly draw from the arts and humanities in pursuit of these much needed new directions in the leadership role. In this book we will use as exemplars models of persuasive leaders drawn from real life and fiction. These models represent guides to our own behaviour. We do want to imitate always as much as it is possible the very best or ideal performers in terms of our own desired future performances. Finally, we want to emphasize our belief that a fundamental drive in almost all human beings is to create a life that is purposeful and meaningful and that encountering good leadership is a key to attaining this end.

This chapter also briefly discussed historical views of leadership as well as more contemporary perspectives. We argue that in all circumstances there must be change in how the leadership role in societies is performed. We promote a greater emphasis for persuasion in all types of societal institutions—business, government, non-profit, as well as in families—the basic social constituent of any society.

END CASE

Marguerite "Mara" Galaty, born in Germany and raised in the suburbs of Washington D.C., was an accomplished leader throughout her career. In high school, she was the first manager of the boy's football team. In college, she raised funds and organised students to fly to Mexico to help small villages to recover from the devastation of a severe hurricane. Later, she worked for a non-profit educational organisation creating a working group of young leaders from the Balkans. Here, she carefully selected and persuaded these individuals with charm and diplomacy to work on disputes and promote peace. Soon after, working for a humanitarian organisation, she developed projects around the world that helped to resolve 150 land conflicts. As an officer for a US government international organisation, she created and managed several programs to assist communities in Jordon where she was assigned. When she started to receive treatments for an illness, thousands of individuals visited her and sent admiring messages from around the world. Her death at 38 created much grief among those who knew her and were inspired by her example.

—From an obituary published in the *Washington Post*

Works cited

[1]   Hill, A.S. (1895) *The Principles of Rhetoric*. New York: Harper & Brothers.

[2]   Burns, J.M. (1978) *Leadership*. New York: Harper & Row.

[3]   Geneen, H. and Moscow, A. (1984) *Managing*. New York: Doubleday & Company.

[4]   Flood, P.C., Dromgoole, T., Carroll, S.J., and Gorman, L. (1998) *Managing Strategy Implementation*. Oxford: Blackwell.

[5]   Peters, T. and Waterman, R.H. (1982) *In Search of Excellence*. New York: Harper & Row.

[6]   Hume, D. (1910) *An Enquiry Concerning Human Understanding* (Vol. 37). Harvard Classics.

[7]   London, J. (1903) *The Call of the Wild*. New York: Macmillan.

[8]   Yukl, G. (1989) *Leadership in Organisations* (Second Edition). Prentice Hall.

[9]   Carroll, S.J. and Gillen, D.J. (1987) How useful are the classical management functions in describing managerial work? *Academy of Management Review*, **12**, 38–50.

[10] Carroll, S.J. (1998) Implementing strategic plans through formalized goal setting. In P.C. Flood, T. Dromgoole, S.J. Carroll, and L. Gorman (Eds.), *Managing Strategy Implementation* (pp. 31–43). Oxford: Blackwell.

[11] Carroll, S.J. and Gannon, M. J. (1997) *Ethical Dimensions of International Management*. Thousand Oaks, CA: Sage Publications.

CHAPTER 2

Using aesthetics and the arts in persuasive leadership

"The painting shows the artist's way of seeing. Our appreciation of it reflects our way of seeing."

—M. Berger

"Design has a spiritual impact whether implied through colour, light, texture, or expressed through architectural replication."

—Charles McClennahan, *American Theatre*, 2003

"Mankind is almost incapable of dispassionate, unemotional thinking. In something which he has recognised as evil man can seldom see also what is good."

—Aleksandr Solzhenitsyn, *The Gulag Archipelago*

"Fiction is art and art is the triumph over chaos."

—John Cheever

BEGINNING CASES

At the death of Ptolemy in 51 BCE, his daughter Cleopatra VII ascended the throne of both upper and lower Egypt. Cleopatra received a particularly challenging education. She focused on the masterworks of Greek literature including the works of Homer, the great poets, as well as the tragedies of Euripides, the comedies of Menander and the art of rhetoric from the speeches of Demosthenes. She learned and spoke many of the languages of her day and could converse in court with many ambassadors from around her world without the aid of translators. In addition to her literary and historical studies, her schoolwork included geometry, astronomy, and medicine. As a result, Cleopatra was a very articulate woman and her extraordinary beauty helped her effectiveness as a great persuasive leader. She ruled very wisely and was a mastermind in political strategy. She was artistic in her dress and manner. Several films have described how when faced with threats from Rome under Caesar and then Marc Antony she used dramatic means to make a significant first impression on both of them. According to one story, she wrapped herself in a coverlet or rug and had herself carried into Caesar's palace where she then emerged dramatically from her cover. For Marc Antony, she refused his invitation to have dinner in his quarters and invited him to her palace where she orchestrated one of the most spectacular feasts of all time. Of course, she then immediately captivated them with her wit, intelligence, and beauty. According to historical literature, she was caught up in political forces in Rome which she could not control and as a result committed suicide (dramatically) at the age of 39. She was a true artist and a great persuasive leader of her people.

—From Edith Flamarion, *Cleopatra: The Life and Death of a Pharaoh* [1]

T.S. Lin, CEO of a Taiwanese company waited in a side room of a large hall occupying more than 2000 managers and Carroll for an annual meeting in Taipei. The hall was decorated with numerous flags and plaques commemorating achievements of quality and various other awards won by the company over the years. Before his entrance, a chorus of female workers from the company sang the national anthem and the company's own anthem. Their singing exuded such beauty that their audience were visibly moved. The CEO entered the hall through a side door about 10 minutes after the meeting was scheduled to commence. The crowd was slightly restive as he made his dramatic entrance, pausing at the door to wave, proceeding slowly through the crowd, and bowing with his hands below his chin in a lotus position. Several managers, on the stage behind the presentation table, stood and initiated applause from the crowd who then stood as a mark of respect. As the applause waned, he moved to the platform in front of the stage.

In a brief and animated talk, he summarized the company's achievements from the previous year, addressing the crowd in an eloquent manner, pausing frequently and enthusiastically emphasizing particularly significant accomplishments. He highlighted the dependency of the nation on its business sector and how the achievements of their own company contributed to the state. He spoke of the bond between the future of their company and the national interest and how this was related to the quality of life for our children in the future. He then turned to the table of managers and acknowledged those managers whose performance throughout the year was of particular note and merit. He spoke of their accomplishments in the form of anecdotal stories and awarded them commemorative pins and certificates and applauded each prize winner.

In the view of Carroll, Lin exactly followed the actions of orchestra conductors of symphonies which he had observed many times. Typically, the orchestra conductor emerges from the audience's left wing of the stage slowly walking to the podium while the audience applauds. He or she bows to the audience a few times, sometimes speaks, and then picks up the baton. The orchestra is respectfully silent and gazes at him intently. He then dramatically moves his body and hand and starts the process of exploring the musical themes and organizing and managing the sounds into an engaging harmonious musical presentation. Following Lin's initial talk, the two external consultants (Carroll and a colleague) gave brief presentations in harmony with the theme of the meeting. In these solo performances they gave variations of the theme of the overall meeting citing their initial favourable impressions of the company and highlighting both positive aspects and areas where added attention was needed to bring the company forward in the coming year. To conclude the ceremony, Dr Lin presented his overall vision for the company by way of new directions and goals and succeeded in actively soliciting support for these from the assembled company members. Organizational members left the ceremony seemingly inspired, at least until they had to confront the cold realities of the actual world.

Teddy Roosevelt was one of the most persuasive presidents to have held office in the US. Many of the most far reaching policies and programs initiated in the US were passed during his administration. His persuasive efforts resulted in the reigning in of economic monopolies and trusts, the establishment of national parks, the attainment of power by labour unions and the establishment of the United States as a naval power. To ensure Congress would implement these, Roosevelt convinced the general public, the intellectual community and the media of the desirability of such programs in his many public speaking engagements and through his writings. Also, his ability to convince the Japanese and Russians to end their war only further emphasises his persuasive leadership skills.

Teddy Roosevelt followed certain aesthetic principles and suggested them to others. He once said that every person is an artist who, in constructing their life, is a playwright, director and actor. He was committed to change for the good of the nation and was adept at creating an attractive public persona. As he intended, US citizens saw him as an appropriate leader of the nation's core values and ideals. He had high credibility because his background corresponded to enduring national values. He had showed strength and character by transforming himself from a frail sickly boy to a strong outdoorsman and warrior. Despite his family being part of the elite in society he criticised the class system. He was dramatically theatrical in his public appearances and often wore his old rough-rider hat from his legendary exploits in Cuba during the Spanish–American war. On one occasion, before delivering a speech, he was shot by a member of the audience. Fortunately, the bullet lodged in the folded speech which he had in an inner pocket covering his breast. He took out the speech, showed the bullet to the audience and continued on talking to the end. This became a legend. He was very well read which contributed to his writing skills and believed in the power of persuasion through a variety of means such as public speeches, writings and face-to-face meetings with influential persons.

—Teddy Roosevelt, *An Autobiography* [2]

Leaders using the arts

The leaders described above used leadership approaches involving the arts or aesthetics to effectively engage the audience and make their messages more memorable. In these examples, the arts were used to further the persuasive process whether they were conscious or unconscious in their efforts. Their expressions were artistic and contributed to a high level of effectiveness in their delivery like actors on a stage. Music, costumes, symbols, and various aesthetic images were used to prime certain desired emotional responses from their audiences. The performances were carefully planned to achieve certain aesthetic reactions and were executed appropriately. Of course, many who aspire to be effective leaders may not be so naturally artful in their approach. Artistic and aesthetic concepts have long been used to sell products and services; however, their value in selling ideas and concepts seems to be insufficiently appreciated. We believe studying the arts with the aim of understanding art may help remedy the absence of natural artistic insight and help us to become more persuasive in our leadership.

What are the arts?

The arts consist of painting, sculpture, performing arts, as well as many crafts and applied arts. Fictional writing and poetry are also considered artistic skills and many perceive writers as artists of language. Paintings of leaders, biblical scenes, myths, and historical events remind us of the truths, lessons, and concepts that can be learned and applied to our own leadership endeavours. A work of art can provoke a thoughtful enquiry to understand what message the artist intends to deliver and entices us to reconsider a presupposed idea or moral. Theatre and film represent an especially useful artistic method of studying leadership and have long been used to illustrate various leadership concepts, perspectives, or recommended actions in business and political science. One principle of communication is to create harmony and integration between the spoken word and body language. Film is especially useful when studying the integration of these communicative means and presents them together in a very comprehensible way. For centuries, plays and stories have been used as a vehicle to promote moral concepts in different cultures around the world. So-called morality plays were performed in Europe for hundreds of years. Live theatrical performances can be useful for teaching and may be especially necessary when a population or audience is illiterate. However, even for highly educated audiences theatrics can be an effective teaching tool. At the home business schools of the authors, theatrics are used today for teaching several subjects including ethics, leadership, and various other topics in organizational behaviour.

Practical use of the arts

Usually, art is used to communicate a truth or possible truth of human life. Early in human existence the arts seemed to represent an attempt to control the fear or stress of potential uncertainties which many faced. For centuries, paintings, statues, dance, musical compositions, and theatre have been created to curry favor with important dignitary figures and gods to persuade them to intervene and help them achieve their goals. Practical applications of theatrics in law show participants in a court case holding mock trials. The intention is to ensure an extra-confident, more effective presentation when under scrutiny during actual court proceedings. Teachers (including the authors) have used the art of role playing in their classrooms with great success for many years. A common method in role playing is to act out the roles of supervisor and subordinate with the intention of providing an actual example of the various emotions experienced when facing challenging interactions. By taking part and observing role plays, leaders can learn and benefit from using different approaches to decision making, problem solving, and methods of effective social interaction.

The aesthetic response

The fundamental objective of the arts is to elicit an aesthetic response from its audience. This involves a human reaction characterized by activation, attention, alertness, stimulated interest, and at times a sense of pleasure or excitement. The aesthetic response is an emotional response—recent studies in neurophysiology/psychology indicate that various aesthetic experiences go directly to the primary emotional location in the brain [3]. On occasion, an artist's intention is to target a set of alternate emotions. Indeed, certain aesthetic responses cannot always be achieved as the outcome is dependent on the quality, perceived sincerity, and nature of the artistic creation. Aesthetics as a focus of study by philosophers, psychologists, writers, and poets has been examined from many different perspectives. Philosophers have often explored the artistic creation itself as is seen in the writings of Aristotle on rhetoric and poetics. Most importantly though is what characteristic of the artistic event is most important in eliciting a perception of beauty? When the Greeks designed and constructed buildings, they would place a great deal of emphasis on physical proportions paying particular consideration to harmony and symmetry of the building. The Greeks were effective in intertwining art and logic. To them, beauty and rationality were to be achieved simultaneously and for the Greeks success in achieving this was an art in itself. Their architecture was not considered separate domains of art and science as is often found today.

What happens psychologically and physiologically to a person who is presented with aesthetic images, words, or music? What emotional states are experienced from the exposure to artistic images, words, actions, or settings? Why do these things happen? Psychologists are interested in aesthetics and have used the arts to stimulate certain aesthetic responses from their clients. Analysis of these responses has provided deeper insights into the psychological implications of art. The aesthetic response is essentially an emotional reaction. Since emotions are typically viewed as the most primitive motivation of human behaviour, Aristotle would say that persuasive leadership and teaching should target emotions to stimulate such responses from their audiences. Once the audience is captivated, the use of reasoning and logic can build upon this captivated attention to deliver their message.

Emotions have a biochemical basis and when humans experience an event a flow of chemicals often referred to as neurotransmitters send messages to the rest of the body. Endorphins or natural opiates produce an emotional "high". Leadership research has found that these emotional highs have been identified in followers' reactions to the words spoken by certain highly persuasive leaders [4]. In fact, emotions have been found to be related to many other human functions. For example, there is a strong relationship between memory and emotional experiences. Transference of emotions from previous experiences into the present is believed to exist in all meaningful relationships. Positive or negative emotional states trigger different memories from the past. Emotions also play a key role in what we remember and forget. Memory is equally important to human survival and is an important characteristic for human evolution. Individuals who could not remember which environmental places are potentially harmful are more likely to perish before passing on their genes.

Aesthetics and human evolution

It is likely that human beings' responses to images of other humans, objects, nature, and events as well as their sounds are based on evolutionary processes. The survival of a legacy of genes seems to be an intrinsically primitive human motivation. Human attraction and appreciation of beauty is favourable for several possible reasons. The mating instinct is one hypothesis. Observations of higher level animals and birds propose that the aesthetic appearance of such creatures in the form of plumage, fur, or adornments suggest health and physical wellbeing and thus, the probability of gene survival. Noticeable behaviours such as mating dances are methods of enticing the opposite sex to reproduce and ensure the survival of their kind. Also, an interest in the allure of other humans, events, and aspects of nature is necessary for survival and thus is favourable to the human evolutionary process. The world is filled with a multitude of various stimuli including sound, colour, shape, and smell to name a few. This stimulus is true of both the living and inanimate world. Human awareness of changes that occur in such stimuli is ultimately related to survival. Those less sensitive to such cues in nature would be more likely to perish.

Human interest in storytelling has been rooted in history. The storyteller is often a person held in high regard by the community in many different societies and there is good reason for such storytelling. Humans have historically depended on stories to illustrate various lessons of survival, morality, and how to achieve enlightenment. Stories help reduce some of the uncertainties of life. For those who resist such stories, there is greater possibility they will struggle to survive in society and less potential to pass on the legacy of their genes to future generations.

Unity among the arts

Although we often discuss the fine arts, applied arts, performing arts, and literature separately, the arts are essentially unified. Musical compositions, for example, are often based on poems and stories. The choral section of Beethoven's Ninth Symphony transposed the poetry of Schiller into music. His famous violin piece *The Kreutzer Sonata* was turned into a dramatic novel by Leo Tolstoy which featured a musician playing the musical composition within the plot of a murder thriller [5]. Later, another composer, Janáček, arranged a piece of music based on Tolstoy's story. Opera which has existed for hundreds of years employs all of the arts together. The art of opera is based on literature and employs instrumental music, singing, painted scenery, costumes, and dance together in an attempt to create a sublime aesthetic experience for the audience. In addition, most operas teach us lessons in human morality. Persuasive efforts can typically begin with a metaphor or story. This approach has continuously proved to be the most effective way to engage the interest of the audience. In truth, all humans are artists, by continually creating themselves as entities and personas in fiction as well as life as illustrated in the cases of Roosevelt and Alexander the Great. In reality, however, one's artistic ability varies just as it does in the world of art.

Performance art

Performance art is perhaps an exception to the above. Through the use of the body or creative dress, the artist intends to make an artistic statement to express a personal impression or communicate a vision or truth. This is sometimes referred to as living art. The objective is to instantly grasp the audience's attention and ensure the message is presented in a dramatic way (i.e., lecturing to a dead rabbit held in the hand or implied messages through the use of symbols, body posture, or facial expression). Performance art has been an effective means of communication for centuries. Many have pointed out that we are all performance artists but typically bad ones. We communicate to others with our dress and body language as well as with our words. Some studies have suggested that when using communication, the spoken word is less important than body language and tone. Many persuasive historical figures such as Alexander the Great, Bishop Sheen, and Teddy Roosevelt were just more consciously aware of this technique than most. The concept of performance art has been extended to not only the way we communicate with our bodies but in the actual achievements we have. Some painters have claimed they are performing artists also because their paintings are a performance in themselves and represent the characteristics and competences and insights of the person who created them.

Leader–managers as architects

The type of artist most often associated with business leaders in literature is probably the architect. Architects design various purpose-built structures and facilitate the use of space in many ways in order to achieve definite and precise targeted ends. These artists often use a combination of scientific and artistic expressions and concepts and work under numerous restraints and limitations. In designing the interior of buildings, one is often called upon to create an aesthetically pleasant environment whilst simultaneously optimising space and safety under restraints of location, costs, client preferences, and functionality. They have to be able to anticipate future factors and contingencies such as changing functions, occupancy rates, weather conditions, and geological factors. These individuals therefore require continual learning to remain knowledgeable of any other advances in the field. Interviews with three architects by Carroll have revealed the importance of persuasive skills in this artistic profession. During a project, it is not only clients who must accept a design but it is the job of the architect to persuade a variety of other stakeholders including the planning authority, builders, and suppliers to accept the proposal. There is some anecdotal evidence suggesting that architectural designs affect behavioural conditions at work. Some claim that a beautiful school building is associated with greater school attendance, less turmoil, and enhanced learning. Similar claims have been made for industrial office buildings and factories. It is quite possible that the quality of the space where one resides or works can influence perceptions of self worth as well as communicate behavioural and performance expectations. It is also likely there exists a relationship between the space in which an event occurs and the potential for one to be more susceptible to being persuaded. For example, certain venues, settings, or environments such as the classroom or court room can elicit certain expectations of one's behaviour.

The orchestra conductor metaphor

The orchestra conductor metaphor can and has been used to illustrate persuasive leadership. We can speak of leaders as well as conductors doing good "baton" work. Conductors are called upon to effectively and concisely direct a set of diverse specialists into producing a desired aesthetic outcome. This role requires conductors to be fully aware of the strengths and weaknesses of individual musicians and, on occasion, respond swiftly to any problems and formulate appropriate modifications. Obviously, conductors need to possess great technical knowledge and keen aesthetic dexterity. They, like architects, can often improve their existing capabilities by continuously studying the work of other conductors and critically evaluating their own performances. Conductors are also teachers; prior to performance when a conductor may not appear to be doing very much they are in fact ensuring the completion of a strict period of rehearsal and training with the orchestra. Leaders, especially of quite complex organizations, behave much like orchestra conductors.

Music in aesthetics

Music is an artistic creation which attempts to elicit certain aesthetic responses that involves the use of many musical talents (e.g., tempo, rhythm, harmony, and contrasts). Music relates directly to human perceptions of time in its passing among other attributes. These characteristics are found everywhere in the natural world. For example, the child in the womb is perpetually exposed to sounds produced by the natural functioning of the mother's body such as the rhythm of her heart beat. Recent research in neuropsychology also shows that a foetus in the womb can be aware of music and other sounds from outside the mother's body [6].

It is also true of our species that different types of music can be discovered in different cultures. Such cultural variations reflect previous histories as well as the isolated experiences of different peoples. Social approval is also a factor in the acceptance of certain sounds. Humans are conditioned to accept certain sounds and sequences which are based on past experiences and social conditioning. This has resulted in an inbuilt system that assists in processing sound and determining whether these sounds are good, bad, safe, or threatening. Music has the potential to create certain emotional feelings as is clear in the extensive use of music in film to communicate certain targeted emotions. A number of psychological experiments have shown that music can predispose an audience to accept or reject certain persuasive communications [7]. There are also many studies indicating the performance benefits of listening to certain kinds of music for certain types of jobs [8].

As humans we are obviously very much oriented especially toward the human voice. Such voices communicate as well as evoke certain emotions. Singers are often the most widely respected individuals in the world. Their recordings sell in the millions and listening to them provokes profound emotional feelings in listeners. The ability of singers to convey emotional feelings about the story or situation of focus seems to be a major factor in their success. We often pay insufficient attention to our voice in spite of its importance to how we are perceived. Speech, as a form of music, has been identified by music specialists as strongly influencing the audience's emotional response. Some voices are more appealing to an audience than others and this has implications for an audience's acceptance of the performer. This phenomenon is not restricted to singers but has relevance for public speakers as well. A TV documentary described an account of a young female lawyer experiencing difficulties with her appeals to juries. A partner in her law firm urged her to obtain voice training to lower her high-pitched voice. The outcome of her training was successful and she was able to elicit more favourable verdicts from future juries. Similarly, there are cases in which political leaders are taught relaxation techniques to change the sound of their voices from a less excited and frantic manner to a composed speech delivery. For example, Margaret Thatcher, once prime minister of Great Britain, received voice coaching to lower her voice from a high pitch to a more commanding controlled delivery. This helped make her public speeches more aesthetically pleasing to her audience [9].

> "She sat listening to the music. It was a symphony of triumph. The notes flowed up, they spoke of rising and they were the rising itself, they were the essence and the form of upward motion; they seemed to embody every human act and thought that had ascent as its motive. It was a sunburst of sound, breaking out of hiding and spreading open. It had the freedom of release and the tension of purpose. It swept space clean and left nothing but the joy of an unobstructed effort."
>
> —Ayn Rand, Atlas Shrugged [10]

Humans as artists

Many artists and writers have pointed out that we are all artists; we all dance through the unique manner of our movements and we are all actors by the way we dress and talk. They contend we are all musicians due to the unique tone of our voice, writers and poets in the words we choose, and painters in how beautiful we paint our lives and careers. In an interview with a former ballet dancer, Carroll learned about her new career as a movement therapist. By teaching clients to move differently she helps them reduce pain and discomfort from different injuries. Also, by coaching executives to think consciously about how they walk and stand they can appear more self-confident and commanding in their environment.

The world is a stage, as Shakespeare once said, and we all perform on that stage as actors. In everyday life, we all create a persona or public self, and as artists we attempt to create a signature self. There is however, a hidden real self in us all and the closer the public self is to the real self the more likely it is that others will be more attracted to us. This congruence between the public and real self suggests a lack of ambiguity in one's character and as such is associated with higher likeability. Many of those in leadership positions attempt to create a public persona which can often be transparent if the leader cannot effectively act out their desired persona. Such falsity can usually be observed and detracts rather than seduces the targeted audience. A leader's public behaviour and actions must appear to be authentic and cannot be obscured by a false representation of the true nature. It appears that many ambitious, aspiring leaders fail for this reason. Also, for those who are naturally conservative or introverted the use of artistic expression can facilitate an effective release of the true person. This is often used as a form of therapy to release an individual's inhibitions and improve self-confidence in public professions such as leadership.

Great artists have the ability to see what is often or even usually unseen. In this, they are often guided by the works of previous artists that they have taken the trouble to study in depth. It's a myth that great artists create great works through their own thinking alone. Reports by great painters and writers indicate they study carefully the previous works of what they consider to be "first class" writers, painters, dramatists, etc. and build upon their insights in creating ground-breaking works of their own. Ordinary but important aspects of our world are often overlooked by most humans who are not artists, poets, or scientists. They call attention to such overlooked issues, events, or behaviours and by so doing make the rest of us aware of such things. This is, however, not always a sufficient rationale for greatness. The artists must also have the ability to use artistic means to create in an audience their engagement, interest, and understanding of the artistic message. Leaders with a true artistic sensibility will likewise have these talents, as many of them do even though they may not see themselves as artists.

Theatrical principles in leadership

Let us revisit theatre. Theatrical principles are widely used in leadership situations. Consider the elaborate ceremonies associated with the coronation of kings and queens and the inauguration of political leaders. There is a clear use of dramatic devices during such events: groups waving flags, staged applause; symbolic settings, and use of famous historic quotes from admirable historical leaders. Similar to the theatre, costumes and traditions are very important to leadership. Leaders may alter their apparel depending on the image they wish to convey. For example, political leaders might pose with guns, military equipment. Military leaders often adopt a signature uniform which creates an image which is immediately recognizable. This uniform may also be suggestive of a leader that has a certain type of human character necessary to fulfil role-specific requirements of a military leader. During World War II, the leading US generals—Eisenhower, McArthur, and Patton—all adopted distinctive uniforms which became their signature. An alternative strategy can be seen in recent political campaigns in the United States. Some politicians posed with a bowling ball or even an open bottle of beer to give an impression that s/he is a typical American citizen and provoke their audience to think s/he is indeed "one of us". Corporate leaders in the finance industry tend to dress one way—an expensive pin-stripe suit and tie.

In contrast, high-technology company executives dress in jeans and open shirts. Identifying these differences and culture-specific trends in each profession prompts a critical question which needs to be considered: How do you want to be perceived by others?

Playwrights and drama directors have many tricks and devices that they use to engage an audience and to keep it engaged throughout a performance. Boredom is to be avoided at all costs. One principle to avoid boredom is to be non-predictable and to avoid what an audience might expect. Surprises should be used. When individuals observe what is not expected their psychological arousal state tends to be high. Their interest can be engaged and maintained when interesting narratives are told or presented with unexpected twists from time to time. All persuasive efforts are likely to be more effective when they follow such principles.

The use of any existing acting skills is increasingly useful when performing a leadership role. Theatre companies now offer acting classes to managers and other leaders in their off-peak seasons. In fact, a number of consultants have long taught acting and theatre skills to managers. Some leaders such as former US Presidents Richard Nixon and Ronald Reagan studied acting formally and have actively employed such skills in their leadership roles. To their benefit, actors improve their dexterity for this art form by carefully observing other actors and imitating them within the confines of their own ability. Also, by continuously seeking out feedback from others they further develop their skills and performances. It is imperative to continually seek introspection in this process to convince an audience of the authenticity of a particular role or character. Once a character is created the actor's speech and movements must be plausible and accurately represent the particular character in all of his or her complexity. Actors are especially skilled in understanding the necessity of behavioural details being consistent. To achieve their ends actors must of course have a clear concept of the character they are to present. Leaders can do the same by studying the behaviour and performance of other leaders to improve their own competences.

Fictional versus actual leaders

Through biography and literature we can learn from the experiences of both fictional and factual accounts of leader's lives and particular meaningful events. Consider, the kings in plays by Shakespeare, Shaw's account of St Joan (one of more than 25,000 accounts of her life), Nordoff and Hall's *Bounty Trilogy* documenting the leadership styles of bona fide leaders (e.g., Captain William Bligh and his First Officer Fletcher Christian) [11, 12]. It is possible that through the study of speech and leadership styles, we can achieve higher levels of effectiveness in various situations. For example, in the *Mutiny on the Bounty* case, Fletcher Christian is challenged by some of his crew as he tries to assume the role of the ship's new captain. Cleverly, through his selection of words and his controlled speech delivery, he disarms those who oppose him. The effective adaptation of a similar approach when dealing with a hostile situation may achieve an equally successful conclusion.

All literature enables us to transcend the limited experiences in our own lives by vicariously experiencing the lives and tribulations of others who are different from us in terms of time, geography, gender, age, ethnicity, class, and so on. By its very nature, literature enables us to transcend the limited experiences in our own lives. Through the various characters in literature, we can vicariously experience different lives and tribulations. Poetry is part of literature and can often express great truths or insights in a very clear and engaging manner. Through poetry and its forms, the enthusiast's attention is captured and this consequently provokes thought. Many leaders quote poets or use poetical devices in their orations and written communications to achieve this level of engagement. By combining the lessons from the study of fictional and factual leaders one can improve their leadership delivery. We must, however, investigate and continually embrace any new research on leadership effectiveness. Leadership research is continuously emerging and is perhaps an area of great interest to non-behavioural scientists.

Behaving like an artist

The best artists have a behavioural pattern which would seem of considerable value for creating exceptional outcomes whether they are paintings, great relationships, or wonderful prodigy. One aspect of great art is the ability to examine very closely the unexamined or the overlooked. It is seeing what others do not pay sufficient attention to and often ignore. Another is the idea that one should look for the harmony in reality since the world is organized according to this principle. Another is a conscious attempt to engage and arouse the viewer no matter what form of art we are discussing. Artists also learn from one another—they build on the breakthroughs that previous artists have made. One quote on a museum wall we read says—"mediocre artists imitate, great artists steal".

SUMMARY

For certain aspects of the leadership process at work and in life, the arts and humanities can provide help and guidance to become increasingly more effective in our efforts. Leadership always has an audience, whether it is one individual or millions. To actively engage that audience and achieve understanding and motivation whilst making the message memorable is a critical aspect of leadership. Persuasive efforts first require that the message or appeal is attended to and then requires that the message and its various appeals and justification are remembered. The fine arts, poetry, literature, music, and theatre can all provide assistance in reaching such sub-goals of the communication process as we have pointed out. Furthermore, many of the most outstanding leaders in fiction and history can provide us with vivid accounts of how such leaders use the arts effectively in becoming unusually successful and memorable leaders. The artistic process itself also provides guides to all of those who want to be effective in leadership and managerial positions. See Appendix A for further discussion.

END CASE

Alexander the Great was certainly one of the most inspirational persuasive leaders in history. Setting out from Macedonia with a diverse army, over a short period of 12 years, he occupied much of the old Persian Empire and beyond. In 332 BC, he conquered and appointed himself Pharaoh of Egypt and was considered the saviour of the Greeks. As a young prince, Alexander was tutored by Aristotle at his Macedonian academy. As such, he was introduced to the works of Homer which exposed him to literature about many diverse and often heroic leaders. He was also taught Aristotle's famous ideas on rhetoric, poetics, and other such studies.

Alexander purposely designed his physical appearance, dress, and manner to imply an image to both his troops and populations he conquered that he was a "god among men". He is said to have employed several image consultants to create art works that would convey this impression to those who had not seen him. In battle, he fought fiercely at the front lines on chariot without a helmet which freed his flowing mane of hair. He was noted to have been a particularly persuasive and motivating speaker. Several films have depicted his short life. One such film portrays him mounted upon a great white horse leading his military units. During such times he would pause to deliver different persuasive speeches to each of his ethnically diverse audiences. In every way, Alexander used principles from the many art disciplines to deliver his historic speeches.

Exercise 2.1

1. Choose several persuasive leaders from history or the present that you admire. Describe how they use artistry to produce greater acceptance of themselves as individuals.

2. For these same individuals describe how they use artistic means to gain better acceptance of their persuasive messages.

3. Now evaluate yourself in terms of the degree to which you employ artistic concepts in gaining greater acceptance of yourself as an interesting and credible person.

4. Now evaluate your typical persuasive communications in terms of their employment of artistic means to make them more engaging and memorable.

Exercise 2.2

1. Think of a time when you seemed to have a success in a persuasive effort.

2. Did an artistic element have a role in this? What was it?

Works cited

[1]   Flamarion, E. (1997) *Cleopatra: The Life and Death of a Pharaoh.* London: Abrams.
[2]   Roosevelt, T. (1913) *An Autobiography.* New York: Macmillan.
[3]   Stirling, J. and Elliot, R. (2008) *Introducing Neuropsychology* (Second Edition). Psychology Press.
[4]   Yukl, G. (1989) *Leadership in Organisations* (Second Edition). Prentice Hall.
[5]   Lessing, D. (2003) *The Kreutzer Sonata/Leo Tolstoy.* New York: Random House.
[6]   Stirling and Elliot (2008) *Introducing Neuropsychology.*
[7]   Carroll, S.J. and Tosi, H.L. (1977) *Organisational Behaviour.* Chicago: St Clair Press.
[8]   Sacks, M. (2008) *Musicophilia.* New York: Vintage Books.
[9]   Thatcher, M. (1995) *The Downing Street Years.* London: Harper Collins.
[10] Rand, A. (1992, first published 1957) *Atlas Shrugged* (35th Anniversary Edition). New York: Dutton.
[11] Shaw, B.G. (1924) *Saint Joan: A Chronicle Play in 6 Scenes and an Epilogue.* London: Constable & Co.
[12] Nordoff, C. and Hall, J.N. (1936) *The Bounty Trilogy.* Boston: Little Brown & Co.

CHAPTER 3

Using words effectively in persuasive speech and writing

"With the right words, one can reach the ear of God."

—Anon.

"The non-aesthetic use of words eschews metaphor, imagery, and ambiguity. The aesthetic use of language thrives on equivocation and the possibility of multiple interpretations."

—Immanuel Kant

"It is wiser to choose what to say than to say what you choose."

—Cicero

BEGINNING CASES

Rachel Carson, born in 1907, entered the Pennsylvania College for Women to study English with ambitions of becoming a writer. She was persuaded in a science course by the eloquence of a teacher to change her major to biology and later received an MA in zoology from Johns Hopkins University. Her first of several books published successfully popularised science in 1941. Later, she published a groundbreaking book *Silent Spring* in 1962 which is credited with starting the conservation movement in the United States.

"There once was a town in the heart of America where all life seemed to live in harmony with its surroundings ... then a strange blight crept over the area and everything began to change ... there was a strange stillness. The birds, for example—where had they gone? It was a spring without voices. On the mornings that had once throbbed with the dawn chorus of robins, catbirds, doves, jays, wrens and scores of other bird voices there was now no sound; only silence lay over the fields and woods and marsh."

—Rachel Carson, *Silent Spring* [1]

"You shall not press down on the brow of labour this crown of thorns. You shall not crucify mankind on a cross of gold."

—Closing line of William Jennings Bryan's speech as a political candidate for the U.S. presidency in the early 1900s. (Two major issues were addressed—rights for labour unions and abolition of the gold standard—this speech gave him the nomination.)

"This is an electronics lynching."

—Clarence Thomas at beginning of his rebuttal of a sexual harassment charge at a US Senate hearing

"With the declining day I slowly rode over the stricken field. Around the breastworks lay a hundred and fifty of the enemy's dead and desperately wounded. We had with us, to keep and to care for, five hundred bruised bodies of men—men made in the image of God, marred by the hand of man, and must we say in the name of God. And where is the reckoning for such things? And who is answerable?"

—Joshua Lawrence Chamberlain, *The Passing of the Armies* [2]

Evolution of language

Language, through the written word or public speechmaking is the most important tool leaders and teachers use to accomplish their desired ends. Many theories propose that language evolved primarily as a social learning aid to permit a higher level of communication and group cohesion among humans. For example, recent psychological research finds that linguistic information facilitates an immediate assessment of new environments to determine its level of safety [3]. This linguistic capacity has evolutionary value as it enables clear communication of one's needs and wants and thus renders a high probability of survival. Some suggest that social learning through the use of language grows progressively more important as the social system increases in size and complexity. Greater communications in such complex social systems through rapid analysis enables the establishment of helpful social relationships rather than competitors. A comprehensive linguistic capacity increases access to diverse audiences as the message can be adapted to suit each audience's level of understanding. This also improves the ability to predict the consequences of certain behaviours and thus maximize survival possibilities. Words are essential to teaching processes and enable the human species to advance in terms of knowledge and understanding.

Importance of word choice

Effective communication is not just limited to drawing on words; the delivery is dependent on the word formulation such as the choice of words, the sequence and particularly the combination of words in certain sentences. Most books on linguistics discriminate among different methods of communicating a similar thought or intention. Great writers clearly know how to effectively draw on powerful words to communicate an insight, observation, or conclusion and most importantly engage the minds of their audience. This ability is illustrated in a beginning case about Rachel Carlson. The words she chooses and their arrangement in sentences demonstrate her skill as a writer and her expertise in translating the lessons of science into compelling narratives. Rachel's superior linguistic skills afford her access to a much wider audience to communicate her ideas and research. The field of science is particularly dependent on effective communication. A very large portion of the general population is likely to have a limited interest or understanding of this specialized subject matter. Consequently, scientists need a wide vocabulary to effectively communicate with their less scientifically minded audience. It appears, for this reason, science teachers are increasingly turning towards the arts and humanities as an aid to communicate with their students and improve their learning. In *Silent Spring*, Rachel wished to persuade the general public of the dangers of pesticides which she identified through scientific studies. However, due to the complexity of scientific vocabulary, Rachel knew this would dilute the value of her message to her targeted audience—the general public. Recognising this, she chose to discuss the consequences of misusing pesticides through accessible language to reach and engage a wider audience pool. Rachel introduced her subject matter in a dramatic, theatrical manner—the dawning of a silent spring. She had a vivid way with words and delivered eloquent and poetic prose which evoked thought in the minds of her audience—"only silence lay over the woods and fields and marsh." She of course wrote other books especially of life under the sea which were also always eloquent and informative and was very effective in using words while being interviewed on television as observed by Carroll.

Clarence Thomas was nominated to be a justice of the US Supreme Court when he was accused of sexual harassment by a former work associate. The country was divided over him. His reference to the hearings as being another lynched African American seemed to electrify the US senators and seemed to turn the tide of opinion toward him. He did win the vote and was elevated to this office. This simple sentence may have been instrumental in his victory.

Power of words to evoke emotion

The power of word is also dramatically illustrated in William Gibson's play *The Miracle Worker* which was later made into a movie. The story tells us of a young girl, Helen Keller, who—as a result of an illness when she was an infant—was blind, mute, and deaf. As a six-year-old child, Helen was introduced to Anne Sullivan a teacher for the blind, who was also partially blind. Anne attempted to teach Helen by spelling words on the palm of Helen's hand whilst placing the child's other hand on a corresponding object or person. Attempts to connect the hand spelling with the related object led to failure, time and time again. However, one day, the most miraculous thing happened, Anne held Helen's hand under a cold running tap and the child remembered one of three words she learned before she was afflicted—"Wa Wa" meaning water. Helen suddenly realized that objects had names in the form of words and these words could be learned through the sense of touch. Now Helen understood her teacher's efforts when she was drawing shapes on her palms and making her touch different objects. At this moment in the play, Anne Sullivan dramatically begins to shout out to Helen's parents "She knows!" According to one report more than half the audience typically begin to cry in response to this miraculous event. In real life, from this small beginning Helen began to thrive in her lessons to such an extent that she graduated from Radcliffe College and actually became a famous lecturer and writer. In all of these achievements she was assisted by Anne Sullivan who has been described by some as perhaps the best teacher in the history of the Western world.

The power of words to evoke emotion is true even if the words are used to mislead and to voice lies and untruths as they often are. We remember seeing a student demonstration on TV in which one student was holding a sign saying "everything in this world is propaganda". It certainly often seems that way when you view TV for a day. Advertisers, politicians, and even TV personalities are very careful to communicate half-truths or even make fallacious declarations. We are often quite aware that certain communications have the objective of manipulating our emotions by using negative or positive words to create certain mental associations with certain actions, symbols, or positions that are being discussed. Unfortunately, this is so common that it has the effect of creating a general feeling of cynicism and disbelief among us even if what is being said is truthful—this is something we need to overcome in our persuasive efforts.

Aesthetic versus non-aesthetic language

There has for a long time been a philosophical debate discussing the use of words for various purposes. The fundamental issue being addressed is the necessity to be very clear about what is being observed (e.g., the appropriate use of scientific facts when communicating scientific knowledge). Kant, one of the most widely cited philosophers and champion of reason, developed some of the most powerful arguments defending the value of non-aesthetic language. In his words "the aesthetic use of language thrives on equivocation and possibility of multiple interpretations." However, most communication does not involve the transmission of fact and even when it does the reader or listener must be receptive to the message. This usually requires aesthetic appeals of some type even if quite limited. In persuasive efforts, the use of aesthetic language is important. From our perspective, there is value in both aesthetic and non-aesthetic language; however, the choice of language is obviously dependent on the content of the speech or writing as well as the context and situation in which the message is delivered.

Function of fictional stories

Men have not lived as women, nor have Americans lived as Chinese, nor have those brought up in contemporary society lived through previous historical events. For thousands of years, the use of fictional writing whether in the context of public speaking, print, film, or stage deals essentially with the narrative. From these fictional stories, people have learned about how others live or have lived and how they have coped with various situations that are at least somewhat universal. Of course, since we have not actually participated in these life experiences that seem so accurately similar to our own lives, we are dependent on our perception of the actual accuracy of these narratives or their plausibility if fictional. Such stories enable us to transcend our limited life experiences. We do this by the process of vicariously living the lives of others. Stories can take us to new countries and cultures that are quite different from our own and into the future or through the past. Stories are engaging to us because most human beings have an inherent curious need to understand the world they live in and the other cultures that share this planet.

Use of stories in persuasion

One fundamental lesson of this chapter is to recognize the persuasive power of effective storytelling and endeavour in our efforts to incorporate these stories in our teaching and leadership roles. The use of storytelling makes technical and scientific knowledge accessible to the wider audience by engaging them and making the message memorable. For these reasons, teaching professionals delivering seminars or classes on English literature recommend the use of storytelling to capture the attention of the audience. Stories are not only effective at engaging the audience but useful for unravelling certain complicated issues as they not only address the fundamentals but also their nuances and subtleties. Carroll remembers well the power of Biblical stories to evoke interest and understanding in the fifth-grade Sunday school class he once taught.

Of course, good writing and speechmaking involves more than just the use of stories. They must be presented effectively in writing or speaking. Writing involves the construction of sentences and great writing requires great sentences. Good sentences often require considerable time and effort to construct, and focus is essential at the beginning and endings of each sentence. To maximize audience attention it is necessary to use stories that are relevant to the message intended, sentences that are clear and short, and opening sentences that grasp attention and close with a memorable ending that serves as a bridge to preceding material.

Delivering words effectively

As identified in the previous section, there are some obvious principles for planning or delivering messages. For example, words must be understandable to the audience.

Generally, this is not a problem when individuals from the same discipline or background engage in a discussion. However, difficulties arise when individuals from different disciplines or levels of education attempt to communicate. A fundamental rule of thumb is one must know their audience and adapt their method of communication to facilitate mutual understanding. A case in the next chapter gives an account of a former professor of classics and linguistics at Bowdoin College in Maine who is now a colonel in the Union Army during the Civil War who is giving a short talk to mutineers just before a battle. By giving several justifications and using words which convey powerful images and symbols he successfully persuades a group of Maine farmers, fishermen, and woodsmen to join him in a military battle. When reading this talk, one can see how he effectively communicates through the use of accessible language and expressions which they can understand and relate to.

Communication through the written word provides opportunities to perfect and assess our intended message and ensure it is suitably adapted to suit the targeted audience. There are formulas or tests that can be applied to the text to bring it to a level to match the reader's academic understanding of the material. For example, Carroll remembers serving on a PhD committee. After a short period of time he soon realized that many of the terms and expressions being used by the others were incomprehensible. This was a result of the difference between his discipline and others in the committee. Formal talk normally works best when sentences are delivered short and precise. Mark Twain once spoke about a sermon he attended and, at first, he was so impressed he decided to put a large bill in the collection plate. However, as the sermon went on and on, it became excruciatingly long and as a direct response he vowed to place less and less into the collection plate. Finally when the sermon ended and the collection plate passed by, he took ten dollars out.

Informal conversation differs from formal dialogue as it is more spontaneous in nature and can be quite receptive to many hours of stimulating thought-evoking conversation. Informal conversation is often an essential part of the persuasion process. It typically follows a formal persuasive effort. It may be the follow-up process in persuasion by the initial communicator or may arise among members of the audience spontaneously. During this phase, initial arguments may be diluted, criticized, or strengthened. In virtually all the persuasive efforts we have seen, this informal conversational follow-up process is very often a critical determinant of the overall effectiveness of such efforts.

A word used effectively is a more complicated matter. Some words and expressions are responded to more favourably than others. Words can communicate disrespect or ignorance as well as meaning. There can be an excessive number of words or too few applied to a sentence. For example, using words in unusual ways as poets do is a way to engage the listener or reader's interest. An audience may tune out when the use of trite expressions or clichés are applied to the message. As soon as they hear phrases like "let's now think outside the box" or "let's walk the talk" they are more likely to throw up than engage with the writer or presenter.

Word experts or great writers such as E.B White encourage us not to use any more words than necessary to clearly communicate a fact, thought, or idea. They also encourage the careful selection of words from many alternatives that will boast maximum impact. To actually carry out such suggestions one must review a message before it is delivered or have it reviewed by someone competent in communications. There are countless people that can perform this function quite well by rewriting, practice, and testing to ensure a more effective use of words.

Recommendation for effective use of language has not changed very much over a long period of time. Among many old books in the home library of Carroll's mother is one entitled *Principles of Rhetoric* by Professor Adams Sherman Hill of Harvard University. Although he addresses many of the points made above, he offers additional suggestions and makes his points quite vividly. He begins by stating the importance of clarity and points out that it is more important for a speaker to communicate with clarity than a writer since a speaker's meaning must be captured all at once. He points out that the interpretation of many words such as charity, virtue, freedom, nature, honour, right, wrong, and evidence will vary according to an audience. Clarity is not the only issue in the use of words, words must be effective for the purpose at hand.

> *"A man whose eyes are shut, or turned away from an object, will not see that object, however clear the atmosphere; he must be made to open his eyes and to turn them to the desired direction. Another man may take little interest in what he sees; he knows but does not feel, and will not act until his sympathies have been awakened, his imagination set to work, or his passions aroused."*
>
> —Professor Adams Sherman Hill, *Principles of Rhetoric* [4]

As indicated above, words must also be chosen on the basis of their "force", and the use of figurative metaphors can greatly increase the power of a communicative effort. Men and women can be described as gods, angels, heroes, types of animals, walls, flowers, minerals, planetary objects, or numerous other living or inanimate things. As he says, "a sentence should contain every word which is necessary to the efficiency to the communication of thought or feeling, but not one word more." Efficiency of communication means that a listener or reader is not burdened more than s/he has to be to achieve comprehension thus freeing up the maximum amount of time for understanding. All forms of verbosity must be avoided. Clearness and force is enhanced by antithesis when something is set against or contrasted as we often see in literature, science, and philosophy. He also indicates that choosing words which conform to good taste is important as well as using language which is elegant. However, modern professors of communication might not accept this last suggestion. To summarize some of Professor Hill's principles we have to use correct grammar (correctness), meaning conveyed with clearness, force, or choice of most expressive words, and lastly elegance or beauty—the aesthetic dimension.

Audience reactions to words

All individuals do not respond to the same word in the same way. The word "god" evokes many different images and ideas to various members of an audience as do simple words like manager, worker, female, male, Frenchman, and so on. Jokes can be a significant hazard to a speaker as we all know. Individuals learn words in particular settings and such words are interpreted in terms of degrees of favourability or sympathy and in terms of a listener's own identity or reference group. Often one does not know the emotional consequences of certain words to their target audience unless they know them well. Both authors, on their visits to Japan and China, have been struck by how the same word evokes very different reactions in different countries. For instance, a positive word in the United States can evoke a negative emotional reaction in China and Japan—which of course differ themselves significantly from each other in their reactions to language.

Words reflect characteristics of the speaker

Words convey thoughts and mental processes into action. The words of a speaker are a clue to that person's mental processes as well as personality. If arguments for a particular choice are presented in a very confident way it may signify arrogance or hubris to an audience with different views. If counter arguments are given in a very dismissive tone, the speaker may be viewed as one who is rigid or uninformed. The words chosen may reflect the speaker's degree of passivity, cautiousness, boldness, rigidity in thought, optimism, conscientiousness, empathy, and many other personal traits and characteristics. A speaker's choice of words creates an image of the speaker which may help or hinder the acceptability of the persuasive message whether presented orally or in writing. The wrong words can immediately open or close the minds of listeners.

Being open-minded in one's communications

Being open-minded can greatly facilitate the receptivity of an audience to a speaker's message. There is really no substitute for testing one's ideas in open discourse. One could say there is a great deal of pleasure in testing one's ideas in two-way conversations. It is critically important for the development of one's thinking to have their initial ideas confronted by those who disagree with them. This approach has been well stated by the famous political and social philosopher John Stuart Mill [5]. We might say in passing that this passage reflects the thinking of many philosophers of all types and inclinations.

> "He who knows only his own side of the case knows little of that. His reasons may be good and no one may have been able to refute them. But if he is equally unable to refute the reasons on the opposite side, if he does not so much as know what they are, he has no ground for preferring either opinion. The rational position for him would be a suspension of judgment, and unless he contents himself with that, he is either led by authority or adopts, like the generality of the world, the side to which he feels the most inclination. Nor is it enough that he should hear the arguments of adversaries from his own teachers, presented as they state them, and accompanied by what they offer as refutations. That is not the way to do justice to the arguments or bring them into real contact with his mind. He must be able to hear them from persons who actually believe them, who defend them in earnest and do their utmost for them. He must know them in their most plausible and persuasive form; he must feel the whole force of the difficulty which the true view of the subject has to encounter and dispose of, else he will never really possess himself of the portion of truth which meets and removes that difficulty."
>
> —John Stuart Mill, On Liberty [5]

SUMMARY

The power of words is immense as philosophers and writers have discussed for hundreds of years. Words have the power to inspire or depress, to elevate or lower expectations and hope, to produce love or hate, to engage or detach. It is important to use words correctly and effectively. There are many guides available for assistance on such matters. Obviously rewriting, practice, and using test subjects or audiences can also be beneficial here. Stories are always needed in effective persuasion and storytelling skills must be cultivated if one is to be effective here.

END CASES

"... and that men shall say of succeeding plantations; the Lord make it like that of New England: for we must Consider that we shall be as a City upon a Hill, the eyes of all people upon us: so that if we shall deal falsely with our God in this work we have undertaken and so cause him to withdraw his present help from us, we shall be made a story and a byword throughout the world, we shall open the mouths of enemies to speak evil of the ways of God and all professors for God's sake ..."

—Governor John Winthrop, at sea on the *Mayflower* to his followers before landing in a new English colony (New England, 1630) [6]

"In 1959, I first encountered the topic of management history in a graduate course that I had chosen to take. This encounter changed my entire life. Because of this, I entered a career in one profession rather than another, married one person rather than another, had a different income level rather than a different one, lived in a certain place rather than another, travelled to different places than I would have otherwise. This one day gave rise to many fruitful experiences in my life at later times. Let me tell you this story of my own encounters with the exciting story of the evolution of management thought."

—A professor's opening remarks to a lecture

Exercise

1. Evaluate your choice of words in speech. How could you improve?

2. Evaluate your choice of words in writing. How could you improve?

3. Evaluate your ability to evoke certain targeted emotions. How could you improve? What can you do to make your speech and writing more engaging and memorable?

4. Evaluate your degree of open-mindedness. How could you improve here? What can you do on a routine basis?

5. In general evaluate your storytelling abilities. What can you do to better utilize stories in your persuasive communications.

Works cited

[1]   Carson, R. (1962) *Silent Spring*. Boston: Houghton Mifflin.

[2]   Chamberlain, J.L. (1915) *The Passing of the Armies: An Account of the Final Campaign of the Army of the Potomac, Based upon Personal Reminiscences of the Fifth Army Corps*. New York: G.P. Putnam's Sons.

[3]   Strunk, W. and White, E.B. (2008) *The Elements of Style* (50th Anniversary Edition). Longman.

[4]   Hill, A.S. (1895) *The Principles of Rhetoric*. New York: Harper & Brothers.

[5]   Mill, J.S. (1909) *On Liberty*. New York: Collier & Son.

[6]   Beardsley, J. (1997) *A Model of Christian Charity: Governor John Winthrop (on board the Arabella)*. New York: Norton.

CHAPTER 4

Persuasive leadership and rhetoric principles

"Persuasion is achieved by appeal to emotions, use of reason and logic, or by force of character."

—Aristotle, Rhetoric

"Minds are very hard things to open and the best way to open the mind is through the heart."

—Jonathan Haidt [1]

"Always speak so that your voice reflects the meaning you are trying to convey."

—Prochnow, H.V. and Prochnow, H.V. Jr. [2]

BEGINNING CASES

"This city of all cities knows the dream of freedom ... The fall of the Berlin wall brought new hope. But that very closeness has given rise to new dangers—dangers that cannot be contained within the borders of a country or by the distance of an ocean ... The greatest danger of all is to allow new walls to divide us from one another. The walls between old allies on either side of the Atlantic cannot stand. The walls between the countries with the most and the least cannot stand. The walls between races and tribes, natives and immigrants, Christian and Muslim and Jew cannot stand. These are now the walls we must tear down."

—Barack Obama, Berlin, Germany (July 24, 2008)

Steve Jobs, one of two founders of Apple Computer Inc., is an extremely persuasive leader and is recognized as one of the founding members of the computer industry as a whole. Jobs had a remarkable ability to persuade lenders to fund his new company and employees to work long hours on the basis of a vision of the company's future. As we have seen on a TV documentary, his message often espoused that they were in the vanguard of a new revolution that would change the entire world. Computers would enable the disadvantaged and the dispossessed to gain access to the world of information and knowledge that had been previously closed to them. "Do you want to be part of the future or part of the past?" he has said. "Do you want to be involved in the creation of the most significant development in human education since the invention of writing?" His usual attire included casual jeans, sneakers, and a T-shirt which seemed to indicate that this was a new kind of executive. A famous, wealthy entrepreneur, Ross Perot, observed one of Jobs' presentations to his employees in this TV documentary and was so taken by it that he immediately called up Jobs and offered him 20 million dollars. Jobs has been described in the business press as one of the most persuasive executives in America. Each year he gives a keynote speech, often introducing new products, to stimulate enthusiasm amongst his employees and investors. He realizes the importance of continually invigorating and exciting his firm's stakeholders. However, Jobs has himself experienced failures—for example, he was fired from the company he started but since then he has bounced back each and every time. He has used these experiences as a mean of improving his outlook and effectiveness. His personal optimism and sincerity shine through his talks contributing to their success.

Persuasion principles from philosophy

Aristotle presented many principles of rhetoric or what he called the art of persuasion in his lectures. These lectures were then summarized in his book entitled *Rhetoric* which remains available today and is recommended by many students of linguistics. During this time, rhetoric was quite important to Athenian society which fully operated as a democracy. Naturally, in such a society, persuasiveness was often the source of progress and power and also key to one's survival. For example, when charged with a crime, there were no lawyers, and defendants were left to defend themselves often before a jury of 501 other Athenian citizens. In 384 BC, Socrates was forced to defend himself before a jury for alleged crimes against the state in the form of corrupting young Athenians. Socrates was a leading Athenian figure, a renowned teacher, and a hero to many. He was tried by an extremely large jury to whom he addressed in some length. This speech was described by his student, Plato, as the Apology [3]. Socrates explained his teaching to the youths of Athens emphasizing the benefits of this education to both his students and the city and refused to make a defence with the purpose of ensuring a not guilty verdict. He refused to abandon his principles in order to save his life. He was consequently found guilty by only a small margin and accepted his punishment of death by drinking a cup of poison hemlock. The death scene with Socrates on his couch surrounded by his weeping students has been the theme of several famous paintings.

In his discussion on rhetoric/persuasion, Aristotle said there were three sources of persuasion that should be used by a speaker. These were persuasion by argument, by character, and by emotion. In another lecture he indicated that the speaker's ability to persuade was influenced significantly by his intelligence, goodwill, and virtue. He stressed the importance of clarity and propriety in effective persuasive speech, putting great emphasis on appealing to the emotions of an audience. Aristotle considered emotions as a basic pivotal factor in the acceptance of a persuasive effort and suggested a speaker should attempt to elicit a particular emotional state by targeting certain emotions. This emotional state could be affected by efforts to suitably engage the audience and then use an appropriate trigger for the desired emotional state. Aristotle discussed at length a variety of possible emotional states to target such as anger, fear, pity, and the possible tactics a speaker could approach to elicit these emotional states from an audience. He discussed how the influence of the speaker's own emotional state can affect the emotional state of the audience. He also stated the importance of using a persuasive tactic appropriate for a specific situation. That is, the amount of emotion expressed by the speaker should not be too much or too little given the circumstances present.

Aristotle's opinion on the structure of communication was extremely succinct. He indicated that the introduction should explain the purpose of the speech and elicit the sympathy of the audience towards the object of the speech—for example, a person wronged. In the next narrative phase, the speaker should present his version of facts and the underlying issues in the case. It was a concern of Aristotle's that the speaker should not overwhelm the audience with too many facts but rather provide proof or support for each premise. The speaker is compelled to prove his side of the argument and thus successfully refute any possible opposing argument. To conclude the speech, otherwise known as the "epilogue", speakers should attempt to leave the audience with a favourable leaning towards their perspective and negatively towards the adversary and thus sway the audience to the intended emotional state. Finally, there should be recapitulation of the argument. When the speaker recaps the speech, Aristotle opined that persuasion is required to appeal to the basic emotions of their audience, and the use of logic is not entirely sufficient in itself. To truly engage the audience, the speaker needs not only the mind but the heart of his/her audience to realize their desired ends. Again, Aristotle preaches the importance of a speaker's ability to sell himself to their audience and convincing the audience that he is credible as a competent and trustworthy person. He highlighted that "knowing your audience" as well as your desired ends was imperative to achieve success. He said that presenting the logic of your position (or strategy) up front was important and should be followed by any counterarguments, which, in turn, you could then rebut. He also discussed the importance of brevity, of the use of appropriate attire or costume as the speaker, and communicating your passion clearly, and proposed a method to deal with such issues.

Persuasion in literature

Literature often presents us with detailed descriptions of persuasive leaders using their ability to address an audience. Although this literature, often in the form of novels or plays, is classified as fiction the protagonist of persuasion within these works would generally have their identity or origin sourced from actual historical figures. For example, in the play *Henry V*, Shakespeare describes the behaviour of this young king throughout his invasion of France in the 1400s. This includes a detailed account of his famous "band of brothers" speech to his troops. Similarly, George Bernard Shaw's play *St Joan* [4] describes a real historical French hero, Joan of Arc. *Mutiny on the Bounty* describes, albeit in fictional form, the behaviour of the leaders involved in an actual mutiny aboard a British naval vessel in the South Seas. The play *Julius Caesar*, also by Shakespeare, describes the aftermath of Caesar's murder by Roman senators several hundred years ago. In the book *The Killer Angels* by Michael Sharra, well-known historical figures are described from the US Civil War including the great northern military hero Joshua Chamberlain [5]. During this historical period, nobody accurately transcribed the precise words and behaviours. Many authors have attempted to reconstruct their behaviours, conversations, and speeches in a compelling, accurate narrative form. Naturally, persuasive talks detailed in fictional accounts by these historical figures are essentially creations of the author. Whilst these accounts are partially fictional, their actions, settings, situations, and conclusions are real. The talks themselves can be useful to study as they represent an ideal approach to persuasive speechmaking and an illustration of the principles of rhetoric we have inherited from those who have studied the subject. These talks incorporate principles from the arts which represent ideal methods of engaging an audience through the use of rhetorical speech, dress, and manner. When presented on film or stage by actors, such monologues can provide further insights into the principles of live communication. Throughout this chapter we will investigate a handful of detailed examples in literature which illustrate outstanding persuasive presentations which can serve as helpful guides to behaviour.

Henry V

In this play, Shakespeare presents one of several kings he fictionalizes which can teach us about the nature of effective and ineffective leadership. This particular play was made into at least two films which have been used by the authors in their persuasive leadership courses. In essence, the story of Henry V depicts how a young 26-year-old monarch invaded France in the mid-1400s and subsequently claimed the crown of France. After several minor victories, Henry's exhausted and ill forces arrive near a French estate called Agincourt. Here, they faced a huge and well-equipped French army. Henry overhears his cousin, Lord Westmorland, express doubts of a potential victory. As a result Henry V is motivated to give his famous "band of brothers" speech.

Westmoreland (speaking to two comrades):

> *O that we now had here*
> *But one ten thousand of those men in England*
> *That do no work to-day*

Henry V (overhearing Westmoreland and climbing atop a large rock):

> *What's he that wishes so?*
> *My cousin Westmoreland? No my fair cousin:*
> *If we are marked to die, we are enow*
> *To do our country loss, and if to live*
> *The fewer men, the greater share of honour,*
> *God's will! I pray thee, wish not one man more.*

By Jove, I am not covetous for gold,
Nor care I who doth feed upon my cost;
It yearns me not if men my garments wear;
Such outward things dwell not in my desires.
But if it be a sin to covet honour,
I am the most offending soul alive.
No, faith, my coz, wish not a man from England.
God's peace! I would not lose so great an honour
As one man more methinks would share from me
For the best hope I have. O, do not wish one more!
Rather proclaim it, Westmoreland, through my host,
That he which hath no stomach to this fight,
Let him depart: his passport shall be made
And crowns for convoy put into his purse;
We would not die in that man's company
That fears his fellowship to die with us.
This day is call'd the feast of Crispian
He that outlives this day, and comes safe home,
Will stand a tip-toe when this day is nam'd,
And rouse him at the name of Crispian.
He that shall live this day, and see old age,
Will yearly on the vigil feast his neighbours,
And say "To-morrow is Saint Crispian."
Then will he strip his sleeve and show his scars,
And say "These wounds I had on Crispian's day."
Old men forget, yet all shall be forgot,
But He'll remember with advantages,
What feats he did this day. Then shall our names,
Familiar in his mouth as household words—
Harry the King, Bedford and Exeter,
Warwick and Talbot, Salisbury and Gloucester—
Be in their flowing cups freshly rememb'red.
This story shall the good man teach his son:
And Crispin Crispian shall ne'er go by.
From this day to the ending of the world,
But we in it shall be remembered—
We few, we happy few, we band of brothers;
For he to-day that sheds his blood with me
Shall be my brother; be he ne'er so vile,
This day shall gentle his condition;
And gentlemen in England now a-bed

Shall think themselves accurs'd they were not here,
And hold their manhoods cheap whiles any speaks
That fought with us upon Saint Crispin's day.

Act IV, Scene III

Henry's army, although significantly outnumbered, wins the battle decisively. The use of archers using a new weapon in warfare, the long bow, enables the army to overcome the French mounted knights. This was achieved by a rain of arrows from above striking the horses on their less protected backs. After this battle, Henry takes command of much of France. Unfortunately, Henry dies of an illness in a few years. This sets the stage for the emergence of another inspirational leader—Joan of Arc. We shall discuss her later.

Julius Caesar

In the play and film, Brutus, Caesar's friend who participated in his assassination arrives to greet the assembled crowd of Roman citizens. Brutus expected to be lauded for overthrowing the dictator; instead the crowd is sullen and even angry. Brutus is aware he needs to defend himself and does so very eloquently using rhetoric techniques from Aristotle's principles. The crowd is inspired by his words and accepts his arguments.

When Marc Anthony is required to address the crowd, he enters dramatically with the body of Caesar covered in blood in his arms. He gently lays Caesar down on the steps. He refutes the arguments of Brutus and condemns the killing of Caesar and also cleverly uses rhetorical principles to convince the crowd that the murder was unwarranted and a terrible injustice. He shows them the wounds on Caesar's body. As a result, he succeeds at turning the crowd against Caesar's killers.

Brutus:

Romans and countrymen!
Hear me for my cause and be silent, that you may hear:
Believe me for my honour, and have respect to my honour,
That you may believe, censure me in your wisdom
And awake your sense that you may the better judge.

(he defends the assassination of Caesar—although I loved Caesar, I loved Rome more—he offers to use his knife on himself if the crowd wishes—they shout "No")

Marc Anthony (enters carrying Caesar's bloody body and lays it gently down):

Friends, Romans and Countrymen—lend me your ears

Act III, Scene II

Marc Anthony shows them the wounds on Caesar's body and ridicules the arguments of Brutus one by one in a mocking tone. He ends by telling the assembled Roman citizens that Caesar has included all of them in his will after he uses guile to trick them into asking him about the contents of this will. The crowd starts to weep and soon start to riot. Anthony looks with pleasure on the success of his talk.

Joshua Chamberlain

Lt Col Joshua Chamberlain is making a speech in a glen in the woods near Gettysburg, Pennsylvania. He stands in front of a tree facing a group of 138 mutineers from Maine that he has just been given responsibility over. He is unhappy with this burden just before an important battle. He is the leader of a Maine regiment that he himself formed with volunteers from the state and wants to persuade them to give up their mutiny and join the battle. As a former professor of rhetoric at Bowdin College he is an effective speaker. He speaks to them in a low, controlled voice with a continued seriousness often hesitating between the words and sentences he chooses. The phrasing and timing of his words and sentences is perfect.

Chamberlain:

> *Gather around me men*   (long pause)
> *Private Bucklin has told me about your PROBLEMS.*
> *There's nothing I can do about them TODAY.*
> *As soon as I can, I'll do what I can*   (pause)
>
> *I've been ordered to take you men with us.*
> *I've been told that if you don't come, I can SHOOT YOU!*
> *Well, you know that I'm not going to do that*
>
>   (speaking in a low dismissive voice while shaking his head)
>
> *... maybe somebody else will, but I WON'T*   (pause)
>
> *If you are going to come with us, there are a few things*
> *I want you to know.*
> *This regiment was formed last fall, back in Maine.*
> *There a thousand of us then.*
> *There are not three hundred of us now*   (shrugs with resignation)
>
> *Some of us volunteered because we believe in the union.*
> *Some came in because they were bored and this looked like fun.*
> *Some came because they were ashamed not to.*

Many of us came because it was the right thing to do.
All of us have seen men die. (tone of regret)

This is a different kind of army (voice rises)
If you look back at history you'll see men fight for pay or
some other type of loot.
They fight for land or because a king makes them or just
because they like killing.
But we're here for something new (pause)
I don't. This hasn't happened much in the history of the world.
We're an army going out to set other men FREE!
This is FREE ground (bending and picking up dirt)
It should be free from the Atlantic to
the Pacific Ocean (with great emotion)
In this land no man has to bow.
No man born to royalty.
Here we judge you but what you do, not by what your father was.
Here you can be something.
Here's a place you can build a home.

It isn't the land.
There's always MORE LAND.
It's the idea that we all have value, you and me;
we're worth more than the dirt.
What we're all fighting for, in the end, is each other.
The whole Reb army is camped up there,
This is no time to talk about this stuff.
If you want your rifles for this fight you'll have them back
and nothing will be said.
If you won't join us, you'll still be coming under guard. (pause)

I think if we lose this fight the war will be over.
So if you come with us,
I'll be personally grateful (spoken very slowly)

(According to the book 130 out of 138 mutineers picked up their rifles.)

They fight bravely, suffer many casualties and some say, turn the tide of the battle in favor of the northern forces. Chamberlain later receives the Congressional Medal of Honour for his valour here and in many subsequent battles. After the war he is elected Governor of Maine three times and then is appointed as President of Bowdin

College where he had been a professor before the war and later writes a famous book about the war entitled *The Passing of the Armies*, which was quoted in the previous chapter.

—From the book *The Killer Angels* and the film *Gettysburg*

Discussion of speeches

All three monologues are excellent examples of Aristotle's principle of rhetoric. The speakers had high credibility as they were highly ranked persons in their respective societies and expressed compelling noble sentiment as a purpose to their speech. All speakers took a moral stance and perspective and emphasized values that would resonate most with their audiences. For example, Henry V's values were fundamentally patriotism, valour, brotherhood, and enduring glory which are salient issues with military forces even today. Brutus emphasized patriotism—the protection of the free society of Rome and also condemned evil in politics—"the illegal seizure of power." In contrast, Marc Antony focused on reciprocal love and justice—"I have proof that Caesar loved you and he was unjustly murdered." Joshua Chamberlain discussed the importance of preserving an America as a role model of freedom and liberty for the entire world. His speech also promoted the importance of a society that was free from a social system based on class as a set of inherited privileges and instead advocated a system based on merit. This would have had great attraction for the very independent Maine fishermen, farmers, and lumbermen addressed in his speech. This audience was not made up of professional soldiers as such, so his emphasis was on the audience as citizens of a great nation with certain ideals just as Marc Anthony's address—"Friends, Romans, and Countrymen".

The speakers wore attire that conveyed their high rank and confirmed their competency credentials. All speakers sold the value of their worth exceptionally well, particularly Brutus who demanded they respect his nobility and honour. All four speakers had to be persuasive enough to overcome serious resistance to their message. Aristotle discussed the importance of building a bias to accept the emotional feelings that were the target of the persuasive leader. During military expeditions, Henry lived in similar conditions to his officers and soldiers, as a member of the army rather than a privileged king. Chamberlain was seen as a fellow citizen of Maine and not as a professional soldier from elsewhere. By not exerting their authorative entitlements or commanding their audience to obey against their will, these speakers showed respect for their audience. For example, Henry said he would not force soldiers to fight and he was willing to even pay for their transportation back to England. Chamberlain asked the mutineers to volunteer for battle and Marc invited the Roman citizens to resist the seizure of power by the fellow senators of Brutus.

All speakers would premeditate the wording of their speeches extremely carefully as would an effective poet or writer. They spoke their words with a suitable level of emotion and feeling. The words were extremely important and specifically chosen to ensure the purpose was clear to the audience and the words would engage both their hearts and minds and thus be memorable (i.e., "you're my brothers", "his terrible suffering", etc.). As Aristotle espouses, each monologue was brief and used powerful clear arguments to engage the audience's interest. Brutus flourished his dagger threatening to stab himself if the crowd wanted him to. Marc Antony made a dramatic entrance carrying Caesar's body. Chamberlain, when he talked about America, stopped to pick up soil from the land and let it flow through his fingertips. All chose a stage to perform on, which in itself, was selected for its dramatic effect (i.e., a high battlefield rock, steps of a temple, a hollow beside a tree facing a hill where the audience was seated on the grass).

In particular, Chamberlain's speech presents a wonderful depiction of Aristotle's principles of rhetoric. The mutineers are faced with great uncertainty and stress and it is suggested that those consumed with anxiety and faced with multiple options would tend to opt for a conclusion most likely to reduce that stress. If the mutineers were to continue their rebellion they faced the probability of being shot. Chamberlain eased their stress by ensuring he would not personally shoot them, but also suggested that they could potentially be shot be someone else. Therefore, by siding with Chamberlain, the mutineers felt safer. Consistent with the principle of reciprocity, when an individual receives helpfulness they consequently feel a responsibility to repay that "favor". Chamberlain showed them kindnesses through altruistic favours such as feeding them, listening to their grievances, and by giving them respect before his talk thus priming them to receive what he said favourably. As a result, they felt bound by a moral obligation to repay him by returning a favor in the way of picking up their guns and marching with him into the battle. This response is said to be harnessed from a feeling of psychological debt which is a unique human behaviour.

Many psychological experiments demonstrate the importance of social pressures in behaviour—in cases of doubt we look to our peers for behavioural guidance. At the final stage of Chamberlain's monologue, when the first few soldiers began to pick up their guns the remaining and uncertain soldiers are encouraged to follow suit. Psychological research clearly demonstrates the importance of behavioural modelling, particularly when faced with uncertainty [6]. If one has not encountered a particular situation before, one tends to look to the approach of their peers for guidance or an appropriate model to achieve a successful conclusion. As individuals are similar in certain behaviours, it is likely their reaction to experiences will be equally similar and thus a relevant role model to learn from will be beneficial to their survival. Again, Chamberlain was a "Mainer" as were the mutineers, and therefore would be perceived by his audience to hold similar values to theirs. Chamberlain's experiences of war and conflict provided further credibility to his role model potential whilst also drawing from benefits associated with his former respected position as a professor. This experience enabled Chamberlain to discuss other relevant conflicts and war through-out history in combination to his own war experiences, thus allowing him to empha-size a connection between all men in history and emphasising the brotherhood concept.

Social psychology identifies the importance of contrasting human thought [7]. Chamberlain explains that despite entering a comparatively dangerous and uncertain future, that they instead will be freed from their current potential as prisoners with all its associated hardships. Psychological experiments suggest that individuals assess the importance of an event or behaviour based on their real or potential consequences. The mutineers could have faced imprisonment and death; however, Chamberlain states that if they choose not to join war the potential costs to America and humankind in general were very great indeed. In his narrative, Chamberlain primarily uses reason to discuss his premise. This argument plays to what some clinical psychologists have discovered among individuals facing a very high risk of death—if they die they want their life to have had meaning (see Viktor Frankl [8]).

SUMMARY

Philosophy through people like Aristotle has provided future generations with a guide of persuasive principles of rhetoric which appear to be just as valid today as they were in ancient times. They emphasize that an audience is persuaded by the perceived character and credibility of the speaker in addition to the logical soundness of the message. This is combined with the speaker's ability to create the targeted emotional state that will lead to the acceptance of the actions, beliefs, or attitudes requested rather than ordered. All of these principles are needed in a situation where an authoritarian suggestion is probably insufficient given the nature of the audience and where persuasion therefore is necessary.

"The first essential of leadership is knowing how ... Much of the quality of leadership rests on a conscious or unconscious knowledge of the instinctive and emotional springs of action, since men are more motivated by emotion and instinct than by reason."

—Henry Dutton, *Business Organisation and Management* [9]

Exercise

1. Evaluate yourself on a five-point scale (excellent to poor) with respect to your credibility as a source of advice to various others you wish to persuade.

2. Evaluate your ability to use reason in your persuasive oral and written communications.

3. Evaluate your ability to evoke certain targeted emotions in your persuasive communications.

Works cited

[1] Haidt, J. (2005) *The Happiness Hypothesis: Finding Modern Truth in Ancient Wisdom.* Basic Books.

[2] Prochnow, H.V. and Prochnow, H.V. Jr. (1942) *5100 Quotes for Speakers and Writers.* Grand Rapids, MI: Baker Book House.

[3] Bertrand, R. (1959) *Wisdom of the West.* Crescent Books.

[4] Shaw, B.G. (1924) *Saint Joan: A Chronicle Play in Six Scenes and an Epilogue.* London: Constable & Co.

[5] Sharra, M. (1975) *The Killer Angels.* New York: Ballantine Books.

[6] Tosi, H.L., Rizzo, J.R., and Carroll, S.J. (1990) *Managing Organizational Behavior.* New York: Harper & Row.

[7] Brehm, S.S. and Kasin, S.M. (1996) *Social Psychology.* New York: Houghton Mifflin.

[8] Frankl, V. (1963, reprinted 1984) *Man's Search for Meaning: An Introduction to Logotherapy.* New York: Simon & Schuster.

[9] Dutton, H.P. (1925) *Business Organization and Management.* Chicago: A. W. Shaw.

CHAPTER 5

Persuasive leadership-planning considerations

"All great speeches and other works of art must start with hope."

—Anon.

"Thorough planning prevents a lot of later grief."

—Carroll and Gillen [1]

"I spent a little more than 5 hours preparing for my five minute film performance."

—A film actor interviewed on TV

"Planning skills were consistently related to managerial effectives in all of the different types of business firms we studied."

—Carroll and Gillen [1]

BEGINNING CASES

John Quincy Adams, the fourth president of the United States had a record of Public service unequalled in American political history. He served as Secretary of State and as an ambassador prior to being elected President. He followed the example of his father John Adams the third president of the United States. He only served one term because of his refusal to engage in petty politics. After his presidency, he was elected to Congress as a representative where he served for 18 years before dying in his seat in the chamber of the House of Representatives in Washington, D.C. The book and film *Amistad* describes the famous case which was brought before the US Supreme court. In this hearing, he defended a group of slaves who had taken over a slave ship, the *Amistad*, bound for Cuba which was later captured by the US Navy. He won their freedom despite a particularly pro-slavery bias contained in the courts by the judiciary and US President. His presentation to the Justices of the Supreme Court was extremely well planned by meticulous lawyers. While planning his presentation, he interviewed the slave leader and carefully studied the Justices' decisions in previous cases. The film highlights how, through his persuasive talk, he considered and correctly played to the values and concerns of the Justice. The film accurately portrays his presentation and how he dramatically points to each statue of the nation's founding fathers assuring that they would have agreed with his intent; the freedom of all slaves. Anthony Hopkins, who plays the role of Adams exceptionally well, presents the fundamental components of an ideal persuasive speech through his choice of timing, body language and tone of voice etc. It is fair to assume that this film and others containing court cases provide lessons and models from the performances of the protagonist's persuasive processes [2].

Susan B. Anthony spent her entire life trying to improve justice for women. She fought through many different campaigns over the course of her life; however, she died before achieving her fundamental goal of female voting rights. She was raised in a Quaker faith which, unlike other religions at the time, encouraged equal vocal and active participation of women in their services. Consequently, she was a rather outspoken woman which was unusual for this period in history. Her father had provided her with an excellent education and continually encouraged her to be a success. She first worked in the temperance movement whose aim was to outlaw the many evils associated with alcohol abuse. After meeting Elizabeth Cady Stanton, a fierce advocate for women's justice, she became actively involved in the promotion of women's rights and they became lifelong friends supporting and encouraging each other.

They were effective co-leaders of the women's movement, which led to Anthony assuming the role of the systematic strategist and planner and Stanton the more emotional motivator as she was a superb eloquent speaker. They created the Women's Suffrage Association using Anthony's slogan "Failure is Impossible" and became role models for women at the time. The two women were treated with severe derision and scorned by men for their activities as they were highly unusual for women. Mostly, women were passive as enforced by their husbands, fathers, and society in general. Some of the goals that Susan worked towards included legalizing divorce, having girls and boys learn together in the same classroom, ensuring equal pay for men and women doing the same job, property rights for women, and of course the right to vote.

They travelled all over the US in pursuit of these agendas even into the western frontier states and succeeded in Utah and Wyoming ensuring changes in the rights of women. These western states were more susceptible to contempory social change than the more traditional East. In 1872, Susan Anthony was arrested after persuading two poll workers to allow her to vote who later served five days in jail for their offense. Her arrest received much publicity and sympathy from other women. Her greatest success in life came from the laws that were passed after her death and were instigated by later generations of women inspired by her example. She retired at 80 years of age; however, this was not before there was a trained and capable successor to carry out her legacy: Carrie Chapman Catt, who lived until 1947, managed to see most of Anthony's agenda from women's rights accepted as law in various states. Anthony died in 1906 but could see that public opinion was in favor of the accomplishment of her vision [3].

Studying the prospective audience

A useful starting point on the preparation of your own persuasive communication would be to investigate your audience or proposed listeners. Audiences can be studied as distinct individuals or as more complicated groups. For example, Adams, in the earlier case example, was extremely aware of the needs, values, and current concerns of the Judiciary at that time. There will on occasion be an audience composed of more diverse and complicated ideals. As such, these will pose greater challenges to your preparation as it is more complicated to appeal to the salient values, concerns, and goals of a diverse audience. It may be beneficial to adopt the use of general and vague messages. By our very nature, human beings contain many differing and balancing characteristics. Some rather dark leaders may use their persuasive techniques and monologues to convince their audience to carry out various dishonourable or even criminal activities such as murder or genocide.

Building credibility

Building credibility over time involves demonstrating character and consistency in behaviour or actions which by themselves may not be viewed as significant but together work to progress your image as a suitable leader. This involves building an image which demonstrates character, expertise, and consistency. Most people like consistency in others because it makes them more predictable. People like to have confidence in their assessments about how others will behave or perform in the future whether in the short run or the long. Inconsistency suggests falsity in character and creates doubt in people's perceptions of others. We as humans enjoy the confidence provided by being able to predict or assess the proposed actions of another at any one time. In a recent political campaign for the US presidency, candidates were being criticized for inconsistencies in their deliveries. Despite this, it must be noted that consistency is not always beneficial as the famous speaker and writer Ralph Waldo Emerson said in a widely cited quote [4]. In effect, Emerson opines that being consistent with a previous ineffective approach is a bad idea. If one learns something they did not know before they should change. This will of course be inconsistent with a past behaviour or idea; however, it will ultimately improve their performance in the long term.

Obtain endorsements by influential persons

In the persuasive process, obtaining the support or endorsement from others who are respected figures in the community and audience is very common. By association these individuals act as a promotional tool for the policies, values, and of course for the individual themselves. This favourability and perceived credibility of endorsers often dissolves doubt in the targeted audience about an issue or person. If we do not understand an issue involved in a persuasive effort we often accept it if somebody we admire and trust endorses it. In the film *12 O'clock High*, which is widely used in leadership training, the general played by Gregory Peck is trying to gain acceptance for new approaches to improve the performance of an air squadron. Peck tries to recruit highly admired pilots to endorse his plans. By ensuring their endorsement and through various other approaches, Peck manages to achieve greater acceptance of his goals and plans and then this is followed by much higher performance by his pilots and airship crews. Research in social psychology indicates that in all social identities there are certain individuals who can be labelled "influentials" [5]. Very often the process of persuasion is an indirect path from the persuader to various "influentials" and then to the audience which is the object of the persuasion efforts.

Build competence and coalitions

A successful message delivery to an individual or group may depend on the targeted individual's learning capacity to eliminate previous incorrect behaviours in favor of more effective ones. In the film *12 O'clock High*, Peck begins a detailed review process of each mission and utilizes each squadron member by allowing them to contribute to the decision-making process. Throughout the process he ensures that each mistake is highlighted and gives reasons as to why the behaviour is incorrect. In addition, he uses work assignments as punishments or rewards for effective and ineffective behaviour.

The political process often involves building coalitions of individuals or groups to facilitate the acceptance of a person as a leader and the programmes this leader endorses. The creation of a coalition often involves bargaining with such a group and emphasising the benefits or goals they desire. On acceptance of these terms, the coalition leader can be anticipated to influence their party members. An example of a successful acceptance of coalition is a US governor's effective ability to persuade a teacher's union to lobby and support an initiative to build several gambling casinos by promising to distribute some of the proceeds to public schools.

Gather facts and arguments in favor of goals

Individuals and groups must be convinced also, at least to some degree, by the logical arguments that an individual persuader uses as well as the evidence supporting such arguments. Of course, logic and evidence can support the notion that the persuasive effort is justified for a variety of reasons. The extent to which a persuader needs to emphasize facts depends on the nature and educational background of the audience. Audiences differ in terms of their use and acceptance of rationality as opposed to perhaps more emotional approaches. It could be argued that increasing the use of reason in human decision making is always desirable. In recent years, there has been a greater emphasis on using evidence-based approaches in many professional fields such as medicine and management. This approach imitates the scientific perspective which is of long standing in the sciences. It is beneficial to ensure that you have gathered arguments and data in advance and highlight the positive effect of your proposed change and the consequences if these proposals are not implemented.

Plan for creating arousal/activation and more memorable messages

A message cannot achieve its persuasive goals if it fails to be received or contained by the audience. The audience can become interested in the message if enticed to pay attention which can be achieved by implementing some basic principles. Such principles include creating a riveting personal experience, an engaging story, some interesting facts, poll results, some arresting image in the form of an unusual costume, or the use of graphics. The delivery of a persuasive message is generally intended to ensure the manifestation of a particular intended future action from the audience. As such, the content and message must be memorable. The use of a "take away" or repeatable quote or poetical expression can help. In fact, poetical devices such as repetition, intelligent metaphors, and clever rhymes are proven to ensure the memory of a message. Certainly, many consider the most memorable persuasive communication in American history to be the "I have a dream" speech by Martin Luther King in 1964. King enabled an increased drama for his speech by standing alongside the great statues of Lincoln at the Lincoln Memorial in Washington. The speech began with King making references to the unfinished work of Lincoln by providing freedom to slaves. Also, by repeating the term "I have a dream", the audience left with King's evoking message circulating in their minds and wondering about his proposed ideals.

Planning for message content

A question raised by some in communications is: Which is most important in terms of effective persuasion—the message or the delivery? Research provides mixed conclusions to some degree. In the famous Dr. Fox studies carried out with college students a number of years ago an actor, Michael Fox, was hired to present a lecture which had variety in the content and the delivery [6]. In the two most extreme conditions a very factual lecture was given in a very boring manner whilst on another occasion the content consisted of a lot of nonsense whilst the delivery was very lively and animated. The latter presentation was rated much higher by the students.

In another well-designed experiment at the University of Maryland, a speech was given to MBA students by a business owner in several different ways. The message was varied in that it was compelling and interesting and the delivery varied in several ways ranging from boring to charismatic. In this study, the content of the message was more important than the delivery in eliciting desired responses from the audience. The study concluded that one does not have to have charisma in order to be effective in persuasion [7]. In terms of planning, it seems most wise to plan for both an effective message and an effective delivery. However, how does one define an effective message and delivery? In 2008, this approach to speechmaking came under scrutiny in the US presidential primaries. Here, multiple candidates across the political spectrum competed to persuade the electorate to vote for them to lead the country. It is extremely likely that all the messages needed to be generalized as there are time restraints imposed by the debate format. Also, television broadcasts of political talks are generally very brief due to the limited interest of the viewing public. The delivery aspects of the presentations, how something was said rather than what was said, seemed to vary among the candidates.

Preparation

The actual success of a persuasive effort is likely to depend on a number of previous behaviours of the leader. Again, in accordance with Aristotle's perspective and later research, trust and respect based on credibility for the persuader has the power to significantly create a positive receptivity to a message prior to being delivered. Writings on trust point to various key elements in its creation [8]. One type of trust focuses on the perceived expertise of the communicator in which experience, credentials, and actual performance would be critical factors. For example, a sports coach with a winning record would inspire more of this competency-based trust than a coach with a losing record. Another type of trust might be called character trust. Does a leader always tell the truth in their ethical dealings with others? The final type of trust might be called benevolence. Can I trust the leader to be concerned with my needs and problems in combination with his/her own self-interests? It is clear that these types of trust are influenced by the actual observations of a leader behaving and performing over time.

Practice

Virtually all actors say that practice is an important element when working towards delivering a good performance, and if possible practising live before a group willing to provide helpful feedback can be valuable. Without such practice, going over your presentation mentally can help. Research suggests that mental modelling will favourably impact a wide variety of future performances [9]. Studying the audience in advance can be critical if one lacks actual experience with the audience. Looking at surveys and talking to individuals with experience with the group can help. However, relying on people who typically are blind to reality can have an adverse effect and be very dangerous to the performance. During preparation, it is very important that the speakers or persuaders sell themselves on their proposals. Audiences appear to place a lot of emphasis on the importance of the level of emotional expression and enthusiasm shown by the speaker.

Choose optimum timing and setting

Research clearly shows that a more positive mindset can be created in an audience as a direct result of greater attention to the setting and timing. Obviously people are more positive at certain times than at others. The core questions persuaders need to address are: When is the audience most likely to be in a good mood? Which setting might work best? Reminding the audience of favourable things, a victory by the group, or reminiscing past happy times can help in the achievement of this goal. The use of photographs, symbols, and other aspects of a setting can help. T.S. Lin, the CEO described in Chapter 2, held meetings in a hall with photographs of the company's facilities all around the world with the many awards won by the company displayed. Carroll remembers giving a brief and focused talk at Black & Decker. He was in a room which held displays of organizational charts of every company unit and their corresponding manager's name in large letters.

Emotional appeals

Aristotle said that persuasive effectiveness requires an appeal to the emotions which are usually the primary response to a person or appeal [10]. Often, reasoning may follow an initial emotional response and may only provide a justification for it. Hume, another philosopher, states that reason is simply the slave to a particular emotion [11]. Aristotle believed the persuader should know in advance which emotion should be targeted at the audience—anger, guilt, revenge, sympathy, etc. In his principles of rhetoric, he provides suggestions on how to elicit the targeted emotion. Of course, it is important that the persuader's emotion is consistent with the emotion targeted and the theme of the message.

Use of dramatic principles in persuasion planning

As previously indicated, we are all actors performing on a stage. A play is similar to that of a professional presentation as we are often trying to appeal to a group in an engaging and memorable fashion. The aim of such presentations is to capture the attention and excitement of our audience and ensure they are more aware of certain issues post presentation. Principles of playwriting can be useful in preparing and designing such presentations. In a play, a story must be told and contain a certain theme or a message. Therefore, a unity of actions and stories around the chosen theme or goal must be deciphered. To sustain the audience's engagement, boredom is to be avoided at all costs; this can be achieved by introducing variation in the structure of the presentation. The closing of a presentation should always be dramatic and memorable.

Creating an engaging character—yourself

In a play, actors must create a character through their own behaviour. Although playwrights describe such characters and give them scripts, they know ultimately that the actor's conception of the character gives it life and vitality. To achieve this, the actor must have a sense or perception of the character and embody the finer traits of the character's behaviour if s/he is to be considered credible. The actor's basic energy and ability to communicate emotional states accurately through facial expressions and body language is important. To do this, a precise conception of a character on the part of the actor is necessary. Different actors have different approaches for achieving such ends. Actors put themselves in the appropriate emotional mood using a variety of methods depending on the features of the character the actor assumes. Some may recall a similar emotional situation in their own life or imagine a comparable situation which could elicit a similar emotional response. Some actors or speakers can simply convince themselves about the truth of a message they will deliver. Whatever the process, if the speaker is viewed as being insincere, false, or untruthful, the message will be rejected.

In ordinary life, if we want to make ourselves into an interesting and appealing character we must also ensure our behaviours, words, and other actions are consistent. Also, one needs to communicate one's emotional feelings about various issues or perceptions both accurately and transparently. Of course creating yourself is not an easy task and usually requires the help of others for assessment purposes as it is often difficult to see yourself in an accurate way. Feedback from therapists or friends acting as therapists may be necessary.

Learning acting skills

Observing actors on a stage or in films can provide many ideas on how to present our own ideas and selves more effectively. As Shakespeare and numerous others have pointed out, we are all actors and always perform on the stage of life. We can learn a multitude of acting skills and techniques in the form of voice, diction, inflections, timing, and the use of hands and expression of emotions by watching actors perform. After all, reports from successful professional actors indicate this is how they learned their skills (i.e., largely by observing their predecessors). Actors often practise in solitude in front of mirrors and before a small test audience to learn a character or role so that it becomes natural. Many actors try to master the emotions that would be natural to a particular character, thus allowing the actor to reproduce a proposed emotional response at certain times throughout the character's life. Being able to express such emotions in a variety of ways is important. People are drawn to those who honestly express their feelings or emotions. Being uncertain of another renders them suspicious or rejecting of that person. However, it needs to be noted, acting doesn't mean being false, it means being true. We are all called upon to play various roles in our lives and we can learn to perform them more successfully through careful observation and practice.

Process of planning

Management studies carried out by the authors indicate that managers do not necessarily plan by sitting down alone with paper and pen consciously drawing up a detailed plan. They, like all of us, carry around a mental agenda of things we would like to do or achieve in the near or far future. Then in their hours awake (and sometimes in their sleep) useful ideas pop into their minds which relate to various items in their mental agendas. Such ideas are often created from exposure to information through social contact, from material read, experiences observed, or even from exposure to various types of TV programmes. The wider the world that individuals expose themselves to, the more ideas they tend to have. Of course, exposure to sources of information of doubtful competence, expertise, knowledge, or intelligence may turn out to be more harmful than useful.

Using the arts in planning

Again learning from the arts involves a study of some aspects of aesthetics. The dictionary definition of aesthetics is directly defined as the study of good taste or beauty. Aesthetics has been the focus of research in various fields of philosophy and attributes sensations of beauty to different characteristics of what is being experienced. Psychologists also study aesthetics and often attribute it to learned responses. B.F. Skinner, the famous psychologist, once said that an impression that something is beautiful is merely a reflection of other emotional feelings such as goodness, correctness, awe, and is the result of conditioning or learning [12].

The word "beautiful" is used to describe objects, images, or events and this association is then stored in the brain's memory. Many psychologists claim there is an inherent human attraction towards harmony, symmetry, and colour. Evolutionary psychology provides an explanation that this attraction may be related to the libido and the desire to mate with a healthy, stable person to continue the reproductive process. These studies suggest that "beauty" is an influential factor in mate selection and triggers the desire of genes to reproduce for the survival of future generations.

When one perceives a "beautiful" person, action, object, or event it naturally arouses attention and interest and is thus retained in the memory for future encounters. There are also aesthetic responses to words. Combinations of words and their expression can convey images and thoughts which are processed as especially engaging or beautiful. For example, the word "sublime" reflects a person's deep aesthetic response and is often used in response to various literatures or short stories about particular events in a person's life. As such, aesthetics plays an important role in the performance of the persuasive leadership process and in the achievement of desirable ends. New research on leader effectiveness is always emerging and leaders should keep up to date about new perspectives of leadership as they evolve. Hopefully this book can contribute to the education of current leaders performing their role responsibilities both at work and in life. In subsequent chapters we shall describe some of the ways that the arts can help accomplish the end intentions of our persuasive efforts.

Stories have always engaged us, and they especially do so when they follow certain formats, as courses in literature tell us. In drama often a first act describes how different characters are influenced by circumstances and how they move steadily upward into a conflict situation. These situations are then interestingly presented. The conflict is then often resolved in a second, third, or later act. A principle to follow here is a unity of action and a unity of climax. Unity and harmony are essential aspects of all of the arts and of aesthetic responses to artistic creations of various types. Of course it depends on what type of drama it is. Aristotle made a distinction between tragedy and comedy. Carroll remembers a teacher suggesting a rule for a short story to be presented was "get them into trouble and then get them out of it at the end." Stories can be very brief (e.g., a joke told by a comic). As the story progresses tension is induced in the listeners and they anticipate an end with a set of expectations. This is debunked in the surprise punchline and the tension suddenly explodes in mirth (hopefully). The authors and most others have enjoyed mysteries perhaps because they also end with surprises—with what was not anticipated. Of course stories should have characters which are vivid and interesting to the particular targeted audience and the dialogue should have poetic power. Stories about human relationships can have great power since human relationships themselves can be viewed as beautiful to observe. The persuasive leader in creating stories that will help to persuade must remember some of the principles for storytelling which we admit as authors we often neglect ourselves.

SUMMARY

A great deal has been written about some of the principles of interpersonal persuasion. This material is in the form of research findings and also principles derived from observations of effective and ineffective persuaders. There is much written on the disciplines of speech and especially public speaking. These are guides to planning the persuasion process. Both of the authors have been exposed to these subjects and this chapter represents our opinion on the more important practical implications of this material.

END CASE

Huey Long was a charismatic politician from Louisiana during the 1930s. He gained wide political support through his speeches over the entire United States, however, and with a very populist theme. He carefully planned his speeches to make them appear dramatic and appealing and often referred to local situations and problems. In the 1930s, he threatened the re-election of Franklin Roosevelt. However, the threat was averted when he was assassinated in 1936 by a disgruntled physician constituent in his home state.

"I believe that everyman is a king but nobody wears a crown."
"How many of you own 4 suits, 3 suits, 2 suits, 1 suit? You know how many suits Vanderbilt (a very rich man) owns? He has a hundred suits."
"Under this very oak tree here in Louisiana, Evangeline (subject of a famous poem) waited all her life for her husband to return to her to no avail. The people of this county have waited under this tree for even a longer time. They have waited in vain for better schools, decent roads, and decent employment opportunities but your tears have flowed to no avail."

—Richard White, *Kingfish: The Reign of Huey P. Long* [13]

Exercise

1. Observe the persuasive communications of various leaders in life or at work and reflect on the planning considerations that are likely to have taken place to make this an effective or ineffective presentation. What can we learn from examining these chosen presentations?

2. Evaluate some of your past persuasive communications. List what worked well and what did not. On this basis make a list of recommendations to yourself on what you should do in the future.

Works cited

[1]   Carroll, S.J. and Gillen, D.J. (1987) How useful are the classical management functions in describing managerial work? *Academy of Management Review*, **12**, 38–50.

[2]   Jones, H. (1988) *Mutiny on the Amistad: The Saga of a Slave Revolt and Its Impact on American Abolition, Law and Diplomacy*. Oxford University Press.

[3]   Lutz, A. (1976) *Susan B. Anthony: Rebel, Crusader, Humanitarian*. Zenger Publishing.

[4]   Emerson, R.W. (1836) *Nature*. The University of Michigan.

[5]   Tosi, H.L., Rizzo, J.R., and Carroll, S.J. (1990) *Managing Organizational Behavior*. New York: Harper & Row.

[6]   Ibid.

[7]   Ibid.

[8]   Smith, K.G., Carroll, S.J., and Ashford, S.J. (1995) Intra- and interorganizational cooperation: Toward a research agenda. *Academy of Management Journal*, **38**, 7–23

[9]   Tosi *et al.* (1990) *Managing Organizational Behavior*.

[10] Hill, A.S. (1895) *The Principles of Rhetoric*. New York: Harper & Brothers.

[11] Hume, D. (1910) *An Enquiry Concerning Human Understanding*. Harvard Classics Vol. 37.

[12] Skinner, B.F. (1953) *Science and Human Behavior*. New York: Macmillan.

[13] White, R.D. (2006) *Kingfish: The Reign of Huey P. Long*. Random House.

CHAPTER 6

Audience characteristics

"There comes a time in the affairs of men, when they must be prepared to defend not their homes alone but the tenets of faith and humanity on which their churches, their governments, and their very civilization are founded ...
This generation has a rendezvous with destiny. To us much is given; more is expected. This generation will nobly save or meanly lose the last best hope of earth."

—Franklin D. Roosevelt

"A Roosevelt victory will mean that grass will grow in the streets of a hundred cities."

—Herbert Hoover in election campaign in the US 1932

"I always paint my figures with their eyes closed. I do this because I believe most individuals are blind to the humanity of others."

—An American painter

BEGINNING CASES

Napoleon as a young commander in Italy

(to his generals)   *We are vastly outnumbered and more deficient in arms but we will triumph because we have an effective strategy.*

(to his ordinary soldiers) *I know you are tired, hungry, and cold but I will take you south to great fertile plains where you will have everything you want and need.*

(to the Italian people)   *I am here to break your chains.*

—From the film *Napoleon*

"Russia needs a leader who is strong and wise because that fits national instinctive characteristics. A strong hand is more important than institutions. That is why Stalin is considered a hero—he did necessary things."

—Vladislav Surkul, *The Economist* (November, 2007)

Audience characteristics

The reaction of an audience to presented material has long been a concern of the arts. A playwright, for example, ancient or modern, knows that he or she must present their work to an unknown future audience. Such an audience is likely to have diverse characteristics and preferences. Shakespeare dealt with this issue by the use of several levels of languages and themes which would appeal to individuals from different social classes. Successful modern playwrights also are aware of their prospective audience's preferences. In today's world, to ensure a successful outcome to any persuasive effort, its content must be in tune with the characteristics of its targeted audience. If this is not the case, a persuasive communication may not be successful. First, the audience must be aroused, must understand the message, accept the message, and finally must be able to comply with what is being requested. The message should be designed to facilitate the various needs, values, intellectual levels, and situational characteristics (e.g., time, resources, and authority) of the audience. Of course, with a diverse audience, the persuasive effort must be tailored to appeal to each different group. For example, Napoleon used different persuasive efforts to appeal to his different audiences. A documentary film about Alexander the Great implied that he was well aware of the necessity to tailor his appeals to his audience. The film presents him upon a great white horse riding down in front of his many culturally diverse military units. As he stops to address each group, he adapts his appeal to fit the cultural values and concerns of each ethnic group. Herbert Hoover's disastrous prediction of his opponent, Franklin Roosevelt, was accepted by his Republican audience but rejected firmly by the larger audience in the population. Roosevelt's constant reference to a particular generation and their unique historical responsibilities had positive emotional effects on his targeted audience.

Similarly, marketing research efforts are carried out to understand the particular problems, concerns, and needs of various audiences resulting in brainstorming and troubleshooting ideas to investigate the credibility of alternative messages. This research can be conducted via telephone or face-to-face interviews, questionnaires, or by focus groups to get feedback on different proposals. Such studies are commonly used to investigate the outcome of political and jury appeals with a certain composition of individuals representative of the actual target audience. Also, on occasion, the study of the actual past behaviours of certain groups can be very informative to anticipate the audience's response in future settings.

Audience to leader effects

There are many examples of how the presence of a live audience can energize leaders and make them perform more effectively. A live audience can stimulate the leader or performer and foster creativity. Musicians often reflect on the difference between their live performance in comparison to how they perform at a rehearsal or studio recording. The Guarneri Quartet, in residence at the University of Maryland one day a month, has been observed in performances and practices for more than 20 years by Carroll. At one particular monthly session after rehearsal, the first violinist mentioned that in their London rehearsals they played horribly for about an hour. However, when a famous cellist, Jacqueline du Pré, came into the auditorium and took a seat they began to play the next piece better than they had ever performed it in their lives.

To illustrate with another example, in a TV documentary on General Eisenhower's memoirs, he mentioned meeting American troops in England before they set off for the invasion of France [1]. He reported his pessimism and his gloomy projections about the likely success of the invasion. However, when he met and spoke with his soldiers who appeared ready for battle, he experienced a significant elevation in mood which lifted his optimism and self-confidence. Before retirement, the first author in his last honours course liked to start off the class with a very difficult question. His best student sat in the middle row of the classroom and from her expression was clearly confident of a good answer while the other students were unsure. To her credit, she would always give others an opportunity to address the question first and if that did not happen, she would then give a wonderful answer. Her enthusiastic presence in the classroom each day stimulated the teacher to escalate the level of material discussed that day. There are countless examples of managers and school principals who have demonstrated effectiveness by adopting a management-by-walking-around philosophy. This denotes the importance of not remaining confined to one's office throughout the day but rather promotes the value in walking around and meeting subordinates, employees, and students on an unplanned face-to-face basis. This simple process not only enables the leader to determine what is really going on, but places humanness to any directives and plans. Adopting this style of management allows one to become acutely aware of the competences and motivation of the human organization he or she is managing. In one private school known to Carroll, there was a contrast in the management approach between an older retired principal and a new principal who did not like to leave the confines of her office as she felt more secure and less threatened. Respect and liking for the new principal was consequently much lower compared with the previous principle who still visited the school on occasion.

Use of participation

If a group or an individual is given the freedom to arrive at a decision themselves, it will increase the probability that they will accept the decision. However, the trouble with this proposal is the uncertainty that they will make poor decisions. Over the years a number of approaches for using participation with groups (or individuals) have been recommended. One such system of using participation in leadership situations has been proposed by Norman Maier, a psychologist from the University of Michigan, based on considerable research. Carroll has taught this method for more than 30 years to managers and has found that it has yielded a very good response. Maier suggests that when a leader is making a decision of whether to allow a group to participate in decision making, s/he must first decide whether the issue being addressed is one that relates to the followers' needs or impacts them in some significant way. Another factor which needs to be determined is how important is it for the best solution to be chosen? Is there a quality alternative? Some decisions have high-acceptability requirements but low-quality requirements and others the opposite, where quality is important but acceptability is not. Some decisions have both high-quality and acceptability require-ments and some are low in both of these deciding attributes. If acceptability requirements are high then group participation is necessary. In these cases, if quality requirements are low (how the room is cleaned or which of a group is on vacation at a particular time) the group or individual is given the right or authority to make the decision. If there are high-quality and high-acceptability expectations, then the group or individual may have to be guided towards a good decision. Maier's research indicates that achieving high acceptability will primarily occur [2]:

(1)   when each person involved participates in the discussion;

(2)   when each person gets to talk and present their own ideas;

(3)   when each person involved feels they received a benefit from the choice;

(4)   when each person feels respected by the others;

(5)   when each person involved feels a high-quality choice was made.

Maier's research suggests that obtaining a high-quality decision (a good choice) will most likely occur:

(1)   when there is agreement on what the problem or issue is;

(2)   when the discussion moves from issue, to possible solutions, and THEN to choice;

(3)   when a conflict of ideas is encouraged;

(4)   when all available facts are considered;

(5)   when sufficient time is given to the deliberations;

(6)   when solutions from other different situations are not allowed;

(7)   when the problem or issue is discussed at two time intervals not just one;

(8)   when the group making the decision is not too large.

In teaching this approach, Carroll would use hypothetical role play that he learned from observing Maier in two companies in which he was training leader-managers. In Maier's approach to role playing, the class is divided into smaller groups and individuals are assigned a role in an imaginary situation or case. Each participant is called upon to perform while the group arrives at a decision. Different groups perform this role play differently and their accomplishments are publicized. In this way, the validity of Maier's recommended system is demonstrated through the participation of managers performing as actors in the role play activity.

Audience concerns

An audience may consist of students, family members, employees, and many other types of individuals. Each audience is different and many of these groups have been studied in an attempt to identify their concerns. For example, thousands of studies investigate what factors produce employee job satisfaction. One method used by the authors and many others involves asking an individual to compare a particularly good day in the past year with a particularly bad day in the same period. This approach is rather revealing as it highlights the job occurrences that are especially important to the individual. In a number of such comparisons it was found that the most important events related to having a good day were:

(1)   achieving a high level of performance;

(2)   receiving recognition from others for doing good work;

(3)   receiving an advancement, increase in responsibility, or an unexpected pay increase;

(4)   being given an interesting assignment.

In remembering a bad day in the previous year, employees cited:

(1)   failing to finish a task successfully;

(2)   receiving criticism from others;

(3)   failing to receive an expected reward;

(4)   being given an unpleasant work assignment;

(5)   being treated unfairly.

Psychological needs of the audience

The more fundamental psychological needs of human beings have been studied extensively and there have been many proposed lists pertaining to this subject. There is a general acceptance that such needs are often activated in a certain sequence and may vary in an individual from one period to another. Some of the more early lists indicate that survival needs are the most basic and are followed in order by a need for security or predictability, a social need, a need for respect and self-esteem, and a need for achievement, respectively.

Effect of cultural differences in audience responses

Human beings with different cultural values often differ in their response to various types of appeals. Both authors have carried out research illuminating the consequences of having a high collectivist orientation compared with a primarily individualistic orientation. Those with a higher collectivist orientation see themselves and describe themselves as a person or an identity whose life primarily revolves around performing a social role in a group or society (e.g., father, mother, manager, etc.). Those high in individualism describe themselves with individualistic oriented terms (e.g., optimistic, happy, or ambitious). While societies differ in their average propensity towards one of these orientations (Japan—collectivist; US—individualist), there is also variation within such nations. For example, Carroll found MBA students describe themselves as individualistic whereas military officers, in the same class, were primarily collectivist in their orientation. Of course, various cultures place different levels of respect and importance in higher authority, class and gender differences, religiosity, and other factors. This, however, does not imply that each nation has widespread cultural uniformity on such issues. As such, these factors affect the need for a leader to adapt his/her style to various audiences. An appeal to US and Australian managers might be the same, as many of their values tend to be the same. However, a persuasive appeal to a Japanese manager may have to be different to be effective. Carroll carried out a study which indicated that for US managers a message projecting unethical behaviour is bad for you but could be effective for the company [3].

However, in Japan the more effective message might suggest that unethical behaviour is bad for the company. Thus, collectivist appeals are especially likely to resonate in Japan and with military groups.

Motivational propensities in an audience

In persuasive efforts it is necessary that an audience not only receive, understand, and accept a message but be willing to act upon it. Many different motivational processes have been studied over the years resulting in many philosophies and motivational models. The expectancy model has been frequently studied and used by the authors and it is found to be predictive of taking action towards a goal and actual achievement. There are two basic components or requirements for achieving what is ordered or recommended. The first expectancy is the belief that a person or a group can actually attain the goal. Research indicates that this expectancy is based on previous accomplishments of something similar in the past or observations of somebody who succeeded in a similar achievement in the past. Carroll is a volunteer health counselor to those afflicted with a paralysing disorder. Since this author recovered from the same illness, he simply shows himself moving and walking in a fairly adequate way to create an expectation that this illness is recoverable. This provides motivation in the other to commit to a similar program of physical therapy and exercise to overcome their affliction.

The second set of expectancies focuses on the perceived good or bad consequences of achieving a certain performance level. For example, Carroll, in a study of factory workers, found that, despite being rewarded with greater remuneration, such workers would not attempt to achieve a daily difficult work goal if the achievement resulted in a high degree of fatigue or criticism from fellow workers [4]. However, within the following weeks as the need for money increased the level of worker achievement increased. The implications of this research for persuasive messages are obvious. Despite this, highly persuasive leaders, such as Jack Welch at General Electric, can sometimes overcome these conditions to encourage employees to accept "stretch" goals which are extremely challenging.

Occupational differences

Research has identified that occupational differences exist in values and concerns. Some of the most pressing concerns of nurses and physicians, for example, may be different because of their situation. While both physicians and nurses desire respect, it appears that nurses complain most about not receiving it in sufficient amounts. Many surveys have indicated that managers and engineers often differ significantly in values and orientations. The very popular comic strip "Dilbert" in many US newspapers attempts to highlight these differences with some obvious degrees of over-embellishment. It is interesting to note that the cartoonist receives many of his ideas from engineers who send him e-mails referencing their on-the-job experiences. Research in the form of surveys has also identified value differences, perspectives, and concerns between physicians and psychologists, workers and managers, economists and sociologists, business and government employees, and many other groups. Obviously, persuasion failures are probably more probable when the persuader and the audience are of different occupational groups than when both share occupationally similar perspectives and values.

Gender, ethnic, racial, and age differences

Whilst marketing professionals often use different persuasive strategies with men and women, this may not be entirely justifiable when communicating to men and women.

Research suggests that most approaches and appeals appear to work in the same way for women and men. There is, in fact, a wide variance within each group in terms of abilities, motivations, interests, and values in spite of what is often alleged by various social-political organizations. Over the past 80 years, thousands of research studies have been carried out investigating the link between sex, race, and ethnicity differences on different personal characteristics such as intelligence, personality, aptitudes, and emotional actors. In general, these studies concluded that differences within any such group are almost always greater than the average difference between various groups by a large margin. Of course, there are some differences that can be expected. Women are especially sensitive to sexual harassment issues and sexually oriented humor as many male supervisors have found to their dismay. Ethnic and racial slurs can occur if a particular communicator is not sensitive to this possibility. The majority of these differences are more obvious human differences and are not associated with differences in performance. Usually, but not always, a difference doesn't make a difference.

Individuals who differ in age also differ in many other attributes as well (e.g., career stage, life cycle, etc.). One's marriage situation, earnings, career plans, and job concerns are likely to differ due to age differences. Some recent research found that younger voters were attracted to the candidate associated with change while older voters put a greater emphasis on experience and stability when choosing a leader. Age is often related to differences in religious, political, and economic values and beliefs. These differences may make an impact on the response to certain types of persuasive appeals.

SUMMARY

Both ancient and contemporary authorities on persuasion suggest a persuasive leader/teacher should tailor persuasive appeals to known characteristics of the audience whether aimed at an individual or a group. Aristotle indicated that in persuasive messages certain emotions should be targeted. Obviously the current emotional state of the audience would have to be considered. We have identified some audience characteristics that might be most salient in doing this. These include values and attitudes, decision-making characteristics, motivational propensities, experience differences, cultural differences, sexual differences, age differences, and others. Of course, just knowing an audience's makeup is not sufficient. One can have incorrect assumptions about the characteristics of that audience. As a result, a pilot presentation on a hypothetical audience who are representative of the actual audience is typically recommended by persuasion experts.

END CASE

"Persuading a business audience of the advantages of going into bankruptcy would likely elicit quite different responses in a Japanese audience as compared to an American one. In Japan, going into bankruptcy is considered a social sin and bankruptcy would destroy the ability of the Japanese firm to stay in business in the future. This is not so much the case in the U.S. where firms who have gone into bankruptcy often function quite well after this event."

—Carroll and Gannon, *Ethical Dimensions of International Management* [5]

An American professor described to a diverse audience some of the excesses that took place in China during the Cultural Revolution in the 1970s. Later a Chinese student wrote a letter to the Dean complaining about how this teacher had slandered the Chinese people. The Dean was quite used to this type of problem as several groups of women had complained to him in the past of what they felt were insults to women made by male professors during lectures in the form of jokes or comments. In addition, conservative and liberal students had at times complained about the political bias of some of their professors. The Dean felt that his faculty probably was not sensitive to the fact that their present student audiences were not sufficiently appreciative of the fact that their audiences were more diverse today than in the past. He noticed that most of the complaints he had received from students were in classes taught by four or five of the most senior male professors.

Exercise

1. List the various audiences that you have in the past targeted for some type of persuasive effort. Rate your success on a five-point scale on how effective your typical persuasive effort for each audience has been.

2. Make a list of what you might do to increase your credibility and influence with each of these different types of audience members without obviously pandering.

Works cited

[1]   Eisenhower, D.D. (1948) *Crusade in Europe.* New York: Doubleday.

[2]   Maier, N.R.F. (1963) *Problem Solving Discussions and Conferences: Leadership Methods and Skills.* New York: McGraw-Hill.

[3]   Carroll, S.J. and Gannon, M.J. (1997) *Ethical Dimensions of International Management.* Thousand Oaks, CA: Sage Publications.

[4]   Tosi, H.L, Rizzo, J.R., and Carroll, S. J. (1990) *Managing Organizational Behavior.* New York: Harper & Row.

[5]   Carroll and Gannon (1997) *Ethical Dimensions of International Management.*

CHAPTER 7

Leader–follower emotional ties

"You make, —a wonderful rainbow, —and a beautiful light, —and you appear in my life, —just like a star in the sky, —as bright, —as you can be, —and a beautiful sight."

—Anaya Patterson, aged six, *Washington Post* contest winner

"Related to this is the practice of so many people to sanctify the kings whom they have chosen from among themselves. They are not content with honouring them: they need to worship them."

—Michel Montaigne in *Four Essays*

"When Bobby Kennedy was assassinated I cried every day for a year."

—Woman, in her fifties, in conversation with the brother of Steve Carroll

Gandhi was the greatest leader in India and is considered one of the greatest leaders throughout history. He was an extremely persuasive leader who convinced millions of Indians to accept his non-violent peaceful strategies for gaining independence from the British Empire without the use of seniority. He was sincerely loved by the masses as shown by their great reverence for him through-out his career. Also, it should be noted that Gandhi achieved his outcomes without enforcing his authority or offer of rewards, threats or punishments. He trained as a lawyer and was very theatrical in the way he presented himself to his people and to the outside world. He wore a simple loincloth which he made himself on a spinning wheel. He frequently invited arrest and imprisonment, engaged in dra-matic courtroom confrontations, fasted, and made hundreds of engaging and memorable speeches before being assassinated by a Hindu extremist shortly after succeeding in gaining independence from the British Empire in 1946. Some Hindus had resisted Gandhi's great efforts to integrate the Hindu and Muslim populations which he himself considered his greatest persuasive failure. He was unfortunately unsuccessful in attempting to persuade people that there should be no "them" versus "us" mentality. His characteristics, leadership approach, social and political philosophy, and everyday behaviours are described in many biographies and in the award-winning film *Gandhi*. These all describe how he was able to obtain his persuasive power and love of his people from the great masses of his countrymen and the leading politicians to social leaders of his time.

Gandhi, unlike most political leaders in his day, lived and travelled among the masses listening to their problems and concerns. As such, they were able to gain a natural affinity towards him as they believed he understood and loved them. They identified with him and returned his respect for them with devotion and allegiance. Unlike many if not most leaders, Gandhi did not pursue material riches and grandeur; he lived very simply not wishing to live more grandly than the ordinary citizen. To his people, Gandhi's words were the essence of wisdom and his philosophy resonated with them for example:

"If we all accept the idea of an eye for an eye, the whole world will be afflicted with blindness."

"Wherever you are you will always reside in my heart."

Gandhi made spiritual appeals rather than appealing to self-interest, and placed importance on spiritual gain. This perspective has historically found favor with the majority of people; however, there are some who reject this approach. He proposed a doctrine of non-violence to combat the strength of the British Empire which to his counterparts and sub-leaders appeared wise and potentially effective as power differences were enormous. Gandhi had a habit of listening with sincere respect for those he would converse with. However, he would equally reject what he considered bad advice with rational arguments which added to his effectiveness to lead and his endearing nature. He embodied a kind of "tough love" not uncommon among effective persuasive leaders and naturally his personal nobility and ethical orientations added considerably to his stature. His behaviour is not entirely unique and is similar to many other effective and persuasive leaders throughout this book.

—Gandhi, Mahatma, *Gandhi: An Autobiography* [1]

From humble beginnings, Sam Walton built one of the largest retail businesses in the world. After a period of owning several so-called "five and dime" stores, he opened the first Wal-Mart in 1962. Thirty years later when he died, he owned hundreds of stores in the United States and across ten nations. His stores had many innovations including checkout counters at the store exits, profit sharing for all employees, extensive training in customer relations, and a very large variety of goods sold at low prices made possible by purchasing in bulk from suppliers around the world. Walton travelled the nation visiting his stores and those of his competitors and adopted a dramatic signature public persona and leadership style which became immediately recognizable. As observed in a documentary by Carroll, he drove a pickup truck and was outfitted in a baseball cap, blazer, tie, and slacks. Arriving at a store he would walk around greeting and shaking hands with employees often calling them by name. He would then have them gather around while he gave a short speech persuading them in a folksy manner to fully implement his policy of pleasing the customers not only by variety, and low prices, but most importantly through staff friendliness. His talks often took the following format:

"Hallaloola!—I hope all of you are as happy to be here as I am ... In this company we recognize that each customer is very important because they are ... The most powerful person in this company is the customer. They can fire any one of us from the chairman down by withholding their business ... Now I want you to raise your hand and commit yourself to looking each customer in the eye and greeting them warmly."

Despite appearances, Walton was a well-educated and very well–read man and had been a successful leader throughout his life in multiple situations. He listened to others and in fact took his wife's advice to extend the profit-sharing system for managers to all 1.5 million employees. For example, one early worker said that his portion of profit sharing at retirement was three quarters of a million dollars.

Leader–follower attraction

The case of Gandhi and many other leaders leaves no doubt that followers have not only respect but often great love for certain leaders and teachers. In the United States, the funeral processions of Abraham Lincoln, Franklin Roosevelt, and John Kennedy and other leaders were accompanied by deep expressions of sorrow and intense grieving by millions of citizens. Over the years Carroll has read different personal memoirs, which contained testimonies of former students concerning past teachers they considered memorable. Underlying the various accounts of such teachers, there appears to be two fundamental aspects critical to students' favourable reactions to their teachers. One was that students felt these teachers not only respected them but actually loved them. The second was that these teachers were able to guide them to more positive thinking and self-belief in their own abilities to achieve performances that they themselves would never have believed without their teachers' support. These were the essential factors behind strong student–teacher emotional ties.

While leaders need to nourish their followers emotionally, in certain cases the emotional bond between follower and leader can be too strong and even unhealthy when a state known as transference develops. This state can also manifest itself in the leader–follower attachment relationship.

The recent political campaign for presidency in the US has illustrated the strong emotional ties that many followers often have for their leaders. The appearance of a leadership candidate in an auditorium is often followed by almost a mass hysteria of joy, love, loyalty, and frenzied attempts to touch or at least attract the attention of their chosen leaders. In addition, there is often the expression of contempt for their opponents. In psychotherapy, the love for a leader or therapist is often referred to as transference. This involves transferring a past emotional feeling towards previous authority figures (e.g., parent, teacher, or mentor) to a particular and current leader. This is a bond built on emotions rather than reason although one can attribute rational reasoning as justification for such feelings. Of course, these strong emotional ties may result in unrealistic expectations, excessive dependence, and obedience on the leader. In which case, as many scholars have pointed out, this can create increased dependency and conformity.

The word "love" when used in a non-romantic way is associated with various other terms as any dictionary indicates (e.g., adore, cherish, idolize, like, revere, worship, etc.). Various studies and experiments suggest that we all need a minimum amount of affection, particularly from parents, to develop emotionally and socially into adulthood as a secure person. It has been argued that leadership relationships are not dissimilar to intimate relationships and thus draw on the certain needs for adequate amounts of love and affection.

Leader–follower bonding

There is a bonding process that helps to create such mutual affections between leaders and followers. Doing things together, facing common dangers, and providing mutual help can trigger the creation of such emotional ties particularly when accompanied by affection. A poem by the Nobel Prize–winning Irish poet Seamus Heaney describes how such bonds are forged from even simple activities done together [2]:

> When all the others were away at Mass
> I was all hers as we peeled potatoes ...
> I remembered her head bent toward my head
> Her breath in mine, our fluent dipping knives—
> Never closer the rest of our lives

Using the example of family throughout any discussion on leadership is certainly appropriate. Our parents are our first authority figures or leaders, and thus our identities are significantly shaped by the amount of nurturing and helpful persuasion in the teaching we receive from them. Political leaders are often described in parental terms, similarly leaders and teachers often conceptualize their followers or students as their adopted children. A much loved CEO of a Taiwanese company almost always described all employees in the company as "our" children. This did not suggest he viewed them as infantile or deficient—on the contrary, he believed them to be capable and independent entities that, with the appropriate development and nurturing, could be groomed to be high-performing employees. As teachers, the authors themselves have maintained life-long affectionate relationships with certain students whom they appear to have unofficially adopted into their extended families.

Narcissistic behaviour

Affectionate ties between followers and leaders may be blocked by personality factors. One psychoanalyst, who has had a number of CEOs as clients, reports a large proportion of them suffered from narcissism perhaps as a result of the allure of power. The self-loving narcissist seems not to have the ability to love others which is probably a result of a number of reasons. Lowen, author of the book *Narcissism* believes:

> *"The denial of feeling characteristic of all narcissists is most manifest in their behaviour toward others. They can be ruthless, exploitive, sadistic, or destructive to another person because they are insensitive to the other's suffering or feeling. This insensitivity derives from an insensitivity to one's*

own feelings. Empathy, the ability to sense other people's moods or feelings, is a function of resonance. We can feel another's sadness because it makes us sad; we can share another's joy because it evokes good feelings in us. But if we are incapable of feeling sadness or joy, we cannot respond to these feelings in another person. When we deny our feelings, we deny that others feel" [3].

Attraction to morality

As we have indicated previously, the most loved leaders have historically been individuals perceived to be higher in moral or ethical principles—witness the world's religious founders and leaders. Of course, only fools expect perfection from other human beings. What accounts for this attraction to morality and what is morality anyway? Morality does not mean a rigid conformity to a doctrine of ideals—rather, for the purpose of this argument morality is adhering to principles of justice and fairness when dealing with others and in not putting one's selfish interests before the interests and needs of others. There are good reasons for morality from the perspective of human evolution. Obviously, it is safer to encounter individuals or groups which are considered essentially good rather than evil or bad. In addition, evil and excessively selfish behaviour is a threat to group cohesiveness and solidarity in the face of danger. Those individuals who are a threat to the existing social order in society due to their anti-social behaviour are typically ostracized by various means in human and animal groups. We are trained from birth, in most cases, to be moral and good citizens. This training comes from our parents, schoolteachers, religious leaders, the literature we read including early fairy stories, and from the films and TV programmes we watch. In addition, throughout our journey into adulthood we witness reinforced examples of acceptable moral behaviour by observing the good deeds of our parents, peers, and the leaders in groups we join. It is therefore natural that after receiving such extensive training that individuals expect and seek out role models who exemplify these esteemed behaviours. Essentially, these role models represent ego ideals for us which shape our behaviour throughout our lives.

Attractiveness versus behaviour

Beauty is highly valued by human beings and, thus, is a basis for emotional attraction and interest in another. It is often stated that there are evolutionary reasons for this as our instincts naturally associate beauty with health. Therefore, beauty obviously plays an important role in mate selection. A study carried out by Carroll many years ago established the importance of handsomeness in men for receiving managerial job offers and in other promotional offers [4]. Nevertheless we all know that desirable or undesirable behaviour can and usually does, after an initial attraction period (or honeymoon phase), override beauty in terms of likeability. A well-known writer, Anais Nin, describes her own reactions when meeting a very beautiful woman for the first time:

"Her beauty drowned me. As I sat before her, I felt I would do anything she asked of me ... She was colour and brilliance and strangeness. By the end of the evening I had extricated myself from her power. She killed my admiration by her talk. Her talk. The enormous ego, false, weak, posturing. She lacks the courage of her personality, which is sensual, heavy with experience. Her role alone preoccupies her. She invents dramas in which she always stars. I am sure she creates genuine dramas, genuine chaos, and whirlpools of feelings, but I feel her share in it is a pose. That night in spite of my response to her, she sought to be whatever I wanted her to be. She is an actress every moment" [5].

As previously stated, we are all actors and our public persona is constructed to a certain degree. However, we have also mentioned that this persona must be consistent over time and true to our natural inclinations, or it will be impossible to be viewed as a reliable, honest, and authentic person. This beautiful woman's behaviour was so false and changeable depending on the audience that the lack of integrity was apparent to the discerning observer.

Similarity

Individuals are attracted to others who are like them for certain reasons. Evolutionary forces have developed humans to feel safer with members of their own group or insiders than with members of other groups or outsiders. There is, of course, often good reason to fear members of another group. This is certainly true at an emotional level, although reasoning and contemplation can override such inclinations. However, what percentage of the world's population actually uses reason extensively for their attitudes and actions? Even within a group, individuals with similar thinking patterns, interests, and abilities are more likely to enjoy each other's company. We are more likely to respect others with a similar mindset since they can help validate our own chosen identities. Skilled leaders can always find some personal inclinations, prefer-ences, and personal historical events which are similar to those in a targeted group.

Openness and attraction

Perhaps the most common and obvious reason for attracting dislike to oneself is a lack of respect for others. We have previously discussed the key nature of respect before. Most individuals have come to terms with their imperfections and respect themselves. When others treat them in a manner which indicates an impression widely divergent from their own, they naturally reject this opinion and also reject the person who expresses such an opinion whether openly or apparent. In the case of nations, clans, mafia, or gangs, they often go to war. Empirical research conducted with thousands of managers from different organizations, case histories, and leader and teacher biographies indicate that openness to ideas and inputs from others is related to being more liked, appreciated, valued, and respected [6].

Optimistic and hopeful leaders

Leaders are often perceived as a means of reaching desirable ends. As such, leaders who seem confident or optimistic about the possibility of succeeding are more valued than those expressing pessimism. Leaders who help individuals achieve these goals, or at least attempt to, are especially cherished by their followers. The current US president has written a book entitled *The Audacity of Hope* which postulates and develops this ideology [7]. He stresses these themes during his speeches and talks which seemed to be received well by the live audiences addressed. Looking back on leaders throughout history, we find that those who became most memorable typically expressed hope and optimism for the future. Pessimists are more likely to be reacted to negatively even if it turns out that they are correct in their predictions.

Respect for differences

All human beings possess individual differences that make each of us unique—even siblings from the same family differ. Leaders will differ from followers not only in relation to the dynamics of the group but on an individual level. Followers are mostly attracted to leaders who respect and accept such differences in personality, interests, aptitudes, and personal philosophies. However, it is not always recognizable that an individual can be a quite different person from one time to another. Certainly, changes in mood can be triggered by a wide variety of events in that person's life at any one time. Of course, it is also true that all of us can be several individuals within one skin. These different selves or projected identities can often be in competition with each other for supremacy at any one time. To a large degree, a leader will be more highly regarded if s/he respects and accepts such differences within reason [8].

SUMMARY

Likeability, affection, and even love for a leader and vice versa can obviously greatly facilitate the process of persuasion and teaching. Of course, leaders and followers vary on such measures; some leaders and followers are hated and some loved. Typically, a leader or a follower may be both loved and disliked by different groups or individuals. We have discussed briefly some of the antecedents and correlates of being liked or liked to various degrees. These are not a mystery to most. Most individuals seem aware of what behaviours and traits these are, having encountered other human beings all of their lives who varied in likeability. The positive value of integrity, consistency, similarity, openness, respect, and other factors were discussed. Liking for others can obviously change as a person changes, as we change, or as the situation changes. This was observed by Carroll while in Japan where groups or individuals having problems may be taken out by others to a bar where alcohol therapy is used. Certain types of group therapy are also sometimes effective in changing the relationships among individuals or groups. Sometimes, all of these events can occur at the same time. Excessive self-love may be a barrier to love of others. Research evidence suggests that a major determinant of ineffectiveness in CEOs is excessive self-love. Narcissism as a characteristic may change over time. Of course, one can have too little self-love, self-confidence, or self-esteem. One needs to feel efficacious in the tasks that one is confronting to even try.

END CASES

"I couldn't breathe without love in the air. I'd choke. I ceased to exist when not in love. The radiance within blotted out so that nothing would happen inside ... I can truthfully say that I never lifted a hand unless for someone; never took up a brush or pen, a sheet of music or spade, never pursued a thought without the motivation of trying to make someone love me."

—Sylvia Aston-Warner

A voice echoes throughout the lands
Many have heard it, but few believe it
It rings with the church bells
It cries with the mourners
And it triumphs with the victors.
It is quelled by greed.
But never has it been forgotten.
The worst of people need it but do not want it.
The best of people use it for themselves and for all.
And in the darkest of times it is needed the most.
But in the highest of times it seems not to be needed.
But it always is.
And it always will be.
For every beginning needs it.
Every end wants it.
And every middle shuns it.
It is hope.

—Brian Welch (aged 12), *An Unknown Necessity*,
from poetry contest published in the *Washington Post*

Works cited

[1]   Gandhi, M. (1957) *Gandhi: An Autobiography—The Story of My Experiments with Truth.* Beacon Press.

[2]   Andrews, E. (1988) *The Poetry of Seamus Heaney: All the Realms of Whisper.* London: Macmillan.

[3]   Lowen, A. (1985) *Narcissism: Denial of the True Self.* New York: Collier Books.

[4]   Carroll, S.J. (1969) Beauty, bias, and business. *Personnel Administration,* **32**.

[5]   Nin, A. (1948) *Under the Glass Bell.* Swallow Press.

[6]   Yukl, G. (1989) *Leadership in Organisations* (Second Edition). Prentice Hall.

[7]   Obama, B. (2006) *The Audacity of Hope: Thoughts on Reclaiming the American Dream.* New York: Random House.

[8]   Tosi, H.L, Rizzo, J.R, and Carroll, S.J. (1990) *Managing Organizational Behavior.* New York: Harper & Row.

CHAPTER 8

Creating positive emotions in sub-leaders and followers

"It's wonderful when we can work at something we like. Otherwise it is slavery."

—Gorky

"The easiest way to increase happiness is to lower expectations."

—Daniel Gilbert, *Stumbling on Happiness*

"Words with me are instruments. I wish to impress upon the people to whom I talk the fact that I am sincere, that I mean exactly what I say and that I stand for the things that are elemental in civilization."

—Theodore Roosevelt

BEGINNING CASES

At the end of the Spanish–American war in the 19th century, the Surgeon General sent a medical team to Cuba to investigate the cause of death of many soldiers which had occurred due to yellow fever. The medical team leader was a well-known doctor, Major Walter Reed. He had three assistants—James Carroll (who had recently received his MD from the University of Maryland), and two other young MDs: Jesse Lazear and Aristedes Agaramonte. They began their investigation by looking for a causal bacterium but were unsuccessful. Whilst in Cuba, the medical team visited a physician from Havana, Dr Carlos Finlay. Dr Finlay, who contrary to other beliefs, believed mosquitoes were responsible for the transmission of this illness. After Reed was called back to Washington, the three young physicians bred mosquitoes and allowed them to feed on patients. They then applied the mosquitoes to their own skin and to the skins of two volunteer soldiers. One day in late August, Carroll placed a test tube containing one of these mosquitoes on his arm to feed. Within three weeks, he had contracted yellow fever while the others did not. During the treatment of a patient Lazear was accidently bitten and five days later contracted yellow fever and died after a further seven days. Carroll, however, did not die immediately but went into a three-year period of lingering illness before his body succumbed to the illness and died. Further investigations were carried out when Reed returned to Cuba in October, with the intention to rule out other possible causes of the disease. Reed later received world-wide acclaim for his work. The University of Maryland subsequently awarded Carroll an honorary PhD and commissioned and erected a statue of him in the lobby of their oldest medical building.

"Shukov went to sleep fully content. He'd had many strokes of luck that day: they hadn't put him in the cells; they hadn't sent his squad to the settlement; he'd swiped a bowl of kasha at dinner; the squad leader had fixed the well; he built a wall and enjoyed doing it; he'd smuggled that bit of a hacksaw blade through; he earned a favor from Tsezar that evening and he'd bought that tobacco. And he hadn't fallen ill. He'd got over it. A day without a dark cloud; almost a happy day. There were three thousand six hundred and fifty days like that in his stretch. From the first clang of the rail to the last clang of the rail."

—One day in a Russian labour camp for a prisoner; Alexander Solzhenitsyn, *One day in the life of Ivan Denisovic* [1]

Leading sub-leaders

Leadership researchers have long pointed out that, usually, leaders do not relate to all members of their group in the same way. Different individuals may require a different approach as all parents know. Managers may have a few close confidants that assist them to manage the rest of the group, who serve as the surrogate eyes, ears, and mouth of the designated or elected leader. Teachers may judge the effectiveness of their teaching approaches by paying close attention to the understanding and/or reactions of a small group of advanced students in the class. On occasion, political leaders will heavily rely on certain cabinet or senior staff members to assist them when deciding how to approach certain problems and issues. Whilst the head coach for a sports team usually gets the credit or blame for results, several assistant coaches play a significant role in such outcomes. In addition, athletics coaches point to the importance of certain players acting as sub-leaders during the game in implementing the coach's game plan. The same is true in the military and sciences where the formal leader usually obtains credit for victories over their adversaries. The selection of competent sub-leaders may therefore be an important element to any leader's success. Sub-leaders can represent the important and different constituencies within a group and thus aid in the leader's persuasive process. The autonomy and favourable treatment of sub-leaders is thought to be the primary motivation for them to carry out the leader sub-roles they have been informally assigned. This was obviously one of the more important factors contributing to the creative and energetic behaviours of the young physicians in the yellow fever case. Their incredible motivation made their leader Walter Reed world famous. Certainly part of this motivation can be attributed to the leadership style of Reed.

Sub-leaders and leaders in their random encounters with individual group members must be in a position to react to their follower's individual characteristics and the nature of their previous encounters. In such encounters certain counselling or therapeutic principles may prove useful. Sub-leaders serve as sounding boards for proposed actions and changes. Often the leader overlooks certain factors which are likely to doom the success of an action being considered. The sub-leaders here can act as a brake on rash impulses. When Alexander the Great invaded India he wanted to extend his conquest or sphere of operations; however, his sub-leaders demurred for certain rational reasons. Alexander gave up on his plan and agreed to start taking his army back home thus saving many lives on both sides by taking such action. This scenario is not uncommon in many historical accounts of military leaders. However, Alexander himself never made it home dying of an illness shortly after the quiet revolt of his sub-commanders.

Counselling group members as individuals

Counselling as an area of study and practice in colleges has been in existence since the 1920s as we understand it. However, counselling has actually been in existence for as long as humans have had the capability of speech. In addition to helping individuals deal with emotional, behavioural, and relationship problems, counselling aims to provide learning, increased competence, and changes in thinking as well as behaviour. Counselling can provide exposure to progressive advice, reassurance, a release of emotional tension, open up effective communication, and more realistic perspectives. There are many theories of counselling ranging from the very directive counselor-dominated approach to a very non-directive counsellee-dominated approach. Usually the primary focus of these sessions depends on the client providing information. In a mixed approach, the counsellor or counsellee dominates depending on whose information and evaluations are most required at that time. Obviously, the ability to carefully listen and effectively communicate is equally critical to any counselling encounter. It is essential that one employs a distinct, consistent, and concise style of communication in their choice of words, tone of voice, body language, and emotional stance. Under normal conditions, an effective counsellor will possess the ability to elicit a cooperative and insightful response on the part of the counsellee. Counsellors who are warm, inviting, non-judgemental, truthful, sincere, and possess integrity appear to be more effective.

In directive counselling, the counsellor listens to the counsellee, decides on a course of action and advises the counsellee on how to execute their plan for them. There are inherent problems created through this approach, as it can create an excessive dependence on the counsellor which can affect the intellectual and emotional growth of their client. The non-directive approach involves the counsellor listening to their client's problems or issues, showing understanding, and encouraging the client to devolve a solution to their problem. Of course there is a philosophy in counselling whereby two individuals work together to ensure an amicable solution to the problem. This is sometimes called the cooperative counselling approach. In counselling goals there is a new emphasis, discussed in several popular books, which promotes the achievement of emotional intelligence or emotional maturity. Some of the reasons for including emotional intelligence as a goal is the realization that success and happiness are likely to be higher among those who have higher emotional maturity. This can be defined as possessing greater self-knowledge and knowledge of others as well as caring and sympathy for others.

A beneficial approach to therapy which has been developed for those who suffer from anxiety and depression is cognitive behavioural therapy (CBT). This approach is based on seeking out the main cause of any negative feeling. In many cases, these negative impressions can be attributed to false beliefs in oneself and often in those around them. In these cases, a belief has the power to trigger an emotional state and action which is harmful to themselves, others, and those closest to them. CBT aims to rectify these feelings by ensuring that the person involved will alter and change their "incorrect" beliefs. One method in achieving this goal is to challenge any false asserta-tions with contrary evidence. For example, if an individual says "I am a failure" then the counsellor encourages a discussion on an event when their client was a success. Of course, not all leaders can be effective therapists without the necessary training and development that this would require. Professional counselling simply cannot always be avoided and leaders may favor referring an individual to a certified therapist. Receiving professional help in serious cases is obviously the best solution to avoid major problems developing.

Creating positive emotional states

The authors have encountered many books and articles on happiness over the past several years. These writings often describe many experiments on happiness by psychologists, economists, and others. Much of writing on this subject is conjecture; however, some is based on valid research. For example, research has been facilitated using MRI machines to monitor the brain as research participants are exposed to different stimuli that draw various positive and negative emotional states. Research indicates that most individuals tend to have a constant level of happiness or wellbeing that does change with circumstances but then returns to its normal level. Some of this is believed to be due to genetic inheritance. For example, identical twins that have been separated from each other at birth and live quite different lives, very often have similar levels of satisfaction and even happiness. One study showed very similar levels of job satisfaction between separated identical twins even though they lived in different localities and had quite different jobs [2]. Of course non-identical twins and children of different ages may differ on such wellbeing scales partly because they inherit different genes from their ancestors. Other research shows that individuals have been tracked over time while experiencing both happy and sad events and it has been found that after the event is over they tend to revert to their typical feelings of wellbeing. The effects of having a very happy experience (an increase in money, a promotion, lottery, new house, etc.) tends to be short lived. In addition, we might expect that counselling or therapy is likely to change a person's long-time happiness or wellbeing to a limited degree unless it results in a significant change in the way individuals look at themselves or the world.

A number of strategies and programs have been developed to help individuals replace more negative emotions with positive ones. The cognitive behavioural therapy approach described above is one of the earliest of these. Another more recent approach is sometimes referred to as optimism training and guided optimism. Obviously, optimistic people have a greater sense of wellbeing and happiness than pessimistic people do. Research clearly shows that an individual's optimism can be improved through various strategies and techniques. However, it must be remembered that there are different levels of optimism and very unrealistically high levels can be as harmful as excessively low levels.

Optimism works best when it is realistic. Thus, guided optimism attempts to make such optimism realistic by basing it on facts rather than illusions. Optimism in a way is related also to probabilities. Future states must be and can be predicted imperfectly only in terms of probabilities. For example, with certain types of cancer the probability of recovery depends on the stage of cancer growth—early versus advanced—and the cancer's aggressiveness. A stage 1 cancer might typically result in 85% of those afflicted making a recovery. For a stage two, the probability of recovery might go to 45% of those afflicted and so on. Health counsellors for certain types of paralysis disorders can sometimes make recovery predictions based on the patient's illness history and the symptoms shown. Optimistic predictions are also likely to be affected by the time period involved. Will I recover in one day or two years? Will I survive until tomorrow or for the next 40 years? Probabilities are based on actual past circumstances and statistics. For example, "I will be admitted to the local community college" is obviously far more likely for an average college applicant than "I will be admitted to Harvard University". Helping individuals to recognize realistic probabilities helps them to attain a sensible level of optimism.

Optimism in an individual can be influenced in many different ways. In one approach, individuals who voice unrealistic pessimistic thoughts or beliefs are challenged as in the cognitive behavioural approach described previously. Many health counsellors for specific illnesses have recovered from that illness themselves. Their very presence proves that the illness can be overcome. One approach for increasing optimism is by rewarding individuals for eliminating negative thoughts or by fining them for having such thoughts. Rewards can be in the form of monetary rewards, extra privileges, or simple signs of social approval. There is some evidence that encouraging individuals to write realistic essays about their probable futures has been successful in creating states of realistic optimism. This might be especially helpful when individuals are asked to make lists of strengths and weaknesses as well as assets and liabilities. The discussion can then focus on how to best employ strengths and assets to overcome any identified limiting factors. The authors have had success in encouraging individuals to set goals for their future along with statements about the resources and help they will need to attain the goals. Optimism can be influenced by helping individuals choose realistic social comparisons rather than unrealistic ones (I will be as smart as Einstein). Providing obvious social support can increase optimism—we will stick with you and help you. Also, realistic strategies can help. The following realistic strategy will work for you or for us. Leaders who are admired for their competence can improve optimism significantly and improve self-efficacy in others.

Is happiness a topic of interest to leaders? Yes, we as well as most leadership writers think so. The emotional state of followers often determines their openness to persuasive efforts of all kinds. Emotions play an important role in willingness to perform tasks, attempt to reach goals, to improve knowledge, to recover from illnesses, and to form strong relationships with others. Emotions of all types are not elicited primarily by thinking but rather what our senses communicate to us (e.g., what we see, hear, feel, and smell). Such sensory information draws out positive and negative emotions. Recently, it was reported on TV news that retail stores that are saturated with certain fragrances tend to have shoppers linger in the store longer, thus increasing the possibility of impulse shopping.

A huge number of studies suggest that leaders can influence the emotions of followers and others in a variety of ways. To produce happier and more compliant employees, a leader may first recruit individuals who have a more positive view about themselves and the world. These optimistic individuals seem to have a constant level of happiness irrespective of the conditions they may be exposed to (e.g., some individuals are almost always happy and others sad). Leaders of all types including teachers and parents do not always have the ability to select their followers (teachers in private schools or in Japanese universities are often an exception).

Leaders as role models

Leaders need to recognize that their behaviour and mood is constantly being scrutinized by their followers. In fact, a leader's behaviour is often cited as the primary reason for job dissatisfaction. Leaders do not always have control over their own behaviour and as such can facilitate or hinder a group's happiness, satisfaction, sense of wellbeing, and so on. Typically, positive and negative emotions can coincide or be present at the same time. For example, a research study conducted by Carroll in a mattress factory showed workers typically viewed a workday of consisting of both positive and negative elements [3]. The overall level of motivation and satisfaction in a given day depended on the proportion and relative importance of such positive and negative factors.

From experience, we understand that leaders who show love and respect, treat others with fairness and justice, and foster group cohesion through helping behaviour elicit higher degrees of positive emotions in others. However, research highlights further truths such that happiness estimates are often a case of process-based comparisons with others (see Appendix B). For example, people often assess whether they are better or worse off than others or what a particular day is like as compared with other days. Solzhenitsyn's prisoner in a Russian labour camp showed how the prisoner compared a terrible day with that experienced by others in his society. However, in the same stream of thought he reflects that it is not such a bad day compared with others he has had or may have in the future. Research implies that when a group as a whole becomes more prosperous, the happiness of those who progress at a slower rate than others in the group will be less even though they have more income in an absolute sense [4]. Comparisons and perceived inequities are fundamental in achieving overall happiness or a sense of wellbeing. In a recent study, a change in the level of happiness in four countries was examined when freedom of choice was introduced. Findings suggest that freedom of choice increased the general sense of wellbeing and happiness [5]. Perceived freedom seems to be important for happiness and leadership undoubtedly plays a significant role.

Happiness is a subject that has been not only widely described and discussed in writings by novelists and philosophers from the arts and humanities for thousands of years but has also been the focus of many scholars from the various social sciences. At least in the United States, happiness has been considered a human right since the founding of the nation. It also seems to be the current primary concern of almost every person. A person's experiences with various leaders throughout life (parents, school-teachers, supervisors, and religious and political leaders) have much to do with the achievement of one's happiness goals. Happiness is more likely if we know what determines it. (As space constraints limit a comprehensive review of happiness research, the most important developments to date have been highlighted in a table of findings and observations in Appendix B.)

Positive psychology

One of the most significant movements in the field of psychology in recent years is the creation of positive psychology. For a long time much of psychology has focused on negative states—anxiety, depression, and various psychological mental health issues involving neuroses and psychoses. Research indicates that feelings of helplessness and hopelessness are common to many health, work, family, and relationship problems. Following such findings, studies have found that replacing such negative emotional states with increased optimism, an enhanced self-identity, and a sense of wellbeing can result in many positive outcomes [6]. Carroll's volunteer health-counselling work with paralysis and cancer patients and attendance at healthcare conferences has provided many examples of patients who recovered in a physical sense, but were significantly impacted by the presence of negative emotional states. In addition, there were many case histories documenting the value of positive thinking on illness coping and on actual recovery. Positive psychology focuses on positive emotions in contrast to previous perspectives which centred on a client's negative emotional state. This new approach, developed from research, focuses on learning how to nurture not only positive emotions but positive character and positive institutions. The creation of wellbeing is the primary objective of such efforts.

Research studies have analysed several specific ways of accomplishing these ends through counselling, therapy, and education. It has been found that a sense of wellbeing can be enhanced by encouraging one to focus on learning to master their living environment, being more self-accepting, identifying a purpose in life, becoming less dependent and more autonomous, developing positive relations with others, and dedicating oneself to the goal of personal growth and improvement. Much more specific exercises have been tested with quite positive results. These exercises include making individuals pay a gratuitous visit to somebody who helped them, persuade them to describe and list their blessings, ask them to list their top-five strengths and how they could be more effectively used in life, write out a desired obituary, take the time to savour a daily activity, and develop an active constructive response to hearing good news from another. Some may argue that such interventions are in the domain of psychotherapists only; however, as leaders the truth is we all serve as therapists and counsellors at times.

As we have indicated, counselling skills and interpersonal skills are extremely useful in our everyday lives and we can all learn to be more effective in dealing with others. The objective of positive psychology is to move an individual to greater levels of hope and optimism. Hope and optimism are essential to drive our motivations and accomplish targeted results. Evidence from case studies on paralysis victims indicate that hope and optimism play a fundamental role in motivating a patient through their vigorous exercise regime towards recovery. Many research studies have documented the positive role of hope and optimism in recovery from many serious illnesses. Of course, hope and optimism must be realistic, as building illusions of false hope can be dangerous when the reality of a condition and outcome is less positive. Interventions for increasing hope and optimism have proved successful especially for a procedure termed by its originator, Martin Seligman, as learned optimism [7]. Through appropriate exercises individuals can learn to be less pessimistic and more optimistic. Of course, there are also cases in repressive illnesses where medical intervention must accompany counselling efforts to achieve good patient outcomes.

Positive psychotherapy to a large degree focuses on creating happiness in a person's life. As we have pointed out, happiness has been the subject of a great deal of writing in recent years by not only psychologists but by economists as well. Martin Seligman, who is credited with coining the term positive psychology, describes a state of happiness as involving three types of lives. The first of these is the pleasant life which involves satisfaction, contentment, fulfilment, pride, and serenity. The second type of life is the meaningful life. The third and final one is the realized life.

Optimism in the arts

In the second beginning case (see p. 100) from the novel *One Day in the Life of Ivan Denisovich* we see not only a vivid example that happiness is relative to the situation but an example of actual human resilience [7]. Literature and film in the form of fiction very often have an optimistic theme. Such works often involve individuals or groups overcoming considerable adversity in achieving love, health, career success, or some other desired outcome or achievement. Exposure to such works has the ability to create a more positive and hopeful view of life in spite of its uncertainties. The lessons for persuasive leadership here are clear—positive stories of successful striving can be motivational as well as inspirational and pleasing.

Adversity coaching

In life one is often exposed to some degree of adversity as things do not always go as well as they are planned. Persuasive leaders have the capacity to help others cope with adverse events and consequences by explaining what went wrong and why. Carroll found, in his several years as health counsellor, stories documenting difficult events which successfully turn to reveal positive outcomes are very helpful for inspiring patients. He found that showing an individual that s/he is not as bad off as others helps them to continue their fight against their illness. Also being able to point out a positive trend upward from even a very low level helps. Having a step-by-step plan to achieve success has worked in the past to help confront adversity. All of these increase hope and optimism.

Matching individuals and groups with appropriate tasks

Individuals and groups do get satisfaction out of accomplishment. Our own research indicates that happy days in one's life are associated with success and unhappy days with failure [8]. Appropriate assignments for individuals or groups require careful analysis of the people involved; this often involves assessing their abilities, strengths, interests, and personalities. All those in positions of leadership are human resource managers. The joy that can arise out of work itself for many individuals, especially those in certain occupations is described vividly in the book *The Soul of a New Machine* by John Tracy Kidder [9]. The book describes how a leader, Tom West, led a group of young electronic engineers in an unsanctioned project to design a new breakthrough computer. The book documents how West's young engineers, inexperienced in design, donate incredible amounts of time and energy to this project. They succeed in designing and debugging this new machine and met an incredibly difficult schedule in doing so. Much of their success can be attributed to the fact they found the project to be interesting, challenging, and meaningful. They indicated they did not choose engineering for the money but for the appeal of the work itself. Of course, Tom West was an effective leader of this group since he had high technical competence which gave him credibility and his style matched their management preferences.

Social barriers to persuasion

Many human behaviours are determined by social influence and membership in groups with distinctive goals, values, and mindsets. In some cultures or societies, almost all behaviour and beliefs are rooted in group influences. Often it is impossible to alter this behaviour or thinking of a single individual. Even when successful change initially occurs, an individual usually returns to a social norm which will reinforce, if not physically force, one to revert back to group perspectives. In these cases, in order to sustain new behavioural patterns, individuals may need to be sent into another social system. Alternatively an attempt to change a whole group or social entity can be attempted. Teaching an individual how to resist such social coercive pressures may help prevent a reversion back to any previous dysfunctional behaviours. In recent years, an increasing number of programs for parents intent on improving their parenting techniques have been developed. Parents are taught many counselling and other approaches described in this chapter. In some circumstances, both parents and children receive this type of therapy or training together. New contractual arrangements governing relations may arise out of such training or therapy groups.

SUMMARY

It goes without saying that leaders can be most effective in their endeavours by working with sub-leaders or group assistants. The performance of such persons is critical to any leader's overall success. Such assistant leaders can greatly facilitate the attainment of a leader's goals or hinder their accomplishment. It may be especially difficult to work effectively with such assistant leaders since they are often put in the position of having to do more for little in the way of material rewards or recognition. But the use of gratitude, caring, and other intrinsic rewards is often effective in such cases.

Even though leaders have to deal with groups, the members of that group are individuals and research shows that leaders do and should differentiate among group members in the way they are approached. Various helpful approaches for leaders in dealing with individuals have been described. Some of these have been derived from the fields of counselling and psychotherapy. The recent perspectives on the value of optimism and approaches for influencing and creating realistic optimism can be very useful in performing the persuasive leader role.

Most leaders are interested in doing what they can to have followers with positive emotional states rather than negative. A vast body of research findings are available to leaders to achieve such ends. We have summarized some of the most important of these in Appendix D. Their implications for behaviour and actions are usually obvious. In many ways all leaders are architects of emotions for the groups they lead to some degree. Obviously factors in other spheres of a follower's life can be critical here.

END CASE

Alice McDermott has five children—three girls of 12, 9, and 6 years of age and two boys of 10 and 4. Each child has a distinct personality, appearance, and set of abilities. In general, they tend to have distinctive personal problems and perceptions of themselves and of the world. Alice has many separate encounters with each child during the day and only met with them collectively at mealtime and sometimes when watching TV together. When bewildered at times by the behaviour or emotions of a particular child, Alice often confers with her oldest daughter who tends to be emotionally mature and quite intelligent. The 10-year-old boy seems to require frequent discipline due to his consistent teasing of his siblings, doing stupid things as well as neglecting his homework. The 9-year-old girl is frequently sad and depressed and needs emotional support and many hugs and often expresses strange beliefs about herself and the world which Alice is always careful to correct. The two youngest children seem quite normal for their age. In general, Alice wants for her children what most parents want—to be happy, healthy, cooperative, caring, and live up to whatever potential they might possess.

Exercise

1. Identify sub-leaders in three groups you are familiar with. Rate their effectiveness on a five-point scale and list the reasons for your ratings.

2. Choose a day last year when you were unusually happy. List the reasons for this. Are there lessons here for leadership behaviour? What are they? Do the same for an unusually unhappy day.

Works cited

[1] Solzhenitsyn, A. (1963) *One Day in the Life of Ivan Denisovich*. Harmondsworth: Penguin Books.

[2] Tosi, H.L., Rizzo, J.R., and Carroll, S.J. (1990) *Managing Organizational Behavior*. New York: Harper & Row.

[3] Anderson C.R. and Carroll, S.J. (1980) Predicting performance and operational measures. *Proceedings, of the Academy of Management Annual Convention. Detroit, MI.*

[4] Haidt, J. (2005) *The Happiness Hypothesis: Finding Modern Truth in Ancient Wisdom.* Basic Books.

[5] Ibid.

[6] Seligman, M.E.P., Steen, T.A., Park, N., and Peterson, C. (2005) Positive psychology progress: Empirical validation of interventions. *American Psychologist*, July/August, 410–421.

[7] Seligman, M.E.P. (2002) *Authentic Happiness: Using the New Positive Psychology to Realize Your Potential for Lasting Fulfillment.* New York: Simon & Schuster.

[8] Tosi *et al.* (1990) *Managing Organizational Behavior.*

[9] Kidder, J.T. (2000) *The Soul of a New Machine.* New York: Back Bay Books.

CHAPTER 9

Persuasive leadership and change

"In today's uncertain world the basic task of business leaders is to create members of the organisation who are adaptable and flexible as they can be. This is necessary to avoid failure in a rapidly changing world."

—Carly Fiorina, CEO of Hewlett-Packard in a talk at the University of Maryland

"One must learn not to jeopardise one's power for doing the good that is possible by efforts to correct evils over which one has no control."

—Teddy Roosevelt, 1906

"The activist is not the man who says the river is dirty. He is the man who cleans up the river."

—Ross Perot

"It's not the strategy but its successful implementation that is the key factor in a business success."

—Fred Smith, founder of Federal Express

On July 20th, 2003, Sean P. O'Malley was appointed Archbishop of Boston by Pope John Paul II over Cardinal O'Malley's objections. During his appointment, he faced incredible problems. Priest abuse scandals resulted in 1000 lawsuits against the diocese. Church attendance was declining at a significant rate and an increasing number of members left the Church. The Church had hospitals which were losing $30 million a year and enrolment at many parochial schools was very low. In addition, the Boston Church had lost the support of key Catholics in the area including the city's mayor, other political figures as well as many wealthy businessmen. Lay activist political groups had also been established which levied a constant stream of criticism against Church officials. The lawsuits coupled with other factors including an economic crisis resulted in a 15 million dollar annual deficit and a loan obligation of $20 million on the accounts.

O'Malley differed from his predecessors by wearing a simple robe and sandals similar to a monk's. He moved out of his assigned mansion to a shabby rectory, sold the mansion and traded the archbishop's car for a much smaller and cheaper model. He changed the style of the Church's newspaper and TV station, started a weekly e-mail and became the first cardinal blogger. He sold valuable church property to settle abuse lawsuits for $100 million dollars and closed a fifth of all parishes and a number of schools. He replaced almost all the top managers of the archdiocese and reduced the size of the administrative staff by a quarter. The administrative spending was reduced from $51 million to $35 million and the yearly deficit was cut from $24 million to $2 million. Hundreds of thousands of Church members were given training in abuse prevention and meetings were held with abuse victim activist groups. Throughout his change program, O'Malley dealt with considerable opposition and criticism from those adversely affected by his actions. However, relations with local community leaders were significantly improved after many private meetings with them. In such meetings, he continually reminded others of their responsibilities to the greater community to which they all belonged. It appears his leadership style and mindset seems to have been a significant factor in his success. His role model is St Francis and he has a great

"knack for storytelling, a broad familiarity with literature and culture, and an inerrant sense of comic timing."

Michael Paulson, Boston Globe (2008)

The book and film *12 O'clock High* were written by two war veterans who were former officers in an Air Force bombing unit stationed in England during WWII.

The story is based largely on actual events of the challenges of change in their lives [1]. Throughout the narrative the commanding general, General Savage, is sent to the unit as a replacement for the former much loved commander. This commander was replaced as a direct result of his ineffective performance as measured by his poor bombing success and losses of equipment and men. The film has become a classic tool in leadership training in both business and the military. It describes how the new leader first gathers information highlighting the roots of the problems; for example, training, motivation, morale and in the context of the film—bombing strategies. He follows a leadership approach which focuses on improving performance initially through "tough and autocratic measures" and then works on building high morale and greater group cooperation and cohesion after performance improves. The film then describes how he improves perform-ance and morale by appointing existing and respected sub-leaders to implement his change efforts. Throughout, the film describes his ability to cope with many criticisms and oppositions he received on the road to his eventual change success. Also, during the film, General Savage constantly emphasises the need to behave as professionals and carry out responsibilities to higher authorities such as the military and the people of their nation.

—Sy Bartlett and Beirne Lay Jr in film *12 O'clock High* (1948)

One of the most respected and loved leaders in American history is Benjamin Franklin. From a very humble background, with little formal education he became a very famous and respected scientist, diplomat, writer, and American colonial leader and was held in high regard in other countries such as England and France. His writings included his *Autobiography* and *Poor Richard's Almanac* are still read today. His extreme likeability advanced his own career and the interests of the nation (e.g., his success in obtaining aid from France in the American Revolu-tion). Naturally, he had his detractors, as all human beings do, and the rather cynical and dour John Adams did not admire his style or even his personal morality but hey—nobody's perfect.

Change as a constant

Ironically, "change" exists as a constant in individuals, groups, organizations, nations, and the world. Much of fiction as well as non-fiction document the consequences of such change as well as how individuals or groups successfully or unsuccessfully met the challenges of change. Much of the change we encounter takes place at blinding speed whilst other changes are invariably slower. These changes may be unplanned and beyond the control of ordinary individuals or planned and implemented from an individual to organizational level. Change may be resisted when there is a high level of satisfaction with the status quo; however, when there is widespread dissatisfaction a proposed change initiative is more likely to be accepted. To successfully implement planned change, persuasive leadership in some form is usually mandatory. The most suitable persuasive leader, in such situations, will usually depend on their personal characteristics combined with various change procedures proven to achieve targeted change outcomes. Planned change involves a design element, which of course is an important aspect of all of the arts. This suggests that design has aesthetic implications as well as practical ones although this can be often overlooked by those who are not architects or artists.

Some fundamental causes of resistance to change efforts

A basic reason which explains why individuals or groups may resist persuasive efforts to change is that those targeted feel that the costs of making such a change outweigh the perceived advantages. Another is that those pressured for change do not have the ability or capability of changing even if they wanted to. The basic cost or disadvantage of change may include such factors as the physical and mental strain of exerting more effort, learning new approaches, or coping with the hostility shown by social peers to the change. These factors emerged from a study by Carroll and a colleague carried out on mattress factory workers who resisted attempts by the company's CEO to increase their productivity even if it would result in increased earnings [2]. Some of the mattress assembly workers felt that they were already working at the highest level of performance they could sustain in a day. Carroll felt that interviews with the workers showed many had off-the-job living habits that detracted from their physical fitness. Another study, carried out by Carroll and a colleague, found that many foremen involved in a management training class of a plant manufacturing large exhaust systems resisted applying the training back on their jobs for two reasons [3]. First, they felt that changes in behaviour they were being pressured to make would not result in any improvements in their unit's performance. Some felt their subordinates would not accept new models of behaviour. Of course, once leaders know why a change is resisted, they can take this into consideration in their persuasive efforts. For example, they may be able to demonstrate that the actual change will not result in perceived disadvantages or may increase the benefits for changing to overcome the expected disadvantages. In this instance, one must use rewards that are salient or important to those targeted for change and these opportunities may not be obvious without investigation. Among the mattress factory workers, for example, additional earnings were not much of an incentive because the workers had to turn over all their compensation to family members and could not use them for their own wants.

Importance of feelings of self-efficacy in the motivation to change

A belief that successful change is possible or that an individual or group can accomplish a desired end is critical to motivation, as research studies attest. This is not a general type of self-confidence, rather it is associated with specific tasks or achievements. What can be done to create these feelings of self-efficacy for attaining certain accomplishments? What can a leader do to enhance these? Research indicates that reminding individuals of their own similar past accomplishments is useful. If this approach is not feasible, demonstrating that others similar to themselves were successful in similar circumstances is a very effective approach. Carroll in his volunteer health counsellor activities with cancer and paralysis patients simply has to show up so that present patients can see he and others similarly afflicted did recover from the same illnesses with certain treatments. This often replaces gloom with optimism. The patients realize they themselves can possibly achieve the same result by following similar practices. In addition, knowing that an individual or group will have the support, advice, and help of a respected leader in one's change efforts also helps create a positive feeling of self-efficacy. A recent meeting of entrepreneurs at Carroll's business school involved sharing of experiences. One conclusion was that knowing one will have assistance in the future tends to contribute to the success of new business ventures.

Leader effectiveness versus likeability

Leaders often need to choose whether being liked and being effective is most important to them. Machiavelli, a great social philosopher, once said if a leader had to choose between being loved and being feared it would be best to choose the latter [4]. Being liked and being effective in terms of performance and/or goal achievement does not always complement each other, since likeability is independent of many other characteristics of an effective leader, such as competence and intelligence. Likeability, however, is not necessarily related to being moral; anyone could list a number of very likeable rogues and scam artists; being likeable, competent, and seen as moral presents an ideal combination of characteristics for leaders. It would appear that the two leaders described above, O'Malley and General Savage, possessed all these character-istics. It should be pointed out that actual performance is related to trust, which can be clearly seen in the recent financial meltdown. Many leaders were admired by employ-ees and investors until performance problems arose.

Likeability is obviously something that oscillates and a person's likeability can often range from high to low from one point in time to another. This was the case for the two leaders described above (in the Beginning cases). Savage was so disliked because of his initial actions and manner that his flying crews requested transfers. However, as the group became successful the initial dislike of him and his leadership turned into admiration. This is not surprising considering admiration and even liking towards a leader can be influenced by an individual's or group's level of achievement. Many students report great respect and even love for the teachers that forced them to become better and more successful people later despite an initial hostility towards their leadership approach. There are many factors related to both short-term and long-term likeability and many books are available on methods to achieve the likeability factor. Carroll remembers reading *How to Win Friends and Influence People* by Dale Carnegie more than 50 years ago [5]. Millions have since read this and subsequent books by this author, and courses with such titles are still being cascaded out by companies in the training and self-improvement business. In fact, both of Carroll's children have been exposed to this material in more recent times with positive results. In general, all of these books written on "likeability" emphasize the importance of several character-istics necessary to achieve this level of likeability. For example, empathy is often described as the ability to put oneself in the place or situation of others and feel as they do. Another important quality is the ability to be perceived as truthful or "authentic" by others. Other factors include social sensitivity or intelligence; that is, the ability to understand the interests, concerns, and needs of others and demonstrate accuracy in the perception of these attributes. Certainly, these characteristics are highly related to the success of counsellors and therapists in treating patients. In addition, being perceived as friendly and personable with the ability to communicate at ease with others are other such factors related to likeability.

Leadership and admiration—Benjamin Franklin

Franklin had the ability to be seen in a way that others found admirable. This was apparent in France where he was a much lauded figure almost immediately after arriving from America as a diplomat. Obviously, a person's reputation is based on one's previous actions and achievements. Franklin was considered a significant scien-tist by many as a result of his infamous experiments and writing on electricity which was revolutionary during his period. Also, he was well renowned for his success as an entrepreneur, for his writings, and for his establishment of the first lending library in the United States. Franklin certainly fitted the stereotype of the type of person much admired in French culture at the time. In the Royal Court he dressed simply and presented a witty and humble persona that almost perfectly conveyed the impression of the common, home-spun philosopher. He had a scientific outlook and was an advocate of the use of reason and logic to investigate world and life issues. Franklin had a reputation for being a considerate listener with a forgiving nature, and avoided conflict and holding grudges. His philosophy seemed to perfectly match the fundamental American values of the founding fathers. One aspect of this was his basic optimism and typical expression of positive emotions.

Franklin's targeted virtues

Franklin's self-improvement plan is still quite well known. In his teens he developed a plan for arriving at a state of moral perfection. His natural optimism and high self-confidence gave him the self-belief he needed to attain such heights with sufficient resolve, time, and diligence. After much deliberation he determined "13 virtues" as a necessary or desirable means to achieve his life goals. These 13 virtues, however, had to be placed in a certain chronological order since each one depended on the achievement of the previous virtue at a younger age. These virtues are self-explanatory and obvious to most with reflection, and similar to many other writers in antiquity. In fact, one can still find these virtues in present-day writings without reference to Franklin. Let us now take a look at each of these:

1. Temperance: Eat and partake of alcohol in moderation (he drank little with the exception of water).

2. Silence: Avoid trifling conversations. Speak only of that which benefits you or others.

3. Order: Everything in its place and everything in its time.

4. Resolution: Actually do what you resolve to do.

5. Frugality: Waste nothing. Only do what benefits you or others.

6. Industry: Do not waste time or effort.

7. Sincerity: Use no hurtful deceit. Be just. Think innocently.

8. Justice: Wrong none by doing them injuries.

9. Moderation: Avoid extremes.

10. Cleanliness: Tolerate no un-cleanliness in body, clothes, or habitat.

11. Tranquility: Be not disturbed at trifles or accidents common or unavoidable.

12. Chastity: For good of health and offspring and reputations of self and others.

13. Humility: Imitate Jesus and Socrates.

Franklin rated himself with a black mark when he failed to exhibit a targeted virtue. On each of these virtues, he was unable to achieve a score to satisfy himself—particularly chastity. However, he was pleased to find he did improve on these from initial levels. He found pride was an especially difficult factor to overcome. However, Franklin was, as are most, able to project a humble demeanour which he was rather adept at. Eventually, he was able to feel comfortable that his many successes in life were a result of the focus he placed on these virtues [6].

Using goals in change

Many successful change initiatives involve a process of setting goals for those involved in the program. Goals have been successfully used at individual, group, organizational, and societal levels for many years. In such cases, the goal or a desired end or state is specified. First, goals must be feasible or must be perceived as possible by those who are responsible for implementing change. Next, action plans for goal achievements must be formulated. At this stage there is a great need for creativity and space provided to implement creative ideas. It is then possible that the final goals may be broken into sub-goals or progress points. It is necessary to periodically evaluate goal progress to make corrections necessary during the change effort. Of course, people must be persuaded to accept such goals and the inclusion of others in the decision-making process may encourage them to commit to the change program.

Handling multiple factors in change

An old change technique used by the authors during a number of consulting projects required a group of individuals to initially implement a change. This enables participants to identify factors that may emerge as potential barriers to change and factors that can help or facilitate change. An obvious barrier to change is that the individuals involved are not trained adequately and do not know how to perform their new roles. Carrying out training needs assessments, and providing adequate training can reduce the suppressive pressure of this barrier. Another barrier may emerge as a result of a lack of resources—such as funds, equipment, or time—and the provision of such necessary resources will naturally mitigate this as a negative force. Current rules, regulations, policies, and contractual obligations are also common barriers. Some factors that facilitate change include the sudden availability of new resources, policies, contracts, or widespread discontent with the present system or situation. At any rate, a persuasive leader can identify such forces before a planned persuasive communication and incorporate them into their oral or written presentation.

Self-leadership and change

As discussed in Chapter 1, it is often forgotten that, as individuals, we are capable of leading ourselves. Each individual can consist of several different selves within one skin. We are not discussing multiple personalities but rather the fact that over time and across roles and different situations, we may act as distinctly different persons. If we know these different selves we might choose to change some of them while retaining others. Of course, in addition to our multiple selves we do change over time without necessarily intending to do so. We are actually different individuals at different ages typically. One can re-read a book that one has read at a much younger age and it seems as if the book is different than how we remembered it. But it is who we are that has changed and not the book. Over time, we accumulate knowledge, perceptions, attitudes, and even values that change as a result of life experiences. Hopefully, these changes over time are made in a positive way rather than a negative one but we know from our personal observations of others that this is not always the case.

Psychotherapy as an aid to change

Psychotherapy is a discipline which focuses on individual change. In general, the first step in a change process is the recognition of one's deficiencies which are subsequently translated into change imperatives. The identification of the cause(s) must take place and be as true a reflection of the individual's actual deficiencies as can be determined. Attainable, realistic, and challenging development goals are then required to effectively implement change in an individual. After this, a behavioural goal with intermediate goals and self-assessment is required. The same steps are relevant whether one is focusing on individual deficiencies or group deficiencies.

Creating positive emotions

As we have previously indicated, in a conscious change effort, one attempts to induce a feeling of optimism. Negativity not only produces uncertainty and depression in the audience but in the speaker as well. Starting a talk with a success or a number of successes is a proven approach which Margaret Thatcher, a former British prime minister, adopted when she argued in a political speech it was important to have facts and arguments presented from a staff group. In one of her last speeches she said:

> "Ten years ago, the eastern part of Europe lay under totalitarian rule, its
> people knowing neither rights nor liberties. Today we have a Europe in which
> democracy, the rule of law and basic human rights are spreading ever more
> widely; where the threat to our security from the overwhelming conventional
> forces of the Warsaw Pact has been removed; where the Berlin Wall has been
> torn down and the cold war is at an end. These changes did not come about
> by chance. They have been achieved by strength and resolution in defence, and
> by a refusal to ever be intimidated. No one in Eastern Europe believes that
> their countries would be free if it had not been for those western governments
> who were prepared to defend liberty, and who kept alive their hope that one
> day eastern Europe too would enjoy freedom."
>
> —Margaret Thatcher, The Downing Street Years [7]

How small changes can have big effects

A marvellous book—The Tipping Point—presents a great deal of evidence that small changes can produce large effects [8]. The metaphor used to explain this is the "epidemic" caused by a virus which can spread very quickly through a community or social system and new ideas can have this power. The book also documents the importance of incremental changes which by themselves are not profound, but when added on to an existing state of affairs can tip a system into a new direction. From this, it might be concluded that one must not be daunted by what appears to be great difficulty in making a change. Some of the examples provided in the book are dramatic changes in the crime rate in New York City from small changes in policing and changes in fashion trends among different groups. Adding one more female to a mixed gender group has been demonstrated to sometimes have significant effects on that group's subsequent behaviour. In these, and many other examples given, the effects seem to be out of proportion to the causes. Social contagion is one of the reasons given for the big differences resulting from small changes.

SUMMARY

Persuasion in leadership is almost always necessary when change is required at the level of the individual, group, organization. In this chapter, we have highlighted some of the many factors that contribute to successful change management. Leaders who are liked, respected, and perceived to be competent obviously gain greater acceptance from their followers when implementing change than those who are less reputable in terms of their character, nobility, and technical expertise. There is a large body of literature focused on factors that make a leader respected, competent, and at times even loved. We have chosen to explore this issue from three diverse case studies describing very effective leaders who had to deal with the likeability versus competence issue. In addition to leader characteristics there are many tools available to help achieve change. Goal-setting processes, system analysis procedures, and psychotherapy approaches are among these.

END CASE

In the 1970s, Carroll and a colleague—Henry Tosi—made periodic trips to Black & Decker to conduct basic executive training in the fundamentals of management. During this training, the managers often compared the differences between actual company systems and the more ideal systems recommended by various management scholars. One company system, which created significant dissatisfaction, was the managerial goal-setting and appraisal system. This, however, was not surprising since such systems are very relevant to the personal goals of managers in relation to compensation, promotions, and work assignments. The trainers then asked us to study this system, and top management including the son of one of the founders endorsed the project. With the goal of improving the system, this endorsement along with managerial discontent with the present system created a readiness to cooperate in the investigation of the system's problems. In addition, the managers trusted the trainers after becoming very familiar with them. A survey of 50 key managers was made and the results of the survey were cascaded to an alternate group of high-prestige managers. With the aid of trainers, the existing system was substantially changed by this group of managers. The new system was implemented with new forms and training. After 18 months, the system was evaluated and some new modifications were made. A further 18 months later, the same procedure was carried out and again twice more at later stages by the same trainers. Within the first five years operating under the changed system productivity doubled and sales per employee increased four-fold amongst many other performance improvements during this time. Of course, one cannot assume these system changes completely created these performance improvements; however, management believe this was the case.

Exercise

1. Rate on a five-point scale the degree of success you had with the last four change efforts you initiated.

2. List the reasons for the degree of success you had in such change attempts. What could improve your change success rate in the future?

Work cited

[1] Lay, B. (1981) *Twelve O'clock High!* J. Curley Publishers.
[2] Anderson, C.R. and Carroll, S.J. (1980) Predicting performance and operational measures. *Proceedings of the Academy of Management Annual Convention, Detroit, MI.*
[3] Carroll, S.J and Nash, A.N. (1970) Some personal and situational correlates of reactions to management development. *Journal of the Academy of Management,* **13**.
[4] Machiavelli, N. (2004) *The Prince.* London: Penguin.
[5] Carnegie, D. (1982) *How to Win Friends and Influence People.* New York: Pocket Books.
[6] Skaggs, M.M. (1991) *Autobiography of Benjamin Franklin.* Lincoln, NE: Cliff Notes.
[7] Thatcher, M. (1995) *The Downing Street Years* (p. 859). London: Harper Collins.
[8] Gladwell, M. (2000) *The Tipping Point: How Little Things Can Make a Big Difference.* Boston: Little Brown & Co.

CHAPTER 10

Strategic plans as a persuasive tool

"Soon came the thrilling order. It announced one more leftward movement, but it awoke new courage and inspired confidence. It seemed to take us all into confidential relations with the commander."

— Joshua Chamberlain, *The Passing of the Armies* [1]

"It's not the strategy but its successful implementation that is the key factor in a business success."

— Fred Smith, founder of Federal Express

'Several Japanese companies in the 1970s pursued a strategy of constant innovation so as to bring new products and product changes to market constantly and ahead of competitors. This proved to be a very effective business strategy for a while until many adopted it."

— Tosi and Carroll (1982) [2]

BEGINNING CASES

The German Army at the beginning of World War I adopted a strategic plan to target the French and the Russian armies. They then determined that the French army could be mobilized much quicker, and thus presented a more immediate threat than the Russians. Therefore, they decided to initially disregard the Russians and pursue the French as quickly as possible using trains to speed a battalion to the battlefield. Their successes early in WWI have been attributed to the wisdom of that strategy.

As a general, Napoleon was a key strategist and developed many innovative approaches to warfare which contributed to his many victories. For example, in some of his early successes, instead of arranging his forces as one mass army in a frontal assault, he divided his army into independent divisions which created flexibility, mobility, and opportunistic possibilities to attack the enemy forces in a variety of ways.

I decided after some experimentation with drugs and alcohol in a fraternity setting in college that I had to change if I was to realize my goals of achieving occupational and financial success. I developed a new life strategy, I quit the fraternity and the hedonistic excesses they promoted and moved to a single room. I got up early and ran for several miles. I identified great books and tried to read some of them in addition to those assigned by my professors. I started a part-time real estate career while an undergraduate and applied what I learned in my marketing major to good effect. I have bought with my earnings some recommended stocks that have done well. I will finish my MBA degree in a few months and have already received several good job offers.

—Conversation between an MBA student and Steve Carroll

Jim Sinegal, CEO of Costco the fourth largest retailer in the United States, has received huge media attention as a result of his unique approach to his CEO position. The first distinct element is his salary of $350,000 which is far below the salary expectations of a CEO in a company this size. Moreover, Costco employees receive the highest salaries within the US retail sector. Their wage averages at $17 per hour. In addition, they have 90% of their healthcare costs covered by the company (both full-time and part-time staff). For much of the year, Sinegal visits Costco stores and meets with both employees and customers. From these meetings, he accumulates information to formulate a corporate strategy and policies as well as competitive tactics. His demeanour is always friendly, open, and observant and gives others an opportunity to express their ideas. In an interview he was once addressed the following statement: "Some analysts have argued that Costco's generosity to its workers hurts the company and its shareholders." To which he replied:

"You have to recognise—and I don't mean this in an acrimonious sense—that the people in that business are trying to make money between now and next Thursday. We're trying to build a company that's going to be here 50 or 60 years from now. We owe that to the communities where we do business. We owe that to our employees, that they can count on us for security. We have 140,000 employees and their families, that's a significant number of people who count on us. We owe it to our suppliers. Think about the people who produce products for us—you could probably multiply our employees by three or four times. And we owe it to our customers to offer good prices. Our presence in a community makes pricing better throughout that community because when you have a tough competitor in the marketplace, prices come down."

—Jim Sinegal, from a TV documentary

What are strategies?

Strategies are plans to accomplish certain desirable ends. There are strategies for nations, for organizations, for groups, and individuals. Although strategies are usually discussed with respect to military, organizational, and political issues they are also used by individuals to accomplish certain personal ends—think of the narratives in the novels of Jane Austen or thousands of other works of fiction. In education we often use the term "learning strategies" as well as teaching strategies. Strategies are often formed in light of one's own strengths and weaknesses in light to those of others or competitors. Strengths can be in the form of advantages such as superior financing, technology, knowledge, political backing, alliances and networks, familiarity with an area, motivations, and willingness to sacrifice. Although some successfully use a weakness to their advantage, that is not usually the case.

Importance of acceptance of strategies

In a book entitled *Managing Strategic Implementation*, the authors and others documented that strategies are rather useless unless they are actually implemented correctly [3]. Athletics coaches usually blame their teams' defeats on this problem. The effective implementation of a chosen strategy requires acceptance from those who are responsible for carrying it out. Of course they must have the ability to carry it out which is an issue in the design of strategies. The authors' book on strategic implementation contains many different approaches to improve acceptance of a strategic plan by an organization's members. However, a major factor is the perception that the proposed strategic plan can and should work. Thus, it is fundamentally important that the strategy is perceived by the audience as possessing merit for achieving a given end. This initially requires persuasion and encouragement of later successes as they occur on the march toward the end objective. At the various phases of a strategy, an individual or a group must be persuaded and reassured that they are on the right track for a desired end.

Credibility in the strategic planning process

There is always uncertainty whenever one deals with the future. If strategies are too complex or unrealistic, then the credibility of those who propose and/or endorse the plan can be a major factor in its acceptance. When this book was written, governments all over the world were proposing strategies to cope with the financial breakdowns and economic recessions. Since each nation is unique in terms of the severity, causes, and special constraints underlying national problems, their solutions are understandably different. In each country there is some divergence in acceptance of the proposed plan often because the credibility, capacity, and integrity of those proposing such plans are in question.

Strategic plans and goal setting

Carroll in *Managing Strategic Implementation* wrote a chapter on how strategic visions and plans must elicit increasing support and commitment through a process of persuasion rather than directive leadership. Today's highly talented managers and professionals demand this approach. In addition, an innovative approach to carry out a role in a strategic effort is needed and this demands acceptance of the overall strategic plan. This chapter also discussed how strategic plans in organizations should be converted or broken into group and individual goals to ensure accountability in performing critical steps and track progress. The successful accomplishment of all sub-goals is imperative to the success of the overarching strategic plan. Of course goal setting by itself is no panacea for achieving targeted outcomes. There are effective goals and ineffective goals as well as desirable and undesirable goal-setting processes.

Carroll and others have carried out many research studies which provide guides and principles for setting goals and monitoring progress toward their achievement. These guides and principles are important also for preventing or alleviating some of the many possible negative consequences of using goals to implement personal, group, organizational, or even national goals.

In terms of avoiding bad consequences it seems to be important to avoid emphasizing only individual achievement rather than cooperative goals. Short-term goals that are detrimental to the achievement of long-term goals are obviously undesirable as are goals that can encourage unethical behaviours. Observably providing very high rewards for goal achievement may result in efforts to negotiate easy-to-attain goals. Goals without an action plan for achieving them are less likely to be accomplished. Goals which build on an individual's strengths rather than weaknesses or deficiencies are more likely to be achieved. Goals for maintaining previous performance levels should be used alongside goals for new projects if total performance is to be improved. Severe punishments for goal failures might result in some undesirable behaviour. Whilst too many goals can create problems, for managers no more than six seem to be desirable according to one study undertaken by Carroll. Goals should not be set only for areas where a quantitative measure of progress is available as this limits areas where goal setting might be helpful. Subordinate participation in goal setting is usually desirable for many reasons. One is that the subordinate often possesses important information relevant to the achievement of a desired end that is unknown to others. Also participation in goal setting is usually related to higher goal acceptance especially when other motivations are absent or limited.

Importance of self-perceived efficacy in goal achievement

Research clearly illustrates that one must believe s/he or their group is capable of complying with a suggestion or directive in order to invest high amounts of effort into the pursuit of a particular goal. We are continuously emphasizing this rather obvious fact throughout this book because it is far too often overlooked. The competency of individual actors and groups involved in executing the strategy needs to correspond to specific goals they are assigned to. Such goals are more likely to be viewed as attainable with effort, than a vague and distant future goal shrouded in much uncertainty. Carroll is involved in health counselling for an illness which attacks the peripheral nervous system damaging the motor neurons which causes muscle failure and thus paralysis. Fortunately, recovery is possible for the majority so afflicted, with patience to allow the nerve mechanisms to grow back and with extensive physical therapy. The trick is to convince the patients of such possibilities when they feel so helpless. All counsellors for this disorder have recovered themselves from the illness. As they tell their stories to newly afflicted sufferers, the patients can readily observe the mobility of the counsellors and the belief dawns that they too can recover. In addition, counsellors usually try to manage the recovery expectations of the patients. They achieve this by pointing out that actual recovery is not necessarily a steady upward progress but two steps forward and one step backward. Realizing this helps to maintain self-efficacy perceptions. As an aside, this uneven rate of progress and recovery seems to be the rule for groups, organizations, and nations. At any rate, the importance of self-efficacy perceptions in motivation to achieve targeted goals has been well documented in hundreds if not thousands of research studies.

Visioning and goal setting

In the past, goal setting in organizations of all types had often resulted in an over-formalized planning system. This was acceptable when outside change was limited. However, today in the ever-changing world of the "Third Wave", over-formalized systems of planning can be harmful as recent societal events indicate. Flexibility is now essential and many large companies have now substituted the use of visions for the future as a substitute for the rigidity of past planning systems. Indeed, at Black & Decker the formal planning system, created with some input from Carroll, was changed to a more dynamic and resilient system to good effect by a new incoming CEO in the 1980s.

To be effective, visioning should involve or require several features. A vision should be compelling and attractive, it must be perceived as feasible or possible of attainment, and should be capable of being understood and remembered by all. It is also recommended that the vision or multiple visions should reflect high ideals, standards of excellence, and should reflect the uniqueness of the social entities (individual, group, organization, and nation) involved. Visions for their achievement usually need much repetition and promotion. The use of artistic processes or devices can be helpful here. For example, Jack Welch of GE, when he was CEO, not only established several compelling visions for his company but constantly discussed them with his subordinate managers whenever he could. He often used familiar metaphors in doing this. For example, he talked about the weeds that will not go away until you pull out their roots. Also, he would mention the useless assets accumulated in the "attics" of companies as well as the many company "closets" that needed to be cleaned out. He constantly acknowledged success stories of individual GE managers and units as they applied to the achievement of such company visions.

Follow-up activities in strategic implementation

There is viability in persuasion by nagging. Here leaders keep reminding an audience of a strategic thrust of tasks to be done to implement a vision and so on. As we indicated, Jack Welch was a master of this approach as perhaps many company presidents are. Carroll observed a very effective CEO of Black & Decker in the employees' cafeteria sitting with various workers and discussing company goals with them as they ate lunch together. Of course, he was gathering information about problems they were having as well. These follow-up contacts between upper-level managers and subordinates in which strategic goals and thrusts are discussed are quite common. Sometimes this has been described as "management by walking around". Many of the persuasive leaders described in this book habitually use this approach whether they are managers, school principals, parents, or other individuals in a leadership role. For example, many effective school principals walk around their schools at times talking to students and teachers, and the biographies of the most effective military leaders depict them as talking to soldiers.

SUMMARY

Very often persuasive efforts are carried out to implement a strategic plan for accomplishing a goal or realizing a vision. Acceptance of that plan is key to its successful implementation. The perceived quality of the plan is in itself a major factor in its acceptance. If the plan is not sufficiently understood, the credibility of its proposer and/or endorsers is key to gaining acceptance. The strategic plans of leaders with a past record of achievement are frequently met with complete acceptance without much persuasive effort.

Perhaps the most fundamental factor in an individual's or group's acceptance of their particular role in the plan is the degree of confidence they have in successfully carrying out their role in the larger plan. Since each group or individual may have a different role in a plan they must be persuaded uniquely. Here, the persuasive effort such as the arguments employed, the emotions evoked, and the stories told will be customized for each group or individual.

END CASE

Dolley Madison was the wife of an early famous president and founding father in the United States. She was a very attractive woman with a very good education for the times and had a pleasing personality. She contributed greatly to the advancement of her husband's political career through her personal relationships with the influential elites of her time. After her husband became president, she renovated the White House the official residence and started to hold very frequent dinners and receptions at her home where her sparkling personality and wit was a great attraction to the important domestic political families as well as to the foreign ambassadors. At these social events, she constantly argued in an informal but persuasive way for her husband's domestic and international goals and policies. She was very effective in her efforts here [4].

"As compared to our enemies we are outnumbered and much shorter on guns and supplies but we will win because we have an effective strategy."

—Napoleon to his officers in Italy early in his career (he did win)

President Obama's popularity which is currently quite high will probably suffer significantly if his strategies for improving the economy of the US do not appear to be working. The public wants results ultimately.

—Several newspaper journalists and TV news personalities (spring of 2009)

Exercise

1. Describe three instances in the past known to you where strategies seemed to fail to achieve certain targeted goals.

2. List some of the factors that could account for each such failure.

Works cited

[1]   Chamberlain, J.L. (1915) *The Passing of the Armies: An Account of the Final Campaign of the Army of the Potomac, Based upon Personal Reminiscences of the Fifth Army Corps.* New York: G.P. Putnam's Sons.

[2]   Tosi, H.L. and Carroll, S.J. (1982) *Management.* John Wiley & Sons.

[3]   Flood, P.C., Dromgoole, T., Carroll, S.J., and Gorman, L. (1998) *Managing Strategy Implementation*, Oxford: Blackwell.

[4]   Côté, R.N. (2004) *Strength and Honor: The Life of Dolley Madison*. Mt. Pleasant, SC: Corinthian Books.

CHAPTER 11

Harmful persuasion

"The world is a dangerous place not because of those who do harm, but because of those who look at it without doing anything."

—Albert Einstein

"Look to the things of God; know you are bound to help all who are wronged.
Bound to constrain all who destroy the law.
What else holds state to state save this alone,
That each one honours the great laws of right."

—The mother of Theseus to her son in *The Suppliants* by the poet Euripides

"And now give me leave to say how it comes to pass that this work is wrought.
It was set upon some of our hearts that a great thing should be done, not by power or might but by the Spirit of God."

—Oliver Cromwell, English general in Ireland in 1649 justifying the execution of more than 2500 military troops and many civilians after their surrender in the town of Drogheda, Ireland (the home town of Patrick Flood)

BEGINNING CASES

"Then came Eichmann's last statement: His hopes for justice were disappointed; the court had not believed him, though he had done his best to tell the truth. The court did not understand him: he had never been a Jew-hater, and he had never willed the murder of human beings. His guilt came from his obedience, and obedience is praised as a virtue. His virtue had been abused by the Nazi leaders. But he was not part of the ruling clique, he was a victim, and only the leaders deserved punishment. I am not the monster I have been made out to be."

—Hannah Arendt, *Eichmann in Jerusalem: A Report on the Banality of Evil* [1]

James Jones, a religious leader from San Francisco, moved his flock of believers to the eastern coast of South America to "protect" them from what he viewed to be disruptive influences. When a congressman visited the colony to investigate the alleged maltreatment of community members, the investigators were attacked by security personnel under the control of Jones. Knowing the extent of trouble he was in, the cult leader ordered his followers to commit suicide by ingesting cyanide mixed with Kool Aid. All but a few members did so and over 900 followers died. Jones persuaded a loyal subordinate to kill him with a pistol at the end. His last words to his followers were

"Die with dignity ... Lay down your life with dignity ... Let's get our medications ... If we can't live in peace then let us die in peace ... Your children deserve to be in peace."

—James Jones to his followers in a TV documentary

Doing harm with persuasion

Persuasive leaders are often rather capable of persuading others to act harmfully or use harmful methods to achieve their desired goals. The justification for evil deeds may be the allegation that they are doing the work of God as in the Oliver Cromwell quote above. The targeted ends of such leaders may be considered good or evil depending on their impact on human welfare. There are countless examples of such harmful persuasion not only in human history but even in everyday life. Throughout the Nazi era,

Hitler and his close comrades persuaded thousands of German citizens to kill by design defenceless men, women, and children. Similarly, tribal leaders in Rwanda convinced thousands of tribal members to seek out and slaughter with machetes more than 800,000 men, women, and children from a different tribe. In a similar vein, communist leaders, Stalin and Mao, have been accused of killing and torturing millions of their own citizens. In recent Middle Eastern conflicts, some religious leaders persuaded young men and women to commit murder-suicides targeting innocent non-political citizens. Even some young children have been targeted and murdered in this way. In the news recently there was an article about a mother, a professional in a Middle Eastern country, who said she would never speak to her son again unless he carried out such a suicide-murder. Christians, hundreds of years ago, were murdered for their religious beliefs in certain Asian nations. Also, Christians of different faiths were encouraged and persuaded by their own religious and political leaders to put to death, often in horrific ways, other Christians who differed in their religious beliefs. At present, gang leaders in United State cities often successfully persuade younger members to murder members of rival groups in combination with committing other crimes in their communities as a means of income or for other reasons. The authors have read several autobiographical accounts of these actions.

Types of harm

The negative effects of harmful persuasion are not always necessarily lethal. The persuasion of large groups to engage in less harmful modes of conflict with other societal or political elements may only lead to the suppression of speech and the destruction of individuality amongst followers. In the 1970s, the world was witness to a cultural revolution in China. Throughout this period, millions of young people collectively referred to as the Red Guards roamed the country waving their red books of quotations from Chairman Mao and destroyed art and buildings and attacked those who represented the older pre-revolutionary culture. In China Carroll interviewed a former Red Guard about such activities. He described how they would cut off the clothes of individuals in the street they thought were inappropriately dressed and how they would ransack houses and destroy old art objects they found. Even today, on many university campuses, certain politically active student groups have been persuaded to disrupt classes, shout through speakers, and attack those who have opposing opinions. In all of these situations persuasive leaders are able to manipulate people using their persuasive skills to inflict significant suffering on various segments of the community.

Why do such persuasive leaders act the way they do?

Certainly, arrogance, obedience, narcissism, aggressive instincts, selfishness, social pressures, and simplistic egocentric thinking on the part of the leader and followers play a significant role in influencing such situations. Predictably, the principles of persuasion can be used for good or for evil and it is therefore critically important that principles of morality are adhered to by leaders and followers to avoid such situations. To ensure adequate commitment to morality, persuasive efforts should aim to instil appropriate values, rules, and institutions in any group, organization, and society to advance such desired moral ends. Those, throughout history, who have attempted to achieve such ends are considered true heroes of the human community and deserve our reverence and respect.

Confronting evil

What is an ordinary person to do in the face of evil? Remain passive and do nothing? Throughout history, it seems strange that this problem remains today. In the Greek play by Euripides, Theseus is asked to resolve an injustice which is not of his making. He is reluctant to do so and thus is not required to in his present office. However, his mother reminds him that universal obligations exist to support the laws and rules that make human existence possible and bearable. Laws, rules, and standards are an important aspect to all religions and it is obvious when they are broken. However, it is not clear who should take action against these broken rules and when. In the United States, protection is now given to those who speak out against their employer when they engage in wrongdoings. These individuals are often referred to as whistle-blowers. Several films have been made in recent years documenting the activities of employees who have publicized what they considered to be immoral practices in their business and public work organizations. One thing is certain: nothing will change unless courageous individuals and groups speak up and take action.

Why is harmful persuasion accepted?

Apathy in the face of evil is commonplace and has been certainly revealed in many holocaust investigations. When German armies occupied many European countries, their localized leaders attempted to capture with the intent to murder the local Jewish population. It seems that many citizens of these nations often reacted quite differently and remained apathetic towards the Jewish community. As documented in the stories from Vichy France, Poland, and other nations, many fundamental supporters of Hitler and his burgeoning empire enthusiastically joined in the Nazi regime and pursued the Jewish population. However many individuals throughout Europe did everything in their power to protect and save their fellow Jewish citizens and often did so at considerable risk to their own families and lives. Carroll observed a film documentary in which a former Jewish citizen of Ukraine gave an account of her experience when the Nazi regime took control of her town. She and her young sister were surrounded by German soldiers and fellow countrymen in the early 1940s. Guns were pointed at them with no apparent route of escape. However, taking the hand of her sister, she ran towards the circle of soldiers surrounding them in an attempt to flee from their pending fate. Much to her surprise, two German soldiers not only stepped aside to let them through but pushed them through the crowd which enabled them to run to safety and ultimately survive.

Standing up to injustice

In all countries, there are those who firmly stand up to injustice. For example, in Boston, the central public library has a constantly changing photograph exhibition of a group of sponsors referred to as the "Upstanders". The exhibit contains photographs and a brief history of citizens from the surrounding area who spoke out against injustices and collectively worked towards correcting such wrongdoings. Also, any daily reading of the obituary pages often reveal incredible stories of the lives of courageous, noble, and altruistic individuals.

Helping orientations

Altruism has been extensively studied by social psychologists. If someone possesses this characteristic it can have corrective effects on harmful persuasion and acts of unscrupulous leaders. Studies in the field of social psychology found that altruism or helping behaviour is likely to be higher amongst individuals who see others performing an unselfish act for others [2]. Parents, co-workers, leaders, and even strangers can serve as role models for helping behaviour. In a number of staged experiments it has been found that the typical person is more likely to help a stranger if he has very recently witnessed another person doing so. Of course, the personality characteristics of individuals differ and this can be related to altruistic or helping behaviour. The personal characteristic "empathic concern" is related to helping behaviour. Empathy is an ability to put oneself in the place of another. A classmate of the first author, in a prize-winning PhD dissertation, found that managers with higher degrees of empathy were more effective in carrying out their leadership responsibilities. Altruism is a form of self-sacrifice which some individuals object to—not all believe altruism represents desirable behaviour. For example, Ayn Rand in her prize-winning novel *Atlas Shrugged*, and in her other writings, argues that sacrificing oneself for another can have detrimental effects to the overall good of society [3]. There may be an element of truth in this. Whilst many methods exist to serve society, reason may provide a more useful way of helping society rather than engaging in altruistic behaviour in a particular circumstance.

There can be intrinsic or psychological rewards in such altruistic or helping behaviours. Self-esteem and self-image can be enhanced through such behaviours. Some believe that altruism leads towards a meaningful life, and this has been found to be related to greater levels of individual happiness. When volunteering as an illness counsellor, Carroll met many people who have carried out such activities for dozens of years. The first counsellor he met had a full-time professional job and provided illness counselling on evenings and many weekends. In addition, she spent her weekends sitting with dying patients and their families as a hospice volunteer and despite these surroundings seemed to be an unusually happy person. Clearly over the years this person has served as a memorable role model to many others in the health areas where she is known. On most occasions, one is more likely to help individuals or groups they care for and love. This is often, but not always, family members, close friends, and long-term colleagues. However, one can often become emotionally attached to an individual with whom they do not have a personal affectionate tie, as observed by the authors in hospital, educational, and work institutions. There are such people as the teacher's pet, the nurse's pet, and the protégé who receive special mentoring from older professionals. Research by Carroll and others indicate that one is likely to invest more in individuals who are likely to be of high value or benefit to a society or a professional organization. Also, those returning gratitude or affection or who appear noble may receive more help. A young female English professor played by Emma Thompson lies dying of breast cancer in the play and wonderful film *Wit*. She receives extra attention from her nurse who was portrayed very well in the film. In one scene, this nurse and this patient are sitting on the same bed licking popsicles the nurse has brought. The dying professor asks "do you ever miss your patients who die?" The nurse replies and looks lovingly at her and says "some of them".

Of course, the perceived role responsibility or duty is a major reason for helping behaviours and also acts as a barrier to harmful persuasion. Most social roles require the adoption of responsibilities associated with such roles; parenting is an obvious example. Society is held together by a system of obligations and many have been sanctioned by law, custom, oath, code, and/or contract. Any contracted obligation is not always held to the classic, legally binding contract and can, on occasion, be implemented through tacit agreement. Leaders generally feel an obligation towards their followers and vice versa. In some societies, most roles are heavily prescribed (e.g., Japan and Saudi Arabia). However, in other individualist societies, there can be more variety in the way social roles are carried out.

The role of deception in harmful persuasion

Finally, let us briefly discuss the means by which harmful leadership is implemented. This, we believe, is through the process of deceitfulness and lying. It is acceptable to assume that lying is the opposite of truth and that it involves deception of some type. People lie for various reasons (e.g., to gain political power, for money, promotions, employment acceptance, etc.). Most of us learn the art of lying at an early age. Children's blatant lies tend to often be very transparent; however, they grow more skilful around the age of five years.

Blatant lies are obvious and rarely fool others, whilst lying by omission is a more distorted view of the truth and is communicated by leaving out certain facts or perspectives. This appears to be the most common type of lying for adults and perhaps some who use it are oblivious to their lie. In this political year in the United States, the internet and the media are full of such lies. White lies, however, are lies that may have overall good intentions and consequences rather than bad. Some leaders admit to telling what they call a "noble lie" which is necessary to save a nation, a civilization, or a life. Among the uses of "noble" lies are those attributed to religions and religious leaders in the past and present. Many religious books have quite different perspectives of what they refer to as God's actions and thousands of essays have been written to explain these differences. Contemporary religious and political leaders often say that God has talked to them and appointed them his agent and spokesperson. Obviously, one cannot entirely refute these claims and they are often believed. Of course, lying damages if not destroys trust to some degree and this is one of its biggest evils in terms of their destructive effects on the credibility of interpersonal relationships. The deception of a lie can destroy a leader's credibility and can make their message uncertain, unpredictable, and lack consistency.

A recent TV documentary on US presidents describes Vice President Harry Truman's recollections of Franklin Roosevelt who he succeeded when Roosevelt died. In response to the question "what was he like?" Truman said that after meeting with President Roosevelt for the first time Truman said to himself, "Well, he lies". Truman was referring to Roosevelt professing his good health when in fact it was very bad and he knew it was bad. The documentary then went on to say that all presidents lie at one time or another but mostly their lies are insignificant in worldly affairs. However, it also pointed out that some lies are especially harmful and have caused the deaths of hundreds of thousands and even millions in certain cases (Hitler, Stalin, etc.). Immoral leaders are more likely to generate a massive intricate web of lies. For example, Hitler's persuasion program was designed to influence the thinking of citizens and soldiers to favor the extermination of millions of human beings and was constant and pervasive over many years. The persuasive efforts were largely in the form of media propaganda through radio broadcasts, political posters, films, books, and newspaper articles. Social leaders and military officers also demonstrated the proposed action consequences of these communications. Opinions in opposition to these messages were not tolerated. It was believed that such extensive training and indoctrination of the population would be necessary to overcome the moral training the population had previously received in their homes, schools, and churches. Of course, not all citizens and soldiers were convinced by these political and social persuasive pressures. There are many examples of individuals who refused to refute their previous moral training. There is a museum in Israel with the name *Yad Vashem* which lists the names of 20,000 persons who risked their lives saving Jewish people during the Nazi genocide.

Deceptive messages well delivered

Last evening, while scrolling through the various TV channels, Carroll happened to notice two speakers who were very effective in their delivery styles. One was a famous TV preacher and the other was a very famous political commentator, both had very engaging voices. Their voices were animated and musical and both speakers had arresting body movements. The speakers used pauses effectively and communicated their inner emotions with appropriate voice tones. One jumped up and down periodically and repeatedly stabbed his finger at the audience. The other moved his arms up and down while speaking and slowly pounded the table with a regular beat to emphasize important points he was making. However, to the author's ear the messages they were communicating were not only nonsense but in one case hateful. Bad ideas and false statements can be delivered in very effective ways which accounts for the huge audiences that these two speakers have. Lawyers and prosecutors are often accused of being persuasive but often in a harmful way since true justice is not achieved. If an innocent man is wrongfully convicted or a guilty one wrongfully set free then some would argue that justice has not been achieved to the detriment of society as a whole.

SUMMARY

Harmful persuasive activities by leaders are far more commonplace than most would prefer. Self-interest, selfishness, perceptions of privilege, and empathy deficits are among the many reasons why persuasion can have detrimental consequences for so many. We read or hear countless examples of such harmful persuasion everyday in the popular press. This is why persuasive leadership skills must be coupled with certain moral virtues such as nobility.

END CASE

"That man is flawed, fallible, and roguish and is no surprise to anyone outside of the nursery ... Man has deliberate goals for which they strive individually and collectively ...Private ambitions and public posturing are seldom the same, so it is healthy to be wary of the ostentatiously altruistic."

—William Hoar, *Architects of Conspiracy* [4]

Exercise

1. Think of a time when your leadership behaviours had a mostly bad or harmful effect even though this might not have been intended.

2. What lessons for behaviour does this incident provide?

Works cited

[1] Arendt, H. (1963) *Eichmann in Jerusalem: A Report on the Banality of Evil*. New York: Viking Press.
[2] Brehm, S.S. and Kassin, S.M. (1996) *Social Psychology*. New York: Houghton Mifflin.
[3] Rand, A. (1957, reprinted 1992) *Atlas Shrugged* (35th Anniversary Edition). New York: Dutton.
[4] Hoar, W. (1984) *Architects of Conspiracy: An Intriguing History*. Western Islands.

CHAPTER 12

Self-leadership

"The mass of mankind has not been born with saddles on their backs, nor a favoured few, booted and spurred, ready to ride them legitimately, by the grace of God."

—Thomas Jefferson

"It is easy in the world to live after the world's opinion; it is easy in solitude to live after your own; but the great man is he who, in the midst of the crowd, keeps with perfect sweetness, the independence of solitude."

—Ralph Waldo Emerson

"No finer memorial can a person have than the likeness of children to the goodness of the character of their parents."

—Cicero

Several historians have attributed military victories early in Napoleon's career to the way in which he organized his army. The traditional and internationally accepted form of military organization used three separate groups fragmented by specialization or function (e.g., infantry, artillery, and cavalry). There was, in addition, a centralized medical and supply corp. The coordination of these functions throughout the onslaught of battle posed obvious difficulties. Napoleon broke his army into approximately seven separate units, which contained their independent infantry, artillery, and cavalry functions. Napoleon allowed his commanders to have an autonomous rein over these units throughout the battle. These separate self-contained units had considerable flexibility and speed in comparison with older and more rigid arrangements. Napoleon subsequently developed military strategies and tactics which took advantage of these favourable battle characteristics.

The book, *The Soul of a New Machine*, by John Tracy Kidder [1] is a riveting account of how a technical manager, Tom West, motivated a group of largely inexperienced young engineers to create a high-performing new computer in a limited amount of time. He was able to persuade them that this project would not only be important for the future of the company but would be an exciting and challenging project for them all and a way to prove their worth. This audience was enticed by the process of inventing and creating something new that they could take pride in. The project was successful in large part because of Tom West's ability to isolate this design group from dysfunctional outside influences. The group spirit that was created with its many benefits of collaboration and sharing along with a desire to live up to the expectations of others probably also contributed to the overall success achieved.

"To achieve change, create a reason and then communicate that reason as many times as you possibly can, in as many ways as you can and to as many people as you can. Face-to-face communication is best because you can never communicate enough while going through change. It is amazing how many times you have to say something before it finally hits home. To help people understand, it's important to be able to describe things in way that's relevant and that sparks a level of engagement. Everybody wants to come to work and to do a good job. So, if you can find something, a purpose which they feel really aligned to, then you don't need to do a huge amount of persuading. In our company our focus is on being the best loved brand in Ireland and the

best place to work. Those are the two things that we always keep front-of-mind. To achieve these two things, you have to get a lot right across the business—people respond to that. It's important for our people to be working in the best company to work for and also the best company as recognised by our customers. We all get a buzz from that. So, if you can articulate change in the context of your key objectives, then it doesn't take a huge amount of persuasion to get people to go with you."

—Danuta Gray, CEO, O2 Ireland
(voted most trusted leader in Ireland, based upon employee surveys conducted by the Great Place to Work Institute) in conversation with Patrick Flood [2]

Leadership and self-management

Self-leadership or self-management enables the realms of leadership to stretch much further. Within self-leadership the need to monitor and persuade are reduced as individuals carry out these functions themselves. Through this approach, followers become increasingly competent as they make decisions for themselves and learn from their achievements and mistakes. Self-leadership embodies the historical values of independence and self-control which can be attributed to many historical societies throughout time. Philosophers for hundreds of years have proclaimed the importance of self-management and independent thinking. The famous American social philosopher, Ralph Waldo Emerson, is especially well known for espousing such values in his many writings in the early 1800s. These characteristics are seen as an imperative for employees, family members, students, and citizens contained in the complex societies of today's world. In recent years, several excellent books on self-management and self-managed work teams have been written by Henry Sims and Charles Manz; both authors are indebted to these scholars for the knowledge and insights they have received [3]–[5].

Political liberty

Socrates was an early advocate of democracy. In theory, democracy requires a population of independent thinkers as opposed to a society that is led by certain leaders. Socrates' goal was to educate Athenian citizens with his ideas such as democracy. He would walk throughout the city streets in worn sandals and a threadbare tunic, followed by his protégés and endeavoured to mentally challenge those he found. Similarly, Thomas Jefferson proclaimed in the Declaration of Independence the right of human beings to be free under "the laws of nature and of nature's God" including certain inalienable rights of "life, liberty, and the pursuit of happiness". At the end of his career, shortly before his death in 1826, he expressed his intention that America should remain to the world "the signal of arousing men to burst chains". However, at the time, most African Americans were not free despite the original draft of the declaration condemning slavery. In addition, the freedom of women was limited as were the rights of Native Americans. Of course, Jefferson did not believe that liberty and freedom should be unlimited as he showed whilst in office as US president. Nonetheless, over time a hope for human liberty under certain restraints has been realized in a political sense in many nations around the world. Many still have a vision of a new world in which democracy and freedom will be the prevailing modes of government everywhere.

Freedom in organizations

In economic institutions employee liberties have traditionally been much more limited. However, in the past 60 years, legislation has been introduced to protect the rights of lower-level workers to unionize and has led to the advent of whistle-blower rights and more freedom on the job. Certain leadership theories allow employees considerable authority in the decision-making process and have become increasingly popular in contempory leadership strategies. Amongst these theories are those that include life cycle theory and those that promote self-managed teams. Life cycle theory suggests that the supervision of others can gradually decline as levels of performance and morale improve. When both performance and morale reach a satisfactory level, formal leadership can be significantly reduced. Most parents have long implemented such a model in their parenting efforts. However, the premature abandonment of appropriate levels of supervision can often lead to adverse consequences.

There are many arguments promoting the benefits associated with self-management including higher levels of employee morale which is often followed by lower levels of turnover, absenteeism, and resistance to change. With self-management, decisions can often be made quicker and closer to an organization's operating reality. Self-management can result in higher levels of creativity and innovation, integration and cooperation, knowledge accumulation, the creation of human resources of greater values, and lower levels of required supervision.

Trends in self-direction in several fields

Since the conclusion of WWII, self-managed teams have been used extensively in Japan; however, this does not appear to have caught on in Western society. There are a number of reasons for this. The absolute destruction of Japan's economy forced a critical re-evaluation of traditional organizational management practices. A severe shortage of experienced managers also contributed to the need for new leadership processes. However, self-managed teams are not easy to establish. The available research evidence indicates they require patience and much training as well as significant persuasive efforts to gain acceptance by employees of new work role responsibilities.

Self-direction in parenting and preparation for self-direction

Most parents believe that their role is to develop their children to grow into autonomous, competent, and self-directed adults. However, many do not have the requisite know-how to achieve such results. Obviously, following the teaching, motivation, and persuasive leadership principles described in these pages one can facilitate this process. To practise democracy a nation requires independent thinking and behaviour from its citizens. Many and possibly most people are comfortable living and/or leading under more authoritarian leaders and systems. Fortunately, most public schools are committed to developing graduates who are capable of living and working under a system of freedom where independent thinking and self-management are the prevailing respectable values.

Therapy and other individual change programmes

Over the past 50 years, different types of therapy have recognized that authoritarian instruction is usually a less effective approach for the achievement of individual behaviour change [6]. If a leader does not have the authority to command change it remains that the targets of change must choose to change and take individual responsibility for doing so. For example, one popular method to overcome alcohol addiction is the Alcoholics Anonymous approach. This type of therapy requires individuals to admit in a public forum that they have an addiction problem and then commit themselves to changing this behaviour. In this instance, the strategy for change involves setting short-term behavioural goals as well as accepting help from others.

Cooperatives otherwise known as worker-owned businesses can be found throughout America. These are often created subsequent to the collapse of a privately owned business and employees assume ownership to preserve their employment. According to recent reports, many such businesses operating according to democratic principles are quite successful. Of course not all such organizations appear to employ employees with higher work satisfaction. Their experience in participative management is likely to contribute to a better quality of life for employees and their families as well as possibly enabling them to become better citizens.

Differential degrees of self-leadership and wasted human assets

In many societies, the freedom afforded to its citizens is generally unequal in its dispersion. Tribalism, class, and social systems are vivid examples of self-leadership privileges granted only to select individuals from certain castes or social classes. Many nations around the world frequently subject women to rigid authoritarian edicts whilst their male peers are granted far more freedom. There is no scientific justification for such unequal distribution of personal freedom; however, a desire for power and control is obviously a root cause of such practices. Such discriminatory practices are very costly to any society in terms of wasted human assets.

As leaders accentuate the use of persuasion rather than authority to achieve desirable ends, one may suggest they are helping to produce better citizens and individuals. These individuals should therefore be increasingly capable of meeting democratic ideals as advocated by Socrates and many scholars and philosophers. In any group, organization, or society, free thinking and independent individuals would be a decided asset and represent invisible assets that are capable of adding value to any social entities. Moreover, such individuals are more likely to be effective family and community members.

Self-management and human respect and dignity

To ensure individuals and groups maintain their dignity it is necessary to treat and behave towards others in a way that emphasizes respect for one another. Showing respect for others helps maintain a sense of self-respect. Psychological and sociological studies have found that self-respect is directly related to human happiness and development. It is important not to rely on one's behaviour but embrace as many dynamic behavioural patterns as possible. (Appendix C lists the best and worst behaviours compiled by various managers from executive programmes presented at Syracuse University.)

Self-leadership and the professional

Certain professionals such as artists, scientists, writers, physicians, psychologists, and lawyers have always had to lead themselves. Such self-direction may be subject to politically influenced legal restraints as well as various codes of ethics and principles contained in each profession. Self-leadership for professionals and artists typically involves the creation of a vision and specific goals as well as personal strategies to attain such goals. Such personal strategies can be effective or ineffective; thus, guidance from successful professionals to develop such strategies may be very helpful. This is one reason for the popularity of professional conferences and workshops. In addition, biographies and autobiographies prove especially useful in this regard. The arts and humanities have always been very helpful to those who need guidance from successful models even if serving as a model is unintentional by a particular person.

SUMMARY

The mind and soul of a human being can be held captive by others. Setting individuals free has been a position widely advocated by not only Socrates but also by writers, philosophers, and other intellectuals all over the world throughout history. Human advancement is largely due to the progress made by free minds. Democracy in a nation and also in organizations is conducive to the fostering of critical inquiry. However, either case cannot be absolute but must be carried out within necessary rational restraints in the form of laws and rules.

END CASE

A production manager at Motorola, Carroll's brother, has published a number of papers detailing his experiences in creating such a team at Motorola. The creation of such an autonomous team took place over a three-year period and required extensive training and a slow evolution from authority obedience to autonomy. It required a significant amount of persuasion to gain acceptance from workers to adopt this new and rather radical approach to organizing work. It takes patience to create the necessary degrees of autonomy and competence. This effort resulted in very significant increases in efficiency and quality as well as improved morale and decreased employee turnover. The employees acquired higher levels of knowledge, and thus increased their value contribution to the company. The process followed and the results obtained are presently being written up in a book by this former Motorola production manager.

Exercise

1.   List five times in your past when you were given the power to manage an activity or project by yourself. How did you feel about yourself at these times? What were your emotional reactions?

2.   Think of several times in the past when you could have given a subordinate person more autonomy and you did not. Why do you think you acted in this way?

Work cited

[1]   Kidder, J.T. (2000) *The Soul of a New Machine.* New York: Back Bay Books.
[2]   McDermott, A. and Flood, P. (2010) *Leadership in Ireland.* Dublin: Blackhall Publishing.
[3]   Manz, C.C. and Sims, H.P. (1980) Self-management as a substitute for leadership: A social learning theory perspective. *Academy of Management Review,* **5**(3), 351–367.
[4]   Manz, C.C. and Sims, H.P. (1987) Leading workers to lead themselves: The external leadership of self-managing work teams. *Administrative Science Quarterly,* **32**, 106–128.
[5]   Manz, C.C. and Sims, H.P. (1995) *Business without Bosses: How Self-managing Teams Are Building High-performing Companies.* John Wiley & Sons.
[6]   Feshbach, S., Weiner, B., and Bohart, A. (1995) *Personality* (Fourth Edition). Wadsworth Publishing.

CHAPTER 13

Persuasive variations in different settings

"There are two sets of law in this world, one for the rich and one for the poor. This is not real justice. This is as true of nations as it is for individuals."

—A protestor at a rally

"The field of Medicine has been described as both an art and a science. Physicians disagree on the relative importance of these. Personally I say it is both."

—A physician in internal medicine

"I grew up in a dysfunctional family before there was knowledge of the word 'dysfunctional.' And it was no fun. There was fear, walking on eggshells. There was disarray, there was disruption and dissension. During my teenage years, my father was an enormous success in the business world, but an enormous failure in our family world."

—Daughter of a Texas billionaire, from Chris Hedges' *American Fascists* [1]

BEGINNING CASES

Harry Lee was a biological scientist at the National Institute of Health. In 1987, when his son was 11 and his daughter was 9, he told them that he wanted and expected them to attend Harvard University when they reached college age. As he discussed his goals for them, he told them what it would take to reach this goal: what grades would be required, what advanced placement courses would be required, and what SAT scores would be needed. He had investigated this issue thoroughly. He asked them to commit to this goal and they agreed. He knew they were very intelligent and that the goal was attainable. His only worry was their motivation and conscientiousness. In an effort to instil excitement and enthusiasm, he had sweatshirts made for both children which read Harvard Class of ___. When the sweatshirts became too small he had new ones printed up. He monitored their progress every few months and scheduled family meetings to discuss and resolve any problems the two children were having. Fortunately there were not many of these. In 2005, his son was admitted to Harvard as was his daughter two years later.

Around 1620, William Harvey discovered how blood circulates. Through his surgery on cadavers Harvey showed that blood flowed in a one way direction throughout the body and that the heart acted as a pump that facilitated this blood flow. According to Harvey, the blood then returns to the right side of the heart and is pumped to the lungs where it picks up oxygen and returns to the left side a much darker colour. He demonstrated this theory to his colleagues by tying a thin tourniquet around his arm side and told his colleagues to feel his pulse and observe his veins. By demonstrating his theory to them by example he convinced them of the merit of his theory.

Clarence Darrow, an American trial lawyer, was one of the most persuasive lawyers in a field where high skill in persuasiveness is common. He only attended law school for one year before being admitted to the bar in 1878. Soon after, he became very well known as a masterful debater, public speaker, and courtroom performer. He used language and stories very dramatically by effectively following poetical and literary principles. In May of 1912, he faced trial for jury tampering in a highly publicized case involving union violence. Knowing his reputation thousands of spectators fought to obtain seats in the courtroom to observe his trial. Darrow's defence continued for two days during which he sometimes wept, spectators wept, and even the jurors and the judge sobbed. When the jury returned a verdict of not guilty the judge congratulated Darrow and said he spoke for millions of other Americans in that respect. How did Darrow win when the evidence against him appeared so strong?

In their superb book, *Ladies and Gentlemen of the Jury*, law professors Lief, Caldwell, and Bycel analysed his performance in depth [2]. First, knowing that the audience had limited ability to process information he just picked a central idea or theme to emphasize throughout his long eight-hour summation. He chose to use an emotion-focused approach rather than one which was facts-based. His theme was that of a corrupt system and himself facing a harsh punishment which he referred to repeatedly. He spoke much of his defence of the oppressed and how powerful interests were constantly trying to silence him even with the aid of detectives. He talked straight to the jury as equals "speaking neither above nor beneath them". Finally, he used language very skilfully to create targeted emotional reactions with respect to the case against him, and to his enemies past and present.

"I am a defendant charged with a serious crime. I have been looking into the penitentiary for six or seven months, and now I am waiting for you twelve men to say whether I shall go there or not ... I'm a stranger in a strange land, two thousand miles from home and friends ... I have lived my life, and I have fought my battles, not against the weak and poor, anybody can do that, but against power, against injustice, against oppression ..."

"Detectives to the right of me, Detectives to the left of me, Detectives behind me, Sleuthing and spying, Theirs not to question why—Theirs but to sleuth and lie, Noble detectives? ... And are you ready, gentlemen, in this day and generation, to take away the name and liberty of a human being upon the testimony of rogues, informers, vagabonds, immunity hunters, and detectives ..."

"My life has not been perfect; I have been human, too human. I have felt the heartbeats of every man who lived. I have tried to be the friend of every man who lived. I have tried to help the world ... I have done the best I could ... There are people who would destroy me. There are people who would lift up their hands to crush me down ... If you should convict me, there will be people who applaud the act. But if in your judgment and wisdom and your humanity, you believe me innocent, and return a verdict of not guilty in this case, I know from thousands and tens of thousands and yea, perhaps of the weak and the poor and the helpless throughout the world, will come with thanks to this jury for saving my liberty and my name."

Persuasion in the courtroom

In demonstrating persuasion principles the authors often present film clips about court trials. Courtroom persuasion is a very popular theme in novels, plays, and films. Many lawyers have great persuasion skills and serve effectively as teaching models. When devising a strategy, courtroom lawyers have several audiences to think about. There is the jury, the judge, the press and the general public, and their fellow professionals. Even if they lose a case, if they have done well or do better than expected, they may gain in prestige and obtain many future clients. In this setting, what is a persuasive success and a persuasive failure is not always entirely clear. Many famous lawyers have used dramatic approaches in their persuasive efforts in the courtroom. One story which comes to mind is that of a lawyer whose client was accused of poisoning another. At one point in the trial the lawyer grabbed the bottle of poison used as the evidence and drank from it. The judge immediately ordered a recess at which time the lawyer jumped into a car and sped to a hospital where a prearranged stomach flush was administered and then returned to the courtroom at the scheduled time. As a result of his theatrical demonstration coupled with his persuasive defence his client was freed.

Clarence Darrow certainly drew from the arts in his persuasive efforts as the case illustrates. We discuss his approach in some detail because it is a vivid example of how literature and the other arts, especially the performing arts, can be used effectively (for good or evil) in the persuasive process. In Darrow's own defence, he crafted a story in which he played the very sympathetic protagonist and through a narrative of his choosing he challenged the prosecutor's story. His words often used poetical elements and on one occasion he even used an appropriate poem about the game of whist and how one must play the hand that life deals you as best you can even if it is not what you would chosen. He also, like many persuasive leaders, presented his message as a conflict or contrast between two different forces, perspectives or ideas. This is common in literature. People naturally understand this approach and react to it positively. Indeed the authors in their MBA classes, in discussing human decision making, report research on human thinking which tells us that we tend to reduce higher complexity and a multitude of choices down to a contrasted pair. Thus, this is a proven effective approach in persuasion, as even Aristotle recognized thousands of years ago.

Darrow used similar approaches in his other cases. In one case he defended two boys who killed a younger boy for the thrill of it. The issue being debated was the punishment for the crime as the prosecutors sought the death penalty. In this case, Darrow argued that even though all murders were hateful, some were worse than others. He said he felt that murder resulting in more suffering by the victim was the worst and therefore deserved a harsher penalty. As he put it: "Poor little Bobby Franks suffered very little. There is no excuse for his killing. If to hang these two boys would bring him back to life, I would say let them go, and I believe their parents would say so too. But;

> The moving finger writes, and having writ,
> Moves on; nor all your piety nor wit
> Shall lure it back to cancel half a line,
> Nor all your tears wash out a word of it.
> Robert Franks is dead, and we cannot call him back to life."

Darrow also, in his usual manner, pitted himself and his client against his opponent by saying the state, in some ways, was not so different than his clients.

> "Cold-blooded! Let the State, who is so anxious to take these boys lives, set an example in consideration, kind heartedness, and tenderness before they call my clients cold-blooded."

In spite of strong public sentiment for executing Darrow's clients, Darrow's approach worked and the judge sentenced them to life in prison with parole possibilities. Whilst we have highlighted Darrow's application of literary arts, his victory in the courtroom was also due to his being an effective performing artist like many famous lawyers. It's not just the words that one chooses that elicits certain emotional responses and directions in thinking, it's how those words are spoken—the tone, the pauses, the emphasis, and so on. It's also a lawyer's body language and facial expressions that matter. As in all effective works of art, in the drama that is the courtroom presentation there must be a harmony and congruence between all of its elements.

Lawyers are quite aware that a persuasive approach may be effective for one audience but not for another. In the law one can do a masterful job of persuasion but still fail with a particular jury. Juries are, after all, composed of individuals living in a social community which they must adjust to and live with on a day-to-day basis. In the novel and subsequent film *To Kill a Mockingbird*, the town's leading citizen, a white lawyer, is defending an African American man accused of a sexual offence and assault on a young white woman in a small Southern town in the US during a period of segregation [3]. Atticus, the lawyer, provides compelling evidence that the accused African American man could not have inflicted the assault because of his disability. He then makes a very moving appeal to the jury that the law, as applied to all citizens, is fundamental to a free society and must be colour-blind. Nevertheless, the jury convicts the innocent man despite the lawyer's persuasive efforts. Deeply held social attitudes trumped fundamental American values as they often have in America's history. However, eventually segregation vanished and civil liberties for the local African American citizens improved. This was a very slow process and required a series of incremental steps. Perhaps the persuasiveness in the speech of the lawyer and those like him eventually played some role in this achievement. Persuasion failures may in a certain sense be successful in the long run. Even through an audience may not be receptive to persuasion at one point in time; the message may linger in the minds of the audience until it is ultimately accepted.

The law as a symbol of justice

Many novels, plays, films, and current TV programmes involve descriptions of court cases of the present and past—some real and some imagined. Part of the great interest in the law as a subject in literature, films, theatre, and the popular media is largely due to the great human concern with the subject of justice. Justice has been a source of debate for thousands of years. As Plato said thousands of years ago "the need for justice is a basic human value found in all peoples of the world since the beginning of human history." Even young children cry out in anger "it's not fair" ever so frequently as all parents know. It's not just a concern for justice for individuals either. Groups are easily mobilized around the theme of injustice for their people and even those living under tyranny with little freedom still believe in the concept of justice. Many persuasive speeches and writings begin with the premise that an injustice has occurred for various reasons and to remedy this injustice the audience or readers should favour what is being advocated by the pleader.

Persuasion in the medical community

The medical literature shows that persuasive difficulties vary with the type of audience that the medical professional is dealing with. For example, physicians often have problems persuading certain patients to accept prescribed medical treatments. Moreover, pioneers in medical treatments also have difficulties convincing fellow physicians of the effectiveness of their treatment recommendations. In scientific fields, as well as in many professional disciplines, persuasion is largely done on the basis of experimental evidence or case studies which are designed to validate a particular change intervention. Evidence-based persuasion has a long history in medicine. Of course the validity and reliability of presented evidence is often a matter of dispute. Carroll, as a volunteer counsellor to paralysis patients, frequently has to deal with patients who claim a particular treatment cured their paralysis when in fact 85% of those afflicted from this illness recuperate over time. Some famous medical examples which have tried to use evidence-based persuasion include:

- Jonas Edward Salk, who developed the killed virus technique for vaccination against polio by first injecting it into himself, then into his family and into some friends.

- James Carroll who allowed a mosquito infected with yellow fever to bite him after which he contracted the disease and later died proving how the disease is transmitted.

- Philippe Pinel, a French physician during the French Revolution, was appointed as the government physician at a Parisian hospital which served as a prison and a home for the elderly poor. He had become interested in mental illness when his close friend became psychotic and was locked up, chained, and treated like a wild animal. This unfortunately was the custom at the time. His friend soon escaped into the woods where he was then devoured by wild wolves. Pinel, after many persuasive speeches to Couthon, a leading French Revolutionary figure, convinced him to visit his hospital and throughout Couthon's visit he was appalled by what he saw. Pinel persuaded Couthon to permit an experiment where he would release some of these mentally ill patients from isolation. He, however, was warned he would be guillotined if his experiment failed. Pinel first addressed an English patient, who had been chained up 40 years previously for murder, and told the man he would be allowed to walk in the prison yard if he promised to behave like a gentleman. The man gave his word; however, as he had not walked in 40 years he could only but crawl into the courtyard and cried upon seeing the sky and trees. Pinel later released 50 more violent offenders and all demonstrated a gentle demeanour with this form of treatment. Not a single prisoner re-offended which subsequently resulted in a turning point in how the mentally ill were treated.

—Robert H. Curtis, Great Lives: Medicine [4]

Throughout history, persuasion with proof of evidence has a strong success rate. The authors, along with thousands of other professors of organizational behaviour, often teach principles of behaviour by conducting experiments in the classroom where students can clearly see the validity of whatever theory is being discussed and tested. In fact, we found early on that the surest way to increase our teaching ratings from students was to teach our classes in this way. However, in the past, some famous scientists have had difficulties in persuading others about a particular theory or belief because of the way the communicator behaved. Even with strong documentary evidence, there is a danger of rejection from an established authority. This is illustrated in the case of Michael Servetus who disagreed with the eminent medical authority Galen by asserting that blood flowed through the lungs. By order of John Calvin they tied his manuscripts to his waist and burned him at the stake.

Being humble and not arrogant is important. "If I have seen things that others have not it's because I stood on the shoulders of giants" (Sir Isaac Newton). Simply put, it is not only what is said but how it is framed and presented. Arrogant individuals are typically resisted in all walks of life. A little humility as shown in the behaviour of all the world's past great religious leaders goes a long way towards explaining our reverence and respect for them. Why might we ask is such behaviour all too often so rare among our contemporary religious as well as political leaders?

Persuasion in the home

Much of the arts focuses on issues in family life and describes in great detail how such issues arise and what their consequences are at later periods. Persuasion is sometimes an element in such analyses. Unfortunately, in many homes there is very little persuasion and far too much commanding. As indicated in the first chapter, research shows great variation in parenting practices within and across different countries. Evidence strongly suggests that love from parents is predictive of the willingness of children to accept their parent's persuasive communications. Additionally, the actual role model behaviour of such parents is itself a very persuasive factor for influencing the willingness of children to live their lives in certain ways. In terms of persuasive approaches, parents have many options as they control and influence a child's environments to a significant degree and have daily access on a one-to-one basis to the child. Thus, they can develop persuasive themes or messages and encourage desirable behaviour over and over again. They can also influence schooling to some extent and various aspects of a child's social contacts. Certainly, the evidence strongly suggests that a laissez faire approach to a child's development can be harmful. Treating a child with respect and encouraging them to contribute to various life decisions is valuable in developing competent and mature adults.

A major problem with persuasion in many homes is inconsistency and the often conflicting message delivered from both parents. In the home, to make the persuasive effort successful parents need to emulate the same values, beliefs, and expectations with respect to their parenting approach. Research has clearly demonstrated that great persuasive messages are often nullified by exposure to negative social forces at a later time [5]. In many places, exposure to diversity in thought can be productive in developing new ideas, strategies, or theories. A conflict in ideas then is more useful in some settings and on some issues than in others. This is an age-old problem that has no simple answer. Perhaps we should follow the dictates of Plato for moderation in all endeavours.

Architecture

Architecture is a very competitive business. Midway through the latest recession it was revealed at a national meeting that 30% of the staff at architecture firms had been laid off. Obviously, the economic state of the real estate and financial industries has a significant effect on the prosperity of individuals and organizations in architecture. Public funds available for building are also an important factor. Persuasiveness then becomes an important skill in winning business contracts. Architects must be able to persuade many different types of audiences. There is the client, and these have many diverse needs and values which must be addressed if one is to successfully sell a project. There are also zoning boards, community groups, regulatory agencies, historical preservation and planning boards, as well as artistic advisory groups to appeal to. Artistic standards and trends also constantly shift adding complexity to this problem of professional persuasiveness.

Philanthropic and artistic organizations

Organizations lacking the power of authority require much more skill in persuasiveness than business and government organizations. Here the approach often must be to highly individualistic wealthy individuals or families as well as to the general public. Leaders such as curators of museums or fundraisers who are especially successful often have not only great ability to read such targeted audiences but also must have a great deal of patience as persuasion in these situations requires many contacts over a long period of time. All great museums owe not only their benefactors a great debt but also owe their persuasive curators much as well for their success.

In the political arena

Recent research in psychology has demonstrated that, for a significant proportion of a population, political affiliations are very strong and among such individuals persuasive attempts to change their thinking is very difficult indeed. Experiments conducted with brain-mapping techniques show that strong political identifications can lead to a freezing of perceptions such that opinions contrary to those of an audience do not register at all. Politics and religious beliefs form an essential part of the self-identity of many individuals and as such attempts to change core political or religious beliefs are generally likely to fail. However, other persons or the social environment are part of one's self-identity also, so if it is perceived that like-minded others have changed their views it is likely an individual may look more favourably on a changing perspective.

SUMMARY

Persuasive effectiveness is always related to the fit between the persuasive approach used and the setting or group involved. Different professions have different persuasion requirements, constraints, as well as expectations. Persuasion in the legal setting is quite different than that in the medical setting. Persuasion in scientific units of universities is quite different than persuasion requirements in various departments in the humanities. What is standard and what is expected is key here.

END CASES

"I don't care how smart he is. He is pompous and arrogant and disrespectful to others. He may be right but I don't even bother to listen to him usually. And when I do I often go on line to try to find contrary evidence to what he's saying."

—A professor discussing another professor

"Typically, I have many contacts with prospective contributors over a period of several years before I actually ask them for money. I get to know them quite well and usually can tell when a good time to make my request is and what my best arguments will be."

—A very successful university fundraiser

Exercise

1. Recall a few times in your past when you changed your mind about something that was important.

2. List the persuasive factors that you consider upon reflection to be most important in these instances for your change of mind.

Work cited

[1]   Hedges, C. (2006) *American Fascists: The Christian Right and the War on America.* New York: Free Press.

[2]   Lief, M,, Caldwell, H.M., and Bycel, B. (1998) *Ladies and Gentlemen of the Jury: Greatest Closing Arguments in Modern Law.* New York: Touchstone.

[3]   Ibid.

[4]   Curtis, R.H. (1993) *Great Lives: Medicine.* New York: Charles Scribner's Sons.

[5]   Tosi, H.L., Rizzo, J.R., and Carroll, S.J. (1990) *Managing Organizational Behavior.* New York: Harper & Row.

CHAPTER **14**

Achieving trust
and cooperation

"In human society we depend crucially on each other, much more than other, more self-reliant animals. But by cooperation we can increase our strength, by division of labour our skill and by mutual aid our security from misfortune. To establish these desirable arrangements we set up such institutions as promise-keeping, property and the state."

—Anthony Quinton, *The Great Philosophers* [1]

"Pretty soon, at least for me, it becomes harder and harder to force any member of humanity into a straightjacket, into some rigid form in which you all expect to fit. As I see it, political leadership in a democracy requires seeing past the abstractions and embracing the vast diversity of humanity and doing it with humility, listening as best you can not just to those in high positions but to the cacophonous voices of ordinary people and trusting those millions of people, keeping out of their way ... And the word we have for this is freedom."

—Ronald Reagan

"Put more trust in nobility of character than in an oath."

—Greek proverb

BEGINNING CASES

In a series of military campaigns lasting until 448 B.C., a coalition of more than twenty Greek cities triumphed over the powerful Persian Empire. The success of the Greeks was primarily attributed to the construction of 200 ships used to defeat the Persian navy at Salamis in 480 B.C. The secret of the Greeks' victory was in their conceptualization of ships as projectiles that could ram and sink enemy vessels. To achieve success, the Greek ships required advanced speed and manoeuvrability to defeat the Persian ships they were attacking. This required a high degree of cooperation amongst the ships' rowers. They had to row in virtually complete unison with perfect coordination to outstrip and outmanoeuvre their adversaries. The Greeks' use of training and other methods to induce rhythm and synchronization was critical to attain a high degree of coordination and group effort amongst rowers. However, winning the battle also depended upon the co-ordination of ships at a fleet level to initiate effective attack formations. Without fleet cohesion, Greek ships could have hindered each other and created overall chaos during enemy engagement. The Greek ability to achieve cooperation among city states was a crucial component of the assault strategy employed to defeat the Persian Empire. Much of this cooperation was due to the persuasive efforts of various Greek leaders in different city states. The Greeks were motivated by a common threat which elicited loyalty, integrity and a commitment to a united vision. This cooperative military success was the antecedent for future develop-ment of the Greek culture and its contributions to philosophical, scientific, political, economic and educational systems in the western world.

—Based on information in McNeill [2]

Mutiny on board his Majesty's ship 'The Bounty' in the South Seas of the Pacific Ocean resulted in the tyrannical Captain William Bligh and some of his supporters placed on a small boat and set adrift. Following this revolt, mutineers turned their tyranny towards non-mutineers still aboard the ship. The second ranking officer, Fletcher Christian, self appointed leader of the mutineers, looked upon the scene with burgeoning anger. His eyes ablaze with fury he said to his fellow seamen *"Get about your work Thompson—Burkett, if I have anymore trouble from you, I'll put you in irons and keep you there. That's how it is to be, is it?"* To which Thompson replied *"Well we won't have it, Mr Christian. We ain't mutinied to have you come all Captain Bligh over us!"* *"No by God, we haven't!"* Martin added *"and that you'll find!"* Christian returned a steady fierce glare without speaking. The disorderly men dropped their glances resentfully. Christian looked hard at several seamen standing by, Alexander Smith amongst them. *"Order all men aft—Smith"* said Christian. As they gathered together Christian eloquently turned to face them and said *"There is one matter we will decide once for all,"* he began, quietly, *"and that is who is to be Captain of this ship. I have taken her with your help, in order to be rid of a tyrant* (who beat them and deprived the crew of food and water) *who has been a burden to all of us. We are mutineers and if we should be discovered and taken by one of his Majesty's vessels not a man of us will escape death. That possibility is not as remote as you think ..."* (Christian continues to give a number of logical reasons for this)

"The Pacific is wide and still so little known that we need never be taken except as the result of our own folly. In our situation a leader is essential, one whose will is to be obeyed without question. It should be needless to tell British seamen that no ship, whether manned by mutineers or not, can be handled without discipline. If I am to command the Bounty I mean to be obeyed. There shall be no injustice here. I shall punish no man without good cause, but I will have no man question my authority. I am willing that you shall decide who is to command the Bounty. If there is some man most of you prefer in my place, name him, and I will resign my authority. If you wish me to lead you, mind what I have said. I mean to be obeyed." Churchill, the first to speak, said 'Well men, what have you to say?" "I'm for Mr. Christian" Smith called out. There was an instant enthusiastic agreement on the part of all mutineers with the exception of Thompson and Martin. However, when Christian called for a show of hands, even these two raised their hands with the others. The crew had now formed a new cooperative unit. After eliciting more agreements and commitments from the assembled men, Christian then appointed his officers.

—Nordoff and Hall, *The Bounty Trilogy* [3]

Leadership issues in cooperation

Early social scientists posit that all social systems—families, schools, military units, business firms, government agencies, and nations—are systems of cooperation. Certainly all achievements, even those that appear entirely individualistic, when closely examined involve a certain degree of human sharing and collaboration. Since the end of World War II, there has been budding interest in the importance of cooperation among nations to resolve problems which impact all humankind. International organizations have been established world-wide to help achieve the common goals of all nations. Of course, the creation and effective management of such social entities require appropriate leadership. The establishment of certain authority structures require members to subordinate themselves to some extent. The European Union (EU) is a suitable case of such an international system which requires authority and cooperation to achieve many common goals. Within the EU, multiple states submit themselves to the authority of the EU parliament. The Europol police agency is entitled to issue arrest warrants which are also valid across all other European countries. This facilitates cooperation among member states for the overall benefit of EU members. However, the EU is still in the process of evolution as well as the various international courts and economic agencies that regulate its member states.

Successful collaboration is not easily achieved and requires considerable persuasive leadership efforts to realize effective results. This is often the case for cooperative social systems which can become progressively difficult to sustain when the unit increases in size. In large systems, enforced cooperation is unlikely to sustain successful collaboration as all units operate as independent units to some extent. Therefore, acceptance of the established system is a significant factor needed to facilitate sustainable cooperation. However, if members are to accept the overarching system, most of them will subordinate themselves to the leadership of one or a few units. Rational choice theory provides an interesting perspective on this matter. In order to co-ordinate actions and subordinate oneself to a higher power one needs to evaluate the calculated costs of this action. If the pay-offs outweigh the costs of operating in isolation, then the acceptance of subordination would be a rational choice. To illustrate with our previous example, the European parliament attempts to facilitate this acceptance of leadership by rotating the presidential leadership role every six months. This equal ownership of the larger system creates interdependence and acceptance of a desirable collective goal. As demonstrated so far, there are several critical issues in creating sustainable systems of cooperation which will be addressed in more detail in the sections that follow.

Reactions to authority

Many think that life would be bliss if they did not have to subordinate themselves to an authority figure. If you recall, this was the initial reaction in the *Bounty* mutiny case. However, as most often realize, satisfaction usually deteriorates in groups that are created based on complete rejection of authority. In fact, some groups often founded for social, political, economical, and even religious purposes tend to create more misery amongst members than originally existed. Research focused on religious groups in the US, Israel, and other nations has demonstrated most of these groups fail to sustain group continuity and eventually deteriorate. However, in those that do succeed there is likely to be some element of leadership in operation to coordinate effective collaborative movements. Literature from evolutionary psychology suggests that human beings have a natural propensity towards hierarchical systems and a need for leadership to survive and continue to evolve [4].

Strong leaders provide clear direction which develops inner strength amongst members by reducing anxiety caused by environmental uncertainties. This ultimately contributes to enhanced feelings of wellbeing. Strong leaders help members find purpose in their lives through their contribution to worthwhile group goals and retrieve immense satisfaction as a result of this contribution. The formation of group identity creates feelings of strength and competence, as the burden of achievement is shared with others. People find increased satisfaction and a sense of wellbeing when they have honest leaders, who are aware of reality and see the world as it is rather than the world as many would like it to be. People find fulfilment in a leader who wants to create an environment for living in a just and fair world. Individuals are willing to subordinate themselves and the decision-making power to a strong leader who treats them with respect and acts with competence and character. Leaders are in exchange relationships with their subordinates who are willing to commit themselves to a leader who will meet their needs, or at the very least do the best they can in this regard. It appears to us that the seamen in the *Bounty* case looked at Fletcher Christian in this way and for these reasons granted him authority—they trusted his ability to be a strong, noble, and fair leader.

Origins of trust

Trust, as we previously illustrated, is critical to all human relationships. The development of trust begins very early in life in which parents play a critical role. Children trust their mothers as a result of the strong maternal bond that begins at infancy. They also trust their fathers due to the paternal protective role they play in their development. Of course, with trust comes an expectation of love, nurture, and protection. This infantile expectation is a world-wide phenomenon and has existed since the beginning of recorded history. Violations of this parental trust are major precursors of adult unhappiness. If a child does not receive adequate care giving early in life, it is likely this child will enter into adulthood carrying these emotional and mental disturbances. Transferences of these relational disappointments can cause serious difficulties in maintaining satisfying relationships in adulthood. In adulthood a person is likely to have some expectations of the trustworthiness of others based on previous relationships. In a hierarchical relationship such as leadership, these transferences of emotions and expectations are likely to mirror that of previous significant authority relationships, like that of a parent–child relationship. The extent to which trust is damaged in parental relationships is likely to have huge implications for an individual's propensity to trust future leaders in adulthood. This tendency is well documented in thousands of studies in clinical psychology and experimental social psychology research.

Trust is a very important aspect of the emotional ties that bind followers and leaders. Followers are aware of the power differentials that exist between themselves and their leader. Leaders can make decisions that are harmful to followers such as bad financial or economic decisions. They can antagonize powerful others who will then retaliate against the follower. Leaders who abuse followers' trust can cause the leader–follower relationship to deteriorate and ultimately break down. Certainly there is an awareness of power differences among followers which can lead to anxiety, fear, or in extreme circumstances terror.

Types of trust

There are various types and degrees of trust in a leader's capacity to fulfil the responsibilities of their role. If an incompetent, dishonest leader fails the group, it is likely members of this group will suffer harm. To evaluate this risk, followers assess whether the competencies of a particular leader are compatible with the group's current needs. Many factors influence such judgements including previous leadership achievements, academic credentials, endorsements of others' judgements we trust, and our own perceptions of a leader's trustworthiness, honesty, or integrity. Morality and ethics play an important role in perceptions of trust. Perceptions may also be unfairly based on prejudicial factors such as a leader's gender, race, ethnicity, or age. Some such questions that emerge when followers assess a leader's propensity towards trust include:

- Can we believe what the leader is telling us?

- Is the leader a type of person who has shown s/he is devious, cunning, or underhanded at times?

- Does this person have a sense of justice or fairness in dealing with others— especially those with lower amounts of power?

- Is the leader from my tribe or from someone else's?

- Is the leader willing to consider my needs in the decision-making process?

- Does the leader suffer from selfishness, arrogance, or narcissism?

- Are there laws and rules in place to curb wrongdoings?

- Is there measurement and accountability?

Certainly past behaviour may help us to form such impressions and determine the trustworthiness of potential leaders. Some leaders appear to push their own personal needs or the needs of their tribe above those of outsiders. However, system trust can override personal trust if a regulatory system is in place to protect the wellbeing of group members. Returning to our *Bounty* mutiny case, Fletcher Christian, the self-appointed leader of the mutineers, was well known amongst his fellow seamen. He had a good reputation and because he also participated in the mutiny he risked as much as the others. Before the mutiny took place, he gave his fellow seamen good reason for the possibility of escaping capture—the Pacific Ocean was largely unknown at the time and bestowed many hiding places. His main motivation in partaking in the mutiny was the dishonest and destructive behaviour of their previous captain. He agreed to be a fair leader and follow certain rules in punishment rather than be arbitrary in his approach. Previous performance, as the second in command, confirmed his competency and experience at sea. His fellow seamen had faith in his morality to treat them fairly and his ability to captain the ship. Clearly, he possessed all the different types of qualities the crew needed to trust him, and Christian did not fail them.

Although this book focuses primarily on leader–follower relationships and the trust that exists between them, trust has much wider implications at a societal level and can alleviate some uncertainties we are often exposed to in life. For example, strong families and cooperative communities are based on foundations of trust which enable a more predictable and comfortable life when help and support is provided. However, the changing structure of families and community ties have weakened, resulting in more detached social relationships creating higher levels of anxiety, alienation, isolation, and unhappiness. Trust is a major factor in predicting the quality of relationships between individuals and groups. In the study of labour–management relationships, comparisons have been made between relationships characterized by high trust versus those characterized by low trust. Low-trust relationships tend to involve closer supervision, less autonomy, and more coercive action compared with a responsible, trusting autonomous system. Greater trust generates less surveillance, less dysfunctional conflict, and effective use of resources to maximize opportunities. The same is true of relationships between various sub-groups within a nation and the type of relationships that emerge between them. Research suggests that different cultures and nations possess varying levels of societal trust within nations [5].

Follower and leader needs

Followers differ in their need for obedience and independence. When these needs match the authority system, group sustainability can be achieved. In changing situations and circumstances, followers' needs are in constant motion to cope and adapt to the changing environment. As a result, the interdependence and authority needs of a follower will converge and diverge with the existing authority system over time. Many new leaders who, as a result of their own self-doubt, may act as servant leaders and work towards satisfying the needs and expectations of their followers. However, over time, the allure of power and all it brings can be all encompassing for certain leaders. Later, they can become so intoxicated by power some may become dependent on key followers fawning affirmation and admiration to confirm their authority and grandiose sense of self. However, their followers may pursue a contrary path. In a new leader–follower relationship they may feel personally insecure or uncertain, and therefore are likely to be obedient towards their leader. Over time, their growing self-confidence in their own capabilities and familiarity with their leader's competencies and style may create a desire toward independence and autonomy. This tendency towards independence can be found on a greater scale. For example, nations evolve towards this stage for the same reason. Consider the current relationship between Ireland and the European Union. When Ireland first joined the EU, it was financially and economically dependent on EU funding for economic development. Ireland was extremely economically disadvantaged in comparison with other member states at the time. One reason for this was the nation's division and disintegration of key interest groups—employment, management, state, and the church. Persuasive leadership encouraged these groups to cooperate and work towards a common interest—the improved welfare of its citizens. Leadership guidance from the EU facilitated the application of economic strategies to benefit the future interests of the Irish people. As a result, Ireland reaped the benefits of cooperating with this higher authority and became one of the most economically independent members in the EU.

Explaining and fostering cooperation among group members

To foster cooperation one must first identify the factors that stimulate facilitation and those that detract from it. Thousands of studies have explored human cooperation from different perspectives. Trust takes time to build between individuals and results from repeated positive interactions. Some have likened trust-building to filling up a bucket of trust with a teaspoon. The bucket fills up, teaspoon by teaspoon, but one kick will upset the contents of the bucket forever. The authors consider the following theories the most relevant for fostering trust and cooperation in leader–follower relationships.

Theories relevant for fostering trust

Exchange theories suggest that cooperation will increase when parties see that cooperative benefits exceed the costs of working against or independent of the system or relationship. For example, marriage provides benefits such as financial security, love, protection, companionship, child raising, etc. The calculated costs involve some loss of autonomy, occasionally higher stress, burdensome duties, etc. Exchange theories propose that to maintain cooperation, the pay-offs from operating as a unit need to outweigh the calculated costs of operating independent of that unit. Attraction theories suggest that people are attracted to each other as a result of similar values, compatible needs (power and a need for dependence; information sharing), similar goals (for child raising, performance, earnings, etc.), or just liking based on personality or other personal characteristics. There is extensive evidence that individuals look to others as models to guide their own behaviour. These valued others may be admired because of their status, because they are exemplars, or because they are similar to oneself. If these individuals see their mentors exhibit cooperative behaviour it is likely they will also participate in cooperative activities. Considerable evidence suggests that a lack of cooperation can be caused by feelings of injustice or inequity as a result of reward or power differences between group members. Cooperation is more likely to emerge when treatment and rewards are considered fair and dignified. This does not suggest that rewards and treatment have to be equal, but comparable with the responsibilities and level of commitment to a group. However, excessive power differentials which are unmerited can lead to feelings of injustice and anger and contribute to uncooperative behaviour. Diversity in goals and values can often create political conflict and aggression amongst the group. This is especially true in the event of win–lose situations. Negotiation experts, skilled in resolving such situations, favor methods of working towards the achievement of compromise between both parties to facilitate a win–win resolution. Certainly, this tendency towards compromise is a preferential approach to conflict resolution in free societies.

Rewards aim to stimulate cooperation in competitive environments where division amongst the group fails to produce sustainable performance. Financial rewards can arouse and be made contingent on cooperative trusting behaviour. Rewards are not always in the form of monetary gain. Intrinsic or psychologically based incentives in the form of recognition, gratitude, or approval satisfy deeper motivational needs and are often more effective for sustaining trust and cooperation. Research has demonstrated that outside threats to group survival can enhance internal cooperation and group solidarity [6]. For example, the current instability of our economic climate is forcing organizations to restructure and rationalize their operations. In times like this, organizational solidarity and collective sacrifice is emerging in the form of pay-cuts, voluntary redundancies, and longer periods of unpaid leave. These efforts to share the burden are symbolic of the cooperative behaviours necessary for group survival. However, when such threats cease to exist, internal cooperation often deteriorates to a certain degree. Leaders have always used outside threats in an attempt to decrease internal dissension and increase internal solidarity. An examination of newspapers on any given day will usually present examples of leaders using such tactics. Of course there is the "cry wolf" syndrome where sounding an alarm so many times followed by nothing happening can lead to disbelief in such threats.

Some people have "individualistic" mindsets whilst gravitating towards a "collectivist" attitude. There is a higher tendency to cooperate amongst those in the latter group. Both authors have conducted several research studies on such individuals who differ in their groupthink orientations [7]. One method used to differentiate these groups is to ask an individual to write 20 sentences beginning with "I am" followed by a description of how they perceive themselves. Each answer that reflects performing a social role such as a worker, father, son, etc. receives one point on the collectivist scale. Answers relating to individual personality characteristics such as hard-working, ambitious, optimistic, etc. receive one point on the individualistic scale. Within research, this scale has found national differences emerge which have been attributed to the cultural norms of that country. Generally speaking, Japanese participants' scores tend to be much higher on the collectivist scale than Americans who score higher on the individualistic scale.

Evolutionary theories of cooperation

For many years, scholars argued that the lesson of evolution was that of competition among species and individuals for survival. Those more fit for survival under a certain set of environmental circumstances lived to pass on their genes to future generations this preserving such genes. Years ago Carroll attended a lecture by Ashley Montagu, a famous anthropologist, who wrote a book that claimed the natural advantages for survival of individuals and groups would go to those that had higher degrees of cooperation [8]. This was the result of the advantages of helping behaviour and the strengths that unity and cooperation provide. Economic theories that stress the primacy of the pursuit of economic self-interest in human choices have been criticized, as numerous research studies indicate that many, if not most, individuals do not behave in such ways. Many studies show that altruistic and cooperative behaviour are commonplace. In fact, recent TV news broadcasts have analysed human behaviour when various natural disasters such as earthquakes and hurricanes have occurred. The conclusion was that typically in these actual occurrences a great deal of helping and other altruistic behaviours were observed while the instances of predatory and unlawful behaviours were actually small. A problem in such cases is that the media tends to cite the bad behaviours while downplaying the good thus giving a distorted impression of reality. Good news doesn't sell, it seems, as many press observers have noted. Social learning is important to encourage and sustain cooperative behaviour. Many observers also point out that any social, political, and religious practices that encourage collective actions related to goal achievements provide social value to that group or society.

SUMMARY

Cooperation is a critical factor necessary to achieve leadership effectiveness in a wide variety of situations. Without considerable cooperation the success of group efforts would be next to impossible. This is why leadership time is invested in attempting to obtain advanced levels of trust and cooperation amongst group members—mediocre efforts will not suffice. Cultural factors and individual differences may obstruct or facilitate the attainment of trust and cooperation. These include types of individual reactions to authority, different levels of trust, conflict tendencies, social exchanges, perceived common threats, individual versus group rewards, and fundamental individualistic versus collectivist personality orientations. It has been argued by anthropologists and evolutionary biologists that cooperation is a natural state for humans.

END CASES

My mother grew up on a farm on Cape Breton in Canada, one of several in the family. She had seven sisters and one brother. Her mother and father were somewhat disabled, and as a result the children had to contribute in making the farm a livelihood for the family. Her mother assigned each child a certain task necessary for the survival of the farm. Such permanent work assignments were made on the basis of perceived aptitude and the individual preferences of each child. The children tended to prefer tasks that they had appropriate competencies to match. Over time, the children developed expertise in these areas. My own mother was responsible for making the clothes and later in life she became a well-known dressmaker. One sister did all the cooking and another cleaned. One sister traded farm products for fish at the nearby port and another gathered coal from the nearby mines for fuel. The boy and some of the girls were involved with planting and harvesting. There was a piano in the home and the family often sang together. Of course, the children learned something about music and there were also many discussions of current social and political issues as well as a great deal of teaching not only from parent to child but from older children to younger children. Religious topics were often discussed and the family went to church together. Later in life, three children immigrated to America and most of the others migrated to different sections of Canada usually after marriage. The family members maintained strong emotional bonds with each other throughout their lives and helped each other when this was necessary.

—As reported by the mother of Steve Carroll

In his writings, Thomas Jefferson argued that a man is an active, developing, innately moral creature—a social being. Living with other humans in harmonious small rural communities is part of a fully human life. In such an environment, virtue, intimacy, and humanity can flourish. Occasionally individuals are led astray from what is moral, the unguided intellect can be a problem, but more often than not, the environmental factors of overcrowded cities, bleak working conditions, the absence of economic freedom, and the presence of economic exploitation are what cause the lapse in social behaviour. Consequently Jefferson argues for a distinctly non-capitalistic economic system in which every man will always have the option of sustaining and nurturing himself and his family on a small farm. This pastoral life is based, not on profit, but on science, moderation, and beauty. In general, Jefferson believed in a human society based on cooperation and human sociability.

—Richard Mathews, *The Radical Politics of Thomas Jefferson* [9]

Exercise

1. Think of a time when you were in a situation devoid of trust. What led to this? What lessons does this hold for a persuasive leader's behaviour?

2. Think of a situation in your experience where cooperation was much less than ideal. Evaluate the reasons for this. Identify the lessons in this case for the exercise of persuasive leadership.

Work cited

[1] Quinton, A. (1999) *The Great Philosophers*. New York: Routledge.
[2] McNeill, W.H. (1963, reprinted in 1991) *The Rise of the West: A History of the Human Community* (with a retrospective essay). University of Chicago Press.
[3] Nordoff, C. and Hall, J.N. (1936) *The Bounty Trilogy*. Boston: Little Brown & Co.
[4] Tosi, H.L., Rizzo, J.R., and Carroll, S.J. (1990) *Managing Organizational Behavior*. Harper & Row.
[5] Carroll, S.J. and Gannon, M. J. (1997) *Ethical Dimensions of International Management*. Thousand Oaks, CA: Sage Publications.
[6] Smith, K.G., Carroll, S.J., and Ashford, S.J. (1995) Intra- and interorganizational cooperation: Toward a research agenda. *Academy of Management Journal*, **38**, 7–23.
[7] Ibid.
[8] Montagu, A. (1986) *Touching: The Human Significance of Skin* (Third Edition). New York: Harper Perennial.
[9] Matthews, R.K. (1986) *The Radical Politics of Thomas Jefferson: A Revisionist View*. Unversity Press of Kansas.

15

The noble persuasive leader

"If a man be endued with a generous mind, this is the best kind of nobility."

—Plato

"It is better to be nobly remembered, than nobly born."

—Ruskin

"I recognise the right and duty of this generation to develop and use the natural resources of this land; but I do not recognise the right to waste them, or to rob, by wasteful use, the generations that will come after us."

—Teddy Roosevelt

Nelson Mandela was born in South Africa in 1918 and raised by his uncle, a tribal chief, after his father died. The name Nelson was given to him aged seven by a school teacher and replaced his African name meaning troublemaker. In 1939, he attended college where he taught Bible classes and was elected a student leader. He joined the African National Congress, a civil rights movement in 1947 and became a lawyer in 1952. He was arrested several times for his protest activities and was sentenced to life imprisonment in 1962. Later, he refused to be released unless his people were given basic civil rights. His writings from prison received world-wide attention and after world-wide protests about his confinement, he was released from prison in 1990 at the age of 71 and was subsequently elected president of South Africa in 1994. Together with Archbishop Desmond Tutu, Mandela initiated a program of national reconciliation involving amnesty for those who confessed to earlier atrocities. He left office in 1999 a highly respected leader in the world community receiving many honours from various nations.

—Laaren Brown and Lenny Hort, *Nelson Mandela* [1]

Scott Nash founded his organic food company in 1987 using a $2000 loan from his mother. Twenty years later, the company expanded into a $23 million business. The company's success seems to be a product of a number of contributing factors. One is the founder's ability to make friends and create a large social network of individuals who liked and supported him. Such a network provided assistance at critical periods throughout his business's growth. Also, his ability to recognize opportunities and learn from these experiences helped him greatly in his endeavours. His ability to create and sustain a highly motivated and committed workforce and loyal customer base were significant factors leading to the company's growth. His success is, in part, due to his company's unique purpose of making the world a better place by helping to restore the earth's environment. His core customer pool consisted of people who buy organic food who were typically environmentally aware. His customers were not simply purchasing food but seeking out a meaningful shopping experience. The organization was committed to their customer-focused policies and Nash's home telephone number and e-mail address came printed on grocery bags. Nash's strategic commitment to environmental values resonated through all aspects of his business operations. Prospective employees who were invited to join the organization were selected partly on their environmental values. The store chain uses a long list of environmentally friendly and restorative policies and practices which include careful scrutiny of all products to ensure they enhance the environment (e.g., bio-degradable packing and supplies). The electrical needs of the organization were generated entirely through the use of wind power and the company is an active member of various environmental groups and a lobbyist for environmental causes.

Participative leadership practices were in place at every echelon throughout the organization. Nash emphasized that one thing he would not tolerate was lying in any form within the organization. Nash believed that complete openness, sharing of ideas, feelings, and informative communication were absolute fundamental prerequisites for organizational effectiveness. A key concept which was central to his leadership approach was authenticity. His everyday behaviour was such that his emotions and thoughts were transparent to all. Nash believes that an artistic sense is necessary for key employees if they are to successfully execute their assigned roles. For example, his stores have beautiful displays of organic vegetables and each store is designed to create an aesthetically pleasing shopping experience. At meetings, new initiatives are always presented with great dramatic emphasis with Nash often dressing in outlandish costumes. In his talk Nash acknowledged Anita Roddick [2] of the Body Shop (described earlier in the book), an environmentally oriented CEO, as a leadership role model which he uses as a reference for many of his leadership decisions.

—In a talk at the University of Maryland

In 1932, Willoughby McCormick, founder of the McCormick Spice company, died suddenly. In 1988, his nephew Charles McCormick succeeded him as the new CEO. His uncle died whilst visiting New York where he had been trying to borrow money to save his company which had fallen on hard times. Charles had been groomed for the job by his uncle who had no children. However, many had reservations about his capacity for such a position. As the son of missionaries he spent much of his youth outside of the country and as a result had very limited experience working in the company. However, undaunted by his apparent lack of qualifications, Charles immediately took several dramatic actions to turn the company around. He immediately called a company-wide meeting and explained the exact financial and economic problems they faced. He made it clear that together they could solve these problems. He rescinded a previous pay decrease initiated by his uncle and cut working hours to preserve jobs. He called this program the 40/40 deal—forty hours a week at 40 cents an hour. Sometime later he initiated a junior board of directors programme. This was a fast-track program comprised of talented young managers working towards executive appointments later in their careers who were given the power to investigate any problematic company issue they thought worthy of exploration. The young executives developed a new programme which addressed a major issue they believed required attention. They then presented their proposal to the senior board of directors and implemented the change strategy.

Charles insisted that every person in the company should be on a first-name basis and persuaded all managers to volunteer their services to various charity and community groups in their communities. He also installed a guaranteed employ-ment program in which all employees could receive permanency after a short trial period. When he died, enormous sadness overcame the company, many employees claimed Charles' nature and manner made him the most memorable person they had ever met and for many changed their perspectives on life. He left quite a legacy in the minds of those he had known and hitherto his company remains a dominant competitor in the business world to this day

—Stephen Carroll, *Multiple Management in a Changing World*
(unpublished manuscript)

What is nobility?

Nobility can be broadly defined as the attainment of a high degree of moral functioning. It involves absconding one's own selfish interests in favor of helping others in the outside community. Centuries ago, Aristotle claimed that human beings were by their very nature attracted to virtue and the truth [3]. Other Greek philoso-phers and Romans (Cicero, Seneca) were advocates of the same perspective. They also proposed that the best life including one's own happiness was one that involved a pursuit for nobility. Of course, there are those who help others for selfish reasons—better public relations, to avoid being sent to prison or hell, or as a means of gaining power over others. There is more purity in the motive of nobility. The degree of nobility can vary from one individual to another; some individuals almost always behave in a noble way while others do so only on occasion. Historical literature suggests that nobility is not always recognized at the time it is exhibited and sometimes is appreciated posthumously, as was the case for Socrates, Lincoln, and Jesus.

Roots of noble behaviour

There is speculation that a gene for nobility or religiosity exists. This gene would naturally have some evolutionary or survival value for human beings. It is believed that children can be born with noble tendencies; however, various circumstances can later dissolve these qualities. The Transcendentalists, an influential semi-religious/philosophical group of intellectuals in early America, believed that early impulses towards nobility tended to be suppressed by later social pressures. However, they believed that one can transcend these negative forces with appropriate spiritual and meditative experiences. They advocated the development of a strong relationship within a group of like-minded people usually located in a communal setting. There was such a group established on a farm (Brooke Farm) on the outskirts of Boston. The Transcendentalists believed that membership to such a morality-oriented group could ensure that one remained on the proper path or quest toward the noble life. Certainly, many members of strong and cohesive church groups would endorse this purpose-oriented perspective on life. Thus, nobility can be learned through contact and the study of noble persons.

It may well be that nobility as a goal for life is something that many and perhaps most individuals do not strive to achieve. Many, if not most, individuals seem to be primarily passive when encountering various challenges and opportunities that confront our lives. In behavioural terms, nobility tends to require an active engagement with others and life itself. A great story by Henry James, *The Beast in the Jungle*, describes the wasted life of a man who is neither ignorant nor impoverished [4]. His life was so passive that he waited for something important to happen to him. As a result, he missed out on many possibilities for true happiness. If life is a jungle, the beast in the jungle may very well be you yourself.

Does research support these assertions about the nature of nobility and its benefits? It seems so! A large body of psychological research on altruism supports the above assertions [5]. There appears to be a propensity towards altruism among almost all human beings especially towards those close to the helper. However, some claim noble acts include only those actions that are carried out for the benefit of strangers who are unlikely to ever reciprocate their kindness. Research on altruism supports the relationship between altruism and achieving feelings of higher self-esteem, self-worth, and generally a more positive self-identity.

Religion and nobility

Most religions attempt to progress their members towards a greater sense of nobility. Some examples include Jesus, Buddha, Moses, Confucius, and many other religious founders as well as their millions of teachers and promulgators. Recent studies have emerged examining the effects of religiosity on various mental and even physical states and propose a relationship between religiosity and certain positive emotional states—

such as those of hopefulness, optimism, contentment, and personal happiness—have been largely supported. According to a TV documentary observed by Carroll, this is most likely to happen when the religious follower is active in carrying out some moral imperatives of their religion. We would interpret this to mean that when one establishes a strong self-identity, one which incorporates a moral sense, they are likely then to be content with themselves when they live up to their self-imposed behavioural standards.

Nobility in business enterprises

Can the leaders of profit-making organizations be noble? Again, the simple answer to this question is yes; there are many instances of such noble business leaders shown in the examples we have collected throughout this book. However, nobility is not a finite static state but consists of various degrees of noble beliefs and actions. William and Melinda Gates of Microsoft have received world-wide attention and plaudits for their massive donations (more than $28 billion) to various charities around the world. Such charities are attempting to alleviate various types of human suffering and social problems. For example, Warren Buffet, an extremely wealthy United States investor and entrepreneur, has allied himself with the efforts of the Gates Foundation with a gift of billions of dollars. Thousands of other business leaders have been cited for such noble acts such as maintaining salaries of workers who, due to no fault of their own, can no longer work.

Nobility as a social class

Nobility is also often used to describe the ruling elite in a nation. These are often highlighted as a group of apparent aristocrats who attain their exalted status by birth rather than through honourable deeds or behaviours. Despite being indoctrinated with a sense of noblesse oblige, those born to privilege can often exhibit behaviour which is the opposite of nobility. For example, a recent book describes how King Leopold of Belgium, through persuasive lies, convinced powerful political entities to destroy the lives of millions of inhabitants in the middle of Africa for his own personal gain [6]. Recently, popular media has provided us with numerous examples of people who have attained great corporate positions and used this positional power to enrich themselves at the expense of their employees, customers, and investors. Some of these have been sentenced to prison. As an aside we might mention that an accounting professor in the Robert Smith School of Business who teaches ethics brings MBA students to a white-collar prison in Pennsylvania where imprisoned former executives present talks focusing on their remorse for their past behaviours.

Noble behaviour in the form of altruism and helping

Role modelling is a vital contributor for the development of altruism, virtue, truthfulness, and other components of noble behaviour. Research clearly illustrates that individuals are most likely to perform a noble or helping act just after they have observed others behaving in this manner [7]. Individuals who are considered noble have often referred to the influence of their parents, relatives, mentors, and teachers as a source of inspiration which modelled their own behaviour. When leaders foster helping behaviour they set up a dynamic situation whereby an initial increase in helping behaviour is further improved and so on.

A simple approach for increasing helping behaviour is to show gratitude. Gratitude is ego enhancing for both the receiver and giver and is so simple it is rather surprising that so many refrain from doing it. However, on occasion, some may feel that the other is just doing what they are supposed to do and an expression of gratitude is unnecessary. We argue that gratitude is necessary and just as important when individuals are "just doing their job" as it not only provides a source of motivation but suggests acceptance and satisfaction with their performance. Most people believe it is only fair that their efforts be recognized even if they don't achieve a task completely. Similarly, some may feel if they express gratitude somehow they owe the other a benefit. Some, like the latter group, believe in the rule of reciprocity which acknowledges that gratitude and acknowledgement of cooperation is often the cement that holds all social entities together such as friendships, families, work units and organizations, and nations. If such social entities have truly moral ends, they can provide obvious benefits to humankind.

Other personal and situational factors influence the degree of helping behaviour that occurs and most of these are not surprising. Mood and time play significant roles in a person's tendency to be helping towards others. Social loafing is a term used to describe an individual's reduced effort to offer their help as others are present and available. Individuals are also less likely to help when the situation is ambiguous or uncertain as the need for help is unclear. Of course, one must be aware of how help can affect a positive outcome—for example, leadership by walking around has proven benefits for social systems. In this way, leaders are more available as they are frequently in contact with individuals, often in an informal manner, rather than greet members as part of a formal group. As a result of their tête-à-tête contact, information can be exchanged that may have otherwise been unavailable to them. Subsequently, problems may be identified earlier thus reducing the possibility of a problem growing into a more difficult, complicated one. Such contacts can also signal to a subordinate that the leader is more caring, as they are present and actively involved at every level within the organization. In several organizations, where the authors served as consultants, the president or CEO regularly walked around and, in some organizations, had lunch in the employees' dining room. Of course, these benefits will not occur unless the leader appears sincere in his/her interest in the subordinate as a person and issues relating to their specific job or workplace. Such contact can also be viewed as monitoring or abusive if carried out with a negative mindset, which in many instances unfortunately is the case.

The appeal of noble leaders

Followers are naturally attracted to a noble leader as is attested to by the billions of followers of religious leaders. There is much higher reverence for more noble political and industrial leaders both in the present and in the past. It is generally accepted that leader–follower interactions are influenced by both leader and follower perceptions, beliefs, and behaviours. However, a follower's perception and interpretation of their leader's behaviour is what really matters in terms of judging leadership. Therefore, it seems plausible that a higher reverence for persuasive noble leadership will exist if the perceived integrity of a leader's character satisfies followers' expectations. From our perspective, morality does not mean a rigid conformity to a doctrine of ideals, rather in this context morality involves adhering to principles of justice and fairness when dealing with others and not putting one's selfish interests before the interests and needs of others. The most loved leaders have historically been individuals perceived to contain higher moral or ethical principles. In general, noble leaders are more predictable than their opposites, they are more trustworthy and thus validate the need to believe in a just world which satisfies a follower's need for safety, security, and creates a predictable relationship between individual achievements and rewards. Nobility in leadership is worth seeking and what it means is not really a mystery although many may require some therapy, counselling, or training to identify the need for nobility in oneself.

Immoral leaders

The concept of morality can be troublesome in many situations. Many tyrants have justified their authoritarianism on the basis of their own ideology of morality.

However, they really are looking for conformity to their personal standards of behaviour which may be archaic and barbarous in the extreme. The rest of society may view certain leaders' behaviours as highly questionable and immoral. It is often seen that these leaders have designated groups of people within their society singled out as evil or rebellious to the state. Such leaders may enforce social justifications and sanctions to their programmes and command obedience from them. Followers swear allegiance or sanctions to such immoral leaders just as they often do to moral leaders. In Rwanda over the period of 100 days some 800,000 Tutsi tribal members were brutally slaughtered by their Hutu neighbours in 1994. For the most part, the Hutu tribesmen used machetes to execute men, women, and children. However, whilst the massacre received huge media attention, the rest of the world just watched without intervening and for the most part remained detached from the shocking occurrence. There was a United Nations presence but it remained largely committed to peace missions in line with their doctrines. This is a clear and heinous example of an extreme form of immorality at all levels in human society. Why are such immoral leaders supported? Social pressures were important in the Rwanda case and many others in which an "us versus them" mindset operates. Some followers have low expectations or wants with respect to their leader. A jurist who successfully prosecuted a military dictator for various crimes including murder committed during the dictator's leadership was criticized by his mother for his actions. When the jurist asked her why she so ardently defended him she said that the general went to the same church as she did, was a nice-looking man, and she felt he was protecting her against various evil-doers.

What are immoral practices in terms of morality within organizations?

Some companies subject their employees to dangerous practices in the pursuit of higher profits, lower margins, and higher bonuses for executives. Television reports on a pipe company in Alabama reported an excess of 4000 employees injured on work premises since 1995. On one occasion, approximately 60% of the company's maintenance workers were injured on site. The news broadcast reported that at one time a single worker manned one machine; however, later he was forced to run two or three machines at the same time. An international ethics book by Carroll and a colleague lists numerous cases of extreme unethical behaviour in well-known companies around the world [8]. These involve such practices as bribery, product contamination, tax evasions, untruthful financial and marketing practices, cooperation with criminal elements, employment discrimination, sexual harassment, and nepotism among others.

Moral development

A great deal has been written about moral development some of which is found in the teachings of religious groups and in the writings by certain philosophers. Freud described the development of the super-ego which concerns one's feelings of guilt when there has been a certain moral transgression [9]. Piaget, after interviewing many young children, developed a model of moral development which shifts from a blind acceptance of authority to critical thinking about moral issues [10]. Erik Erickson describes the evolution of moral stages based on the confrontation and resolution of certain life cycle issues (e.g., security versus freedom) [11]. Kohlberg later defined a six-stage process of moral development and proposed that most humans have not progressed further than the second stage (social influence) [12]. Thus, he would argue that the majority of people are unfortunately fixed on the concept that moral behaviour means obedience to contemporary social norms rather than action driven by independent and internal moral reflection. Carol Gilligan proposes gender differences influence moral development and developed a theoretical model of moral development for women which she claims follows a separate path than that for men [13].

SUMMARY

Morality and the search for nobility in life have been discussed for thousands of years globally. Certainly, the moral aspect of a person's identity, as judged by themselves and others, seems to be largely associated with how happy one is with one's self and how others react to that person. It is not surprising that most people prefer to be led by moral leaders than by immoral ones. Trust and the predictability of one's behaviour will be higher for the former than the latter. Several psychological researchers have investigated the moral development of human beings; however, there is room for much more research in this area as it is critically relevant to the future of the world as we know it.

Aristotle advocated that humans admire leaders whose nature and behaviour reflect morality and nobility. They are much more likely to embrace persuasive efforts from such individuals than those with immoral characteristics. There is less uncertainty, greater predictability, and less risk in following noble leaders—other skills and competencies held equal. Such leaders are also more likely to serve as positive role models for others. Their behaviour can help individuals maintain their belief in a just world which seems to significantly impact one's mental and physiological health. Moral leaders are likely to foster moral behaviour in the social entities they manage. Research found that high altruism, helping, good citizenship, and more so-called pro-social behaviour in general is associated with noble leadership. Of course, there are many immoral leaders and organizations which tend to diminish human life along their path of destruction. Rules for morality in everyday behaviour have been widely discussed for hundreds of years by various writers in moral philosophy, ethics, and religion. However, these rules are not always concurrent and this is especially apparent in writers representing different religions and cultures. Nonetheless, some moral values do tend to be universal amongst all human beings and therefore provide a standardized platform from which we can relate to others' moral reasoning.

END CASES

"A prudent prince cannot and should not keep his word when to do so would go against his interest, or when the reasons that made him pledge it no longer apply. Doubtless if all men were good, this rule would be bad, but since they are a sad lot, and keep no faith with you, you in your turn are under no obligation to keep it with them. Besides, a prince will never lack for legitimate excuse to explain away his breaches of faith … Men are so simple of mind, and so much dominated by their immediate needs, that a deceitful man will always find plenty who are ready to be deceived."

—Niccolò Machiavelli, *The Prince* [14]

George Washington was perhaps the most persuasive leader in the history of the United States. He constantly had to persuade his officers, troops, foreign volunteers, government and political leaders, wealthy and influential citizens, as well as the general public to do very difficult things in extremely trying times. A great deal of his success was due to his perceived nobility of character. Of course, he had a very noble appearance and bearing which added to being perceived as a noble leader. A contemporary at the time described his fluid movements, erect stature, and regal bearing in his diary. He was seen to be an extremely truthful person willing to sacrifice himself in many ways for the common good. He showed great respect for others at all social levels and was a model of proper and exemplary behaviour even when victories and successes were few and quite rare.

Exercise

1. List the names of the noblest people you have known on a personal level. List the behaviours which caused you to classify these individuals as noble.

2. List the reasons why each of them might have become a noble person. Do some of these have relevance for you? Which? Why?

Work cited

[1]   Brown, L. and Hort, L. (2008) *Nelson Mandela*. Paw Prints.

[2]   Roddick, A. (2000) *Business as Unusual*. New York: Harper-Collins.

[3]   Lawson, H.C. (1991) *Aristotle: The Art of Rhetoric*. Penguin.

[4]   James, H. (2004) *The Beast in the Jungle*. Kessinger Publishing.

[5]   Tosi, H.L., Rizzo, J.R., and Carroll, S.J. (1990) *Managing Organizational Behavior*. New York: Harper & Row.

[6]   Hochschild, A. (1998) *King Leopold's Ghost*. London: Macmillan.

[7]   Tosi *et al.* (1990) *Managing Organizational Behavior*.

[8]   Carroll, S.J. and Gannon, M. J. (1997) *Ethical Dimensions of International Management*. Thousand Oaks, CA: Sage Publications.

[9]   Freud, S. and Brill, A.A. (1995) *The Basic Writings of Sigmund Freud (Psychopathology of Everyday Life, The Interpretation of Dreams, and Three Contributions to the Theory of Sex)*. Modern Library.

[10] Tosi *et al.* (1990) *Managing Organizational Behavior*.

[11] Erikson, E. (1959) Identity and the life cycle. *Psychological Issues*, **1** 140–141.

[12] Kohlberg, L. (1981) *The Philosophy of Moral Development: Moral Stages and the Idea of Justice*. Harper & Row.

[13] Gilligan, C. (1982)*In a Difference Voice*. Harvard University Press.

[14] Machiavelli, N. (2004) *The Prince*. London: Penguin Books.

CHAPTER 16

Leadership emergence

"If the blind lead the blind, both shall fall into the ditch."

—Holy Bible, Matthew 15:14

"When the blind carries the banner, woe to those who follow."

—French proverb

"I must follow them, I am their leader."

—Andrew Bonar Law

Oprah Winfrey is one of the most admired celebrities in America. There are many reasons for this. She is a wonderful example of someone who became a persuasive leader largely from her own efforts. In this, she exposed herself to arts training. At three years old, she learned to read out loud and perform recitations in her home. After a troubled childhood, she was raised by her grandfather in a disciplined environment. She became a TV news person at 17 years old and then studied communication skills and the performing arts in college. From very humble beginnings she became a TV star with her own show which was the most popular show of its kind in America. She also became a TV producer, an award winning actress, and a business tycoon founding a number of businesses. She became a billionaire from her business enterprises. To various audiences she has shown her great persuasive skills. One such case involved an address to the United States congress and President Clinton, whom she convinced to create and pass legislation relating to a national database of child abusers.

Oprah is committed using her celebrity status to improve society in any way she can. One such approach involves encouraging her audience to be nobler and to live happier lives by carefully selecting guests on her show who exemplify behaviour and characteristics which she finds desirable. Carroll observed one show in which close friends and colleagues appeared. In this case, one of the author's friends—a school nurse—told the audience that one of the teachers in their school found she was going to have a baby that year and also found she had not qualified for sick leave. This was a great problem given her difficult financial circumstances. The nurse then persuaded the school's director to allow the nurse and other teachers to donate their sick leave to the pregnant teacher and to fill in for the teacher when she could no longer work. Oprah found this was a good example of everyday nobility and one which she chose to publicise. Oprah also recommends books which she feels have social value. Many feel that in these ways she is a strong promoter of good citizenship. It seems whatever she recommends on her show *Oprah* tends to emerge as a commercial success.

—Wikipedia, 2009

Some of you are surprised to see me here as your new president. I'm surprised myself. I know that I did have disagreements with several of you in the past when I headed up process engineering. I'm sorry—that was in the nature of that job. I'm in a different job now and I assure you I will behave differently.

We all know that we will have to push hard to make this picture tube company an economic success. There's lots of competition in this business. Our American partner has divorced us without alimony because they did not think we could ever be profitable. As our chairman said we have a sick child on our hands but I know we can make him better. I'm sure that if we stick together we can fly through the dark clouds we are facing into the sunny skies beyond. We must try to please our investors—they have faith in us. Also, Taiwan needs successful companies at the present time. The Americans did not really respect our ability to manage a technical company like this. Let's show them they were wrong.

—New Chinese President of a picture tube company
who replaced an American in a joint venture

Joan of Arc was born in France in 1412 and 12 years later began to hear voices from the angels which she said told her that God wanted her to lead France to victory over the English in the Hundred Years War. After several attempts, she persuaded two local officials to present her, dressed in male garb, to the royal court to visit the uncrowned French king. Claiming divine guidance, Joan persuaded the king and several others to provide her with a horse and armour to join a relief army sent to the besieged city of Orleans in France. Although many military commanders dismissed her, she prevailed in persuading many to attack a fortress at Orleans which was considered impregnable at the time. The French finally succeeded after many assaults with Joan continuously persuading them not to give up. This was a great victory and Joan became a national heroine, winning the allegiance of various new military commanders. She subsequently led a number of French units to several other victories before being captured and sold to the English. Under English capture she was tried for heresy and sorcery. After 14 months of trial, she was convicted of wrongdoing by dressing in masculine garbs and burned at the stake in the Old Market Square at Rouen as a heretic at 19 years of age. As one of the most persuasive leaders in human history she has captured the imaginations of many of the most celebrated writers, poets, dramatists, and musical composers in the world who have been inspired to compose works based on her life and exploits. Carroll visited one person's private book collection at the Boston Public Library where he examined a collection of over 3000 books by his rough count on St Joan of Arc. In the third biography that he read of her life it was indicated that at that time more than 25,000 books had already been written about her including several by world-famous authors such as Mark Twain and George Bernard Shaw.

Choosing leaders

Leaders may be elected or appointed or may inherit their position and at times seize their position in a coup. This latter case is often how dictators are brought to power by the military elite. For example, Saddam Hussein on July 17, 1979 declared himself President of Iraq after a coup. The original head of the coup was placed under house arrest. Saddam also became Prime Minister, Commander of the Armed Forces, and Secretary General of the only political party. He then conducted a purge in which many were executed by firing squad. Of course, more typically leaders may volunteer for such leadership positions or may be recruited, enticed, or drafted. Once in place, they have to perform the expected, desired leadership role and are often evaluated on their performance. As a result of this evaluation, a leader may be retained, discarded, or removed from their position.

Carroll, while acting as a consultant, selected David Liu, the Chinese manager quoted above, from several other top managers he interviewed in a company manufacturing picture tubes for the position of CEO in a Chinese company in Taiwan. David was chosen primarily on the basis of his optimism, openness, truthfulness, and of course his technical knowledge of the industrial processes necessary to advance the company. The author felt that David was, most importantly, capable of articulating a strategy for future success and indeed had already developed ideas along this line. It turned out that there was little additional consulting needed by David in the next several years of Carroll observing him, other than some personal counselling. David was in fact a superb success in turning the company around into a profitable entity. Part of his success was due to his absolute dedication to his job in which he worked seven days a week, was open to new ideas, and constantly encouraged others to suggest innovative process improvements and designs. He was a very honest person and often expressed his views openly which his managers and workers appreciated immensely. He never acted politically in the sense of attempting to use guile and deception to advance his own self-interests. In fact, he was not perceived to have any personal agenda, except to advance his company for the good of the nation as he saw it.

Situational factors in persuasive leader emergence and effectiveness

Both Joan of Arc and David, the Chinese manager, owe some of their successful persuasive efforts to time and situational factors which influenced their suitability for such leadership roles. Although it would seem improbable that a 17-year-old farmer's daughter would emerge as a successful military leader, one must consider the political and social climate in France at the time. France was steeped in a particularly desperate situation with a population mired in feelings of hopelessness. Joan, equipped with her claims of divine guidance, represented a source of hope for the future. It was, however, her role in later victories which gave her credibility. Interestingly, the same was true of David. His company was a joint venture between a leading United States electronics firm and a local Chinese company. When the US company divorced the local company because of financial losses, the Chinese managers who remained were extremely pessimistic about the company's future. Carroll, acting as a consultant at the time, noticed they lacked confidence, most likely because they worked alongside American engineers and managers who were generally arrogant and dismissive of the talents of their less experienced Chinese counterparts. David, however, had spent a year in America working in a large US plant as an engineer and as a result did not have any of these feelings of inferiority and consistently communicated hope and optimism. The authors have interviewed a number of CEOs and members of boards of directors and boards of trustees who have almost universally said that the type of leader needed in any organization varies with the organization's situation at the time, although there are basic commonalities or requirements, which is what we are emphasizing in this book.

Some indicators of leader emergence and success

Research, carried out by organizational psychologists, has shed light on only some of these processes. In general, this research has focused on personal characteristics and behaviours related to the attainment and retention of leaders. Such theories relating to the emergence of leaders have been developed by sociologists and psychoanalysts. Research investigating leadership effectiveness usually focuses on just a few leader characteristics and behaviours. Biographies often represent a form of research that, in our opinion, can be quite useful here as they provide a comprehensive representation of the complexities associated with successful and unsuccessful leaders. Literature is also a very useful method for studying leadership effectiveness as it has the added appeal of making such analysis very memorable. Carroll has never forgotten the business leader described in the Arthur Miller play *All My Sons*, which he saw more than 50 years ago. This play depicts a leader who failed to acknowledge the fact that his moral obligations went far beyond his concern for his family. His moral failures eventually led to his ruin as is so often the case in business.

Again, Abraham Lincoln is an example of a very persuasive leader whose career illustrates such processes. He was born impoverished of a mother and illiterate carpenter father who died when Lincoln was nine years old. In his early years as a handyman, he was fired for excessive reading and thinking. At the age of 20 he left home and worked on a flatboat in New Orleans where he observed a slave auction. Appalled by the experience, he vowed, someday, to do something about this societal dysfunction. Lincoln later obtained a job as a clerk in Illinois which gave him the time he needed for extensive reading and enabled him to earn a reputation for honesty, reliability, and kindness. His later behaviour as a postmaster and soldier added to his popularity and widened his circle of friends. Important townspeople took a liking to him and helped him with his efforts to self-education. This ultimately led to his acceptance to the bar as a lawyer. After attaining political office at state level he became more widely known for his skill in debating with political opponents, his positions for voting rights for women and new significant restrictions on slavery. His frontier and impoverished background, striking appearance, and considerable public-speaking skills eventually earned him the presidential seat of the United States. Once in office, his patience and unswerving dedication to the goal of preserving the union, universal compassion, and highly developed persuasive skills made him one of the most highly regarded political figures in the world. His persuasive skills with the general public, members of the US congress, and members of his own cabinet enabled him to repeatedly overcome extreme adversity.

In terms of leadership emergence, there are a number of personal characteristics associated with success in attaining leadership positions and in adjusting successfully to them. First, the perceived integrity and reliability of a leader are commonly seen as good predictors of the appointment and election of an individual to a leadership position as well as precursors to the maintenance of such positions. Those involved in leadership selection seem to want leaders who speak the truth and perform effectively in a predictable, reliable, and consistent manner. Decisiveness also seems to be a prerequisite for achieving effectiveness in a leadership position. It appears that people seem to want a leader to get things done and take decisive action on opportunities and problems.

Conscientiousness and persistence have also proved to be reliable predictors of leadership attainment, retention, and performance. Of course, these characteristics, which are part of the most fundamental personality traits, seem to be consistently predictive of performance in the entire range of human occupations and activities. Another factor which is consistently predictive of leadership selection and performance is self-confidence. Why should others have faith in a leader's capacity to attain certain desirable ends if such a leader does not have faith or belief in their own merits?

Role value congruence is another aspect which appears to have considerable predictability for leadership emergence, adjustment, and success, at least in America where a long research program on this subject has been carried out [1]. However, these research findings were confirmed in a study of Chinese managers in Taiwan carried out by Carroll.[1] Role value congruence theory assumes that all social roles have certain role requirements based on the actions and behaviour consistent with that role. For example, managers, because they work in a hierarchy, must have at least some respect for higher authority and have a willingness to carry out directives from above. In management, another identified role requirement is instructing or advising others what should be done to achieve goals. If an organizational process needs a leader to be receptive to information and ideas from all levels, then of course that leader requires the characteristic of openness. This is something that Jack Welch of GE has emphasized, as indicated in the first chapter.

Today, a leader's capacity to be inclusive is becoming increasingly important and an expected attribute for future leaders. For thousands of years, human beings perceived one another through a rather simplistic lens as either insiders, people like themselves, or outsiders, people unlike themselves. Such assessments form the basis of human behaviour toward such others. Many cultures, in both developed and developing nations, use different words to describe such insiders and outsiders and usually consider outsiders to be somewhat inferior to insiders. Such an assessment of others can unfortunately persist for very long periods. In Japan, for example, which the authors have visited multiple times, Korean citizens are still not completely accepted by many Japanese despite having lived there for hundreds of years. Similarly, in the US, African Americans, Native Americans, and other minority groups have faced comparable rejections by many for several hundred years. All over the world, women have been commonly considered to be so different from men that they should be excluded from not only leadership positions, but from many types of careers, voting, or in some nations being in the company of unrelated men. Evidence from hundreds of studies indicates that women and various minorities perform equally as well as their white male counterparts who traditionally occupy such positions. It would seem there are effective and less effective ways of achieving successful performance in various fields and despite predictive differences. If one acts in an appropriate manner irrespective of gender, race, ethnicity, class, religious preference, or nationality they will achieve similar results. Of course, social class distinction has always been a source of exclusion not only from activities, relationships, and careers but even from respect.

Recently, important leaders in the United States have been removed from their positions because of evidence or beliefs that suggest they have an excluding mindset. Furthermore, significant numbers of members from previously excluded groups have joined high-prestige occupations such as medicine and law and have since been appointed to high leadership positions in many nations around the world.

---

[1] Confirmed in an unpublished study by Steve Carroll.

Leaders as independent visionaries

Leaders at all levels that are considered truly effective are often independent visionaries. They closely study trends and can see or imagine a different future. They tend to have high ego strength and self-confidence such that they do not follow a "herd" mentality like most human beings who are significantly impacted in their thinking and even basic perceptions by what others around them think and do. Psychological research supporting this perspective is very consistent. When psychologists put confederates in a group and have them deliberately misstate what they observe the rest of the group tend to agree with them even when their own perceptions tell them something different. Often leaders are in fact usually expected to have special insights into the future which is why they are given leadership status in the first place.

Persuasiveness and leader effectiveness

There have been studies of leadership effectiveness published in the past 60 years identifying many different types of leadership-related behaviours and characteristics in different situations and leadership roles. They have not necessarily, however, focused exclusively on persuasiveness as compared with other leadership attributes. Our readings of leaders' biographies seem to support a study of exceptional combat leaders in the Israeli Army. Persuasiveness appears especially critical in a military or combat situation whereby the consequences of various actions may result in death. This particular study has extracted four fundamental behaviours of such leaders [2]. The first of these is supportive behaviour. Perceptions of support from other individuals such as leaders, colleagues, family members, and countrymen is associated with lower levels of stress and fear and a greater willingness to take risks. Thus, it is not entirely surprising to find supportive behaviour as a key attribute for leadership effectiveness. The second factor involves having an ideological emphasis. Followers need good justification for engaging in difficult and possibly dangerous activities or behaviours. A third fundamental predictor is exemplary behaviour on the part of the leader. Human beings tend to accept leaders they admire and respect. Admirable leaders at all levels of human life in the past have possessed the characteristic of nobility. At times, people or followers can be fooled through a leader's convincing impression management. Many toxic leaders have successfully given the impression they possess nobility when in fact behind the scenes their nature is quite the opposite. Finally, the effective combat leader places an emphasis on a collective identity; humans are after all social animals and are therefore motivated to protect those with whom they are bonded by ties of loyalty and affection.

Leader–follower interactions

Leader–follower interactions do influence both leader and follower perceptions, beliefs, and behaviours. There seems to be a great deal of support from military biographies that officers in constant contact with their subordinates are not only more respected but at times loved by their followers and thus have achieved more military victories. Leaders in contact with subordinates are more inclined to care for them, to have information about their capabilities and inclinations, to pursue a particular strategy needed to accomplish military goals. An examination of strategy implementation in other types of organizations seems to support similar conclusions from this military-based research.

In some cases, a leader's reluctance to interact with followers appears to be associated with leader narcissism and hubris. By comparing the behaviour of General MacArthur (arrogant) and General Ridgeway (a soldier's general) in the Korean War one can see how such behaviours are prevalent in real-case histories of leaders at all levels from managers, to teachers, and parents of the harmful effects of being self-centred.

Mindsets of effective leaders

In order to emerge as a successful persuasive leader one has to have or develop the appropriate mindset, or perceptual orientation, about oneself and those around them. The use of stereotypes in place of accurate knowledge about the true nature of others will inevitably create false and ineffective appeals and unsuccessful message acceptance. Arrogance and narcissism are typical barriers to achieving credibility and acceptance which are fundamental requirements to truly convince others of the merits of the message. One has to see merit in others, which in turn makes them worthy of respect. Many observers have identified a lack of respect towards others as a major source of tension and conflict in dyadic and group relationships. The credibility of the source of a persuasive message is especially important when a claim about reality is ambiguous and uncertain, and thus there are uncertainties in the mind of the audience surrounding the justifications underlying the appeal. For example, Iran is said to be building weapons of mass destruction; however, for their global neighbours this opens up a litany of questions that need answers. The ambiguity of the information creates distrust particularly due to poor political relations in the past with some Western countries.

Inaccurate and inappropriate perceptions about oneself, others, and reality can be changed. Many have reported such changes after having significant experiences which may be religious, social, economic, or educational and force one to challenge their existing beliefs. Many types of individual or group psychotherapy sessions aim to provide one with such experiences. As such, training such as sensitivity training has often been used to coach leaders to be more accurate in understanding themselves and others. In training, one is constantly confronted by others who demonstrate inaccuracies in interpersonal perception in vivid and dramatic ways. Literature has described the effect of such upending experiences. A famous short story by James Joyce entitled *The Dead* depicts how an arrogant and self-absorbed journalist receives several such confrontational shocks during a holiday celebration [3]. He comes to realize he has not really understood those very close to him such as his wife and that he has deluded himself about his own nature. He undergoes a mental revolution and pledges himself to have a new relationship with his wife and his country.

What do prospective followers want in a leader?

The United States presidential primaries provided some indication of what followers want in terms of an effective leader. After several months of debate from 2007 through to 2008 the reputation of a number of candidates from both parties diminished significantly. The point of contention for most candidates was related to their integrity often defined as their adherence to a firm set of internal values as opposed to succumbing to the expectations or desires of a particular audience. The primaries also highlighted a number of other important factors and characteristics that candidates need to be successful leaders. Honesty and truthfulness was sometimes discussed in terms of possible misdeeds or alleged association with individuals of questionable honesty and integrity in the past. The electorate also evaluated previous experience associated with competence for this particular leadership role which appeared most important. Interestingly, candidates who appeared most moral in their message and behaviour ultimately emerged on top. One candidate who seemed to attract the most excitement especially among younger, less prejudiced voters employed principles of rhetoric and employed figurative poetic language to a greater extent than others. The message of inclusion and cooperativeness resulted in an enthusiastic, almost celebratory, response

> *"we are bringing people together, blacks and whites, Hispanics and Asians,*
> *young and old, small states and big states, red states and blue states, we are*
> *bringing all into the United States. This is our project, this is our mission."*

Leadership changes

Once a leader is in place there may be pressures to change. These may come from followers, from higher authority levels, or from segments of the general public. Disgruntlement as a result of performance may be one reason, and indeed is a very common cause. At the present time many company presidents, politicians, and athletic coaches have had to step down for this reason. Violations of ethical standards or immoral behaviour obviously cause dissatisfaction with leaders. It might be that a leader chosen for particular knowledge and skills is voted out because those abilities are no longer needed. In the great film *The Treasure of Sierra Madre*, three Americans down on their luck in Mexico decide to search for gold in an isolated mountain country in Mexico. There are two young men played by Humphrey Bogart and Tim Holt and a grizzled, much older man played by Walter Huston. The older man quickly becomes the leader because he is the only one who knows anything about prospecting for gold. After they have found gold and mined a large quantity of it successfully his leadership is challenged especially by the young prospector played by Bogart. Bogart's character is so seized by greed and paranoia that he tries to eliminate his partner and capture all the riches for his own gain. His greed eventually results in his murder, all the gold is lost, and the two remaining prospectors chastened by their experience choose new paths in life which are nobler rather than materialistic. The authors have seen this same scenario played out in some companies in which they had the role of consultants. Competition for leadership positions tends to become especially ruthless when the stakes are very high. However, when differences in reward available to leaders versus sub-leaders are much smaller, this ruthless and sometimes dysfunctional conflict should be lower.

SUMMARY

In this chapter, we have explored the different personal characteristics of leaders necessary for such leaders to be selected and also successful. It is clear that a major precursor to successful leadership is often, but certainly not always, the degree to which they are open-minded, caring, and other-centred in their orientation. Such leaders tend to be loved more often than not, and these traits when combined with overall leader competence produce a rather attractive ideal leader. Followers who have a voice or choice in the selection of their leaders appear to be drawn to honesty, truthfulness, integrity, and true commitment to a set of core values. The perceived competence for the particular leadership role is also a factor. If individuals are competing for political leadership posts, following the principles of rhetoric and using figurative language seems to help considerably.

END CASE

William Barnes, as a young Anglican priest, reported to his Bishop for assignment and was stationed in an old parish which at the time was in considerable trouble. Service attendance had been declining for many years and church members tended to be elderly. In addition, the church had considerable financial difficulties that limited their opportunities to promote and hold church activities. The Bishop told William to just let the parish die a peaceful death. However, William asked the Bishop if he had free reign to do what he thought best and the Bishop granted his request.

Within the space of a year, William transformed the services significantly. He brought in modern music and even jazz and scheduled social evenings for the community. The content of William's sermons were directed at contemporary social issues and as a result he became a strong advocate of providing help and assistance to the poor and impoverished in the community and in other parts of the world. Many younger members were attracted to the church for these reasons in addition to William's show of respect towards them. They viewed the reformed church as a lively and fun place instead of the sedate, rigid, traditional churches they were used to. In fact, it became the fastest growing church in the entire region and other priests came to observe its operations in order to learn how to improve the effectiveness of their own parishes. William became an informal leader in this community based on perceived performance.

Exercise

1.   Describe the two most effective persuasive leaders in your experience.

2.   How were they similar and how were they different? Any lessons in this?

Work cited

[1]   Miner, J. (1965) *Studies in Management Education.* New York: Springer Publishing.

[2]   Eden, D. (1975) Implicit leadership theory as a determinant of the factor structure underlying supervisory behavior scales. *Journal of Applied Psychology,* 736–741.

[3]   Fasano, T. (2008) *The Dead by James Joyce.* Claremont, CA: Coyote Canyon Press.

CHAPTER 17

Handling problems and failure

"Remorse is thinking of heaven and feeling like hell."

—Anon.

"Adversity is wont to reveal genius, prosperity to hide it."

—Horace

"Who errs and mends commends himself to God."

—Spanish proverb

"Perspiration: the best solvent of all for solving your problems."

—Prochnow and Prochnow [1]

BEGINNING CASES

Bay of Pigs Invasion

In 1961, President Kennedy was persuaded to endorse a plan to allow Cuban exiles to launch an invasion of Cuba which was led by the communist leader Fidel Castro. The United States' CIA participated in the planning of this project but no help was provided by the US armed forces. The purpose of the operation was to overthrow the Castro government before it received substantial military equipment and jet fighters from Russia. In April of 1961 some 1400 Cuban exiles landed on a Cuban beach. They were all captured by Cuban military forces three days later and imprisoned for a period until the United States negotiated their release in exchange for millions of dollars worth of medicines and other supplies. This failed mission set the stage for the next Cuban episode—the Cuban Missile Crisis in 1962. However, in this second crisis, President Kennedy was not so easily persuaded by his military and intelligence leaders.

The Cuban Missile Crisis

In October 1962, a US spy plane on a flight over Cuba took photographs of a site where missile launchers were being built. When news of this reached President Kennedy a world-wide crisis was emerging. Having just been elected two years previously, he faced new congressional elections—to put it mildly, the president was not happy with this news. These events presented significant problems to the presidency. Almost immediately the top military advisors attempted to persuade the new president to bomb the missile sites and invade the nation of Cuba. Later analyses indicate that the missiles the Soviet Union were placing in Cuba were SS4 medium-range missiles—capable of reaching Washington D.C. Analyses over the next several days identified longer range missiles with the capacity to reach every American city bar Seattle.

President Kennedy's staff saw this as a failure in intelligence as well as past diplomacy which could result in a global nuclear holocaust as a result of a facedown with Russia. The options available to the president were few—a military option as described above or a diplomatic solution. The problem this presented was that Cuba's nuclear capabilities would be operational in a short period of time. The persuasive pressures on President Kennedy were immense. To him, it seemed as if the military wanted to risk nuclear war for the sake of honour. His civilian staff was divided with some advocating the military option and others saying diplomatic approaches should be explored, even though this presented risks given the time restraints. Several famous intellectuals in the world such as Bertrand Russell, the philosopher, made appeals for the use of reason in this crisis.

Despite many persuasive efforts by the military, President Kennedy chose the diplomatic approach with secret approaches to the Russian leader. After diplomatic attempts and the pressure of a military quarantine of Cuba by the United States Navy, a secret diplomatic solution was made. In return for the dismantling of the missile sites in Cuba the United States agreed to refrain from ever invading Cuba and to dismantle the Jupiter missiles they had in Turkey. Of course, Kennedy also had to persuade Congress and the American public to give him a free hand in resolving this crisis. He did this in public speeches and in secret meetings with influential persons in the United States power structure. By pursuing the diplomatic approach and avoiding the hasty emotional response, the United States was saved—at least for the present. As someone once said at the time of the crisis, "If the sun comes up tomorrow it's because there are men of good will." However, who knows what decision making may bring about in future times.

—Description of events from the film *Thirteen Days*

The Challenger Disaster

Challenger, NASA's space shuttle orbiter was launched by NASA despite warnings from various engineers that weather conditions were unsafe to do so. The shuttle exploded seconds after takeoff killing all seven crew members including a schoolteacher who was assigned to the voyage for public relations reasons. Several investigations were made of the disaster—one by the United States Congress. Many possible causes contributing to the disaster were identified. The managers overruled the engineers because of their hubris, because they saw engineers as typical naysayers, and possibly also because of pressures from political leaders outside the organization who had planned a public relations event for the government tied to the event. NASA made many changes in their flight schedules as a result of this disaster. In spite of such changes, a later loss of a space shuttle created another long period of reflection, analysis, and changes in procedures.

"David stood halfway between the door of the classroom and the hallway at the beginning of the day. He was my student and I ordered him to come into the room and take his seat as the bell had rung. My voice rose in anger. I then more softly implored him to sit down as he was disrupting my class. The students were all staring at him. He hesitated. He wasn't sure what to do, it seemed. Finally he jammed his hat on backwards and walked out of the room. Obviously I had failed to persuade him. Many students applauded him."

—High-school teacher in a letter to the editor of a local newspaper

What are problems and failures?

Problems and failures are generally considered a deviation from what was initially planned or desired. Problems can often be solved while failures often cannot. Of course, many problems and failures identified result from unrealistic expectations. At the high school and university level, we encounter thousands of failures due to such unrealistic expectations of young people who lack experience and maturity. However, all professionals such as physicians, lawyers, engineers, scientists, and professional managers know that problems or deviations from what was wanted and also absolute failures are inevitable.

Problems and failures are common

It is widely agreed that there is no such thing as perfection; all efforts result in setbacks to some degree. There may be just as many failures as successes in persuasion efforts and one can learn much from these. In fact, failures may produce higher rates of learning than successes since they often require a more complete and deeper evaluation of causes and effects. Many organizations and therapeutic agencies now rely upon various forms of retrospective analysis to obtain future behavioural and process change. Because of this, failures can result in greater successes in the future.

Causal analysis in dealing with problems and failures

Learning that takes place as a result of failure will be of little effect if the failure is attributed to a false cause. Because of the common tendency to jump to conclusions about the cause of a failure, this attribution is often very common. Overwhelming evidence suggests that most individuals are not particularly competent in discovering the true cause of failures for a number of reasons. One such reason is attribution error. Much research supports the tendency of attributing one's failures to outside forces including others and successes to oneself and especially to one's virtues and/or abilities. Another common tendency in incorrectly analysing failure or problem is human impatience. We immediately want to clear up a problem and move on so the first possible cause that comes to mind is given excessive weight in one's deliberation. Also, individuals tend to oversimplify a failed situation by not recognizing that a failure may have multiple causes and also that multiple causes may be all interconnected in a very complex way.

Retrospective analysis is used commonly in the military when accidents occur. This form of analysis is not uncommon in therapy or in addiction treatments. Certainly, if we teach individuals and groups to use this approach we are likely to reduce the number of future failures. One very systematic approach to causal analysis widely taught to managers in all types of organizations is the Kepner–Tregoe approach. This approach forces one facing a failure of any type to first list all the possible causes of a failure. Then one must compare each cause with the facts of the situation. The facts of the situation are the exact nature of the failure or problem in specific terms. Then one must describe exactly when and where the difficulty emerged and fully state the extent of the deviation from what was initially desired. To identify change in the quality of a performance, one should look at what changes might have occurred to create the deviation. If a possible cause does not fit the facts, it is eliminated. One goes through all the possible causes until one arrives at a cause which fits. If more than one cause fits the facts then an experiment might be made where a cause is consciously introduced to see if it produces the failure. If no listed possible cause fits the facts then new causes might be identified and tested in the same way.

Failures due to a changing world

Machiavelli, in his very famous book on leadership, *The Prince*, provides descriptions of Roman emperors in terms of their style, acceptance by the public, and actual success [2].

He found that some very good leaders often presided over poorly performing empires while some very bad leaders still produced good results. It turns out that these results were primarily due to outside economic and/or political and military factors and not to the leadership exercised. The learning that comes from this analysis suggests that leadership is not exercized in isolation from the rest of the world. All leaders are subject to events quite beyond their control. Historians who carry out studies of presidents of the United States also conclude that, regardless of the quality of a leader, wars, depressions, recessions, and social upheaval may occur because of factors beyond their control. Given this reality, perhaps what a leader must focus his/her attention on is to build an organization and a workforce that is as flexible and resilient ,as espoused by Carly Fiorina, former CEO of Hewlett-Packard. In this way, they can be better able to cope with whatever an uncertain world and life presents them. Naturally, this is what we want to achieve in our parenting efforts with our children. We hope they are resilient and adaptable and mature enough to handle adversity when it arrives as it surely will in all lives.

—Carly Fiorina, in a talk at the University of Maryland

Causes of persuasion failures

Persuasion failures may also result in performance failures. Persuasion failures can be the result of deficiencies in the approach taken or a result of situational constraints and barriers. If a failure is due to factors beyond the control of the persuader, then changes in approach may not be necessary and in fact may be harmful if a less effective approach is adopted in the future. Thus, persuasive efforts may be effective but performance failures may be the result and vice versa. We can only control very imperfectly the world in which we live. Suffice to say, it is very important in the case of failure to correctly identify the true causes of a failure.

Persuasion failures mixed with successes

A persuasive approach may be effective for one audience but not for another. In the novel and subsequent film To Kill a Mockingbird, the town's leading citizen, a white lawyer, is defending an African American man accused of a sexual offence and assault on a young white woman [3]. Atticus, the lawyer, provides very compelling evidence that the accused African American man could not have inflicted the assault because of a disability he was afflicted with. He then makes a very moving appeal to the jury for justice saying that the law as applied to all citizens is fundamental to our free society and must be colour-blind. Nevertheless, the jury convicts the innocent man in spite of the very high quality of the lawyer's persuasive efforts. Deeply held social attitudes trump the other American values as they often have in the country's history.

Persuasion failures due to competing social cultures

Any individual open to change realizes that he or she is embedded in a social system which may be contrary to aspired behaviours or attitudes. Many individuals have been successfully persuaded to change their life style and behaviours in therapy and addiction rehabilitation programs. However, many failures are common as the changed individual often returns to the environment which facilitated the difficulty in the first place. The field of cultural anthropology has demonstrated, through many studies, that much human behaviour is embedded or programmed in a culture consisting of a large network of rules and behavioural expectations. While such cultures have some universals in common such as myths, legends, a social hierarchy, and behavioural norms, they differ in the finer details of these as forces which shape a culture are often unique to each country.

Again, persuasion efforts that attempt to persuade individuals or groups to behave in ways that contradict cultural expectations are likely to fail. A lack of cultural understanding and its social pressures is a major cause of persuasion failures. Thus a successful persuasive attempt may also fail to result in any actual behavioural change because of the impossibility of implementing the change. This frequently occurs in various types of training and change programmes where the participants are discouraged from implementing the change by social pressures in their home environments. Numerous studies have identified this as a major barrier to successful change efforts. For example, school children in certain neighbourhoods find that the social environment in which they live will not tolerate behaviour or thinking which is antagonistic to the local culture. Managers participating in development programs away from the work site also experience the same problem. For example, managers in a management development course, taught by Caroll early in his career, were more likely to learn a topic and apply it on the job when they believed it could help them solve a work-related problem or when their company encouraged them to apply the concept. However, in this latter case the willingness to comply with a company's wishes was dependent on their positive or negative attitude towards the company.

Politics and persuasion failures

In the film *Breaker Morant* (based on actual events in the Boer War), three Australian officers are charged by a British military court in South Africa with atrocities committed against Boer prisoners under their jurisdiction. The military court is secretly under intense political pressure to find the officers guilty and to execute them in order to facilitate a peace treaty with the Boer rebels. Despite their strong defence by a British military lawyer, they were unfairly found guilty. Two of the three officers were executed the next day while the youngest was sentenced to life imprisonment. In this instance, hidden political agendas triumphed over very capable persuasive skills.

Persuasive failures due to foregone conclusions are also described in a book entitled *Funny Business* by Gary Katzenstein who worked for a major Japanese company in Japan [4]. A meeting is held with the company division managers in attendance along with a few Americans to evaluate a new product line for the United States market. The Americans later find out that their arguments at the meeting are not accepted because decisions have already been made in a previous meeting among key Japanese executives. At this previous meeting the Americans were excluded in large part, because outsiders to Japanese culture are inevitably excluded.

Personal characteristics in reacting to problems and failures

Failures are not only common in life they are inevitable. We all know individuals who have adjusted to life's difficulties and those who have been less successful. In contemporary psychology there has been an increased emphasis on factors such as emotional maturity and psychological resilience. This is part of a trend described previously as positive psychology which is preventive in orientation. By building emotional maturity and human resilience we can enable individuals especially those for whom we have developmental responsibilities to better handle the inevitable disappointments and failures as they occur. Research indicates individuals can be trained to improve on such dimensions, which is an important role responsibility for all developmental leaders. Resilience is perhaps especially important in today's workforces as Carly Fiorina, former CEO of Hewlett-Packard, points out at the beginning of this chapter. Indeed, business-focused books and articles have identified organizational resilience as a major factor in survival in the difficult times of the early 21st century.

Resilience has been dealt with in literature in the writings of Thornton Wilder. His plays and novels focus on human resilience and the capacity to cope with the many catastrophes that have occurred in human history. However, not all his characters have this quality, some do not even recognize catastrophic change and if they do they remain passive towards the new circumstances except to behave in habitual ways. Fortunately for all of us, strong resilient individuals often enable others to survive such challenging times and these are not necessarily the elders either. In his novel *The Eighth Day*, a family survived only through the efforts of a 12-year-old daughter when the mother figure and siblings are unable to cope with the sudden absence of the father figure. In his plays *Our Town* and *The Skin of Our Teeth* he describes families successfully coping with catastrophes of various types.

Role of arrogance and hubris in failures

Persuasion failures are often the result of a perception among subordinates or others that a leader's plan or project is likely to fail because the leader has not taken into account an important factor and thus refuse to accept the proposal. Of course, even with subordinate acceptance, projects and proposals that are not subject to careful scrutiny can fail. The biographies of many leaders throughout history show that they often are afflicted with arrogance and hubris and do not listen to others voicing doubts and scepticism. A common personality of leaders is narcissism which is a form of self-love according to popular understanding. It can be more than this, as described by a psychiatrist who has written about this subject.

"Narcissism describes both a psychological and a cultural condition. On the individual level, it denotes a personality disturbance characterised by an exaggerated investment in one's image at the expense of the self. Narcissists are more concerned with how they appear than with how they feel. Indeed they contradict the image they seek. Acting without feeling, they tend to be seductive and manipulative, striving for power and control. They are egotists focused on their own interests but lacking the true values of the self—namely, self-expression, self-possession, dignity, and integrity. Narcissists lack a sense of self derived from body feelings. Without a solid sense of self, they experience life as empty and meaningless … On the cultural level narcissism can be seen as a loss of human values—in a lack of concern for the environment, for the quality of life, for one's fellow human beings."

—Alexander Lowen, *Narcissism: Denial of the True Self* [5]

SUMMARY

Persuasion is not always effective for a number of reasons. Sometimes individuals may be persuaded but the implementation of a proposal or project may be impossible for a number of reasons. These could include opposition by a strong political force, a secret agreement among powerful interests to block a proposal, or an unstated antipathy to the proposal as a result of strongly held internal attitudes and values. Of course, unanticipated barriers may also emerge. Perhaps these were overlooked as they should have been if they were highly improbable. We must concern ourselves primarily with more likely occurrences given the almost unlimited numbers of things that might go wrong in any particular plan or project. A great deal of research carried out in human decision making by psychologists and behavioural economists show that a typical person has never learned to assign probabilities to possibilities very well. Even if they do they very often fail to create contingency plans if the most probable problems occur.

END CASE

Herbert Hoover was the 31st president of the United States. His father died when he was six years old and three years later his mother died also. After the death of his mother, he went to live in California with an uncle and later worked in his uncle's business. Soon after, he became the first live-in student at Stanford University where he met his wife. They were both Quakers and pacifists opposed to war on religious grounds. He became active in mining operations at 23 years of age and was sent to China by a mining company to supervise operations there. He spent two years in China where he lived through the Boxer rebellion. He had made a fortune in mining and became a world traveller. At the beginning of World War I, he raised millions of dollars delivering food for the starving Belgians and French in German-occupied Northern France and became world famous for these efforts. Later, he became Secretary of Commerce in the Presidency of Calvin Coolidge. While in that office he dedicated himself to promote industry standards in the United States. He did not believe the federal government should order companies and banks but rather persuade them to do such things. In 1928, he was then elected President and early in his administration the United States' economy collapsed where he saw the need for various reforms in the financial system. In this instance, persuasion alone was not successful in obtaining change. He lost the 1932 elections to Franklin D. Roosevelt and was blamed for the economic collapse. He and his subordinates helped to make a successful transition from one administration to another. They tried at this time to rescue the many banks that were in distress and later served as chairman on important government commissions. He is widely considered a great man who was blamed for performance failures which were caused by events out of his control. The recent 2008 financial meltdown has brought back memories of failures that started in the Hoover administration. Much of this analysis has focused upon what caused the successes and failures of both the Hoover and Roosevelt administration. There appears to be a wide divergence of opinions on such issues. In the United States elements of both political parties are already blaming each other for the crisis. The scholars, as usual, have more complex and realistic answers for these events.

—Fausold [6]

Exercise

1. Describe two failures in performance or persuasion you have experienced in the past.

2. Evaluate your reactions to these situations and describe what you have learned from them.

Work cited

[1]   Prochnow, H.V. and Prochnow, H.V. Jr. (1942) *5100 Quotes for Speakers and Writers*. Grand Rapids, MI: Baker Book House.

[2]   Machiavelli, N. (2004) *The Prince*. London: Penguin.

[3]   Lee, H. (1960) *To Kill a Mockingbird*. New York: Harper Collins.

[4]   Katzenstein, G.J. (1990) *Funny Business: An Outsider's Year in Japan*. Prentice Hall Press.

[5]   Lowen, A. (1985) *Narcissism: Denial of the True Self*. New York: Collier Books.

[6]   Fausold, M. (1988) *The Presidency of Herbert Hoover*. The University Press of Kansas.

CHAPTER **18**

Why become a persuasive leader?

"Then I considered all that my hands had done and the toil that I had spent doing it., and behold all was vanity and a striving after wind and there was nothing to be gained under the sun ... All go to one place. All are from the dust."

—Holy Bible, Ecclesiastes 2:11 ... 3:20

"It is a young person's story. It is about growing up and learning how to cope with the cruelty and insensitivity of so many. The music is romantic. The story is harsh. It is our first loves and the cruelty of those teen years. It is about masking innocence but never abandoning it. It is about disguising childhood while being an adult. It's about loyalty, betrayal, and remorse. It is about understanding who we are and where we fit in society. It is about honesty and deception, falseness, and candor."

—Leon Major, director of a famous opera, Eugene Onegin

"Habit is a gift from above to compensate for a lack of happiness."

—From the opera Eugene Onegin

"It's not fear of death but a fear of failure to begin to live."

—Marcus Aurelius

BEGINNING CASES

Christopher Columbus was a leader whose persuasive powers changed the world in significant ways forever. As is usually the case, the changes he initiated were probably beneficial in some ways and harmful in others. He had a dream of finding a new route to the riches of Asia by sailing due west from Europe. He had read and reread *The Travels of Marco Polo* and was much impressed with the riches of Asia and the passages describing the alleged geography of the region. He is said to have seen himself as a discoverer of unknown land forms on the other side of the oceans which had been the subject of sailor stories for many years. He had the ends but needed the means of achieving them and this would require persuasion.

Turned down by the King of Portugal in 1484 he turned to the court of Castile headed by Ferdinand and Isabella. Basing himself in Seville, Columbus set out to gain entry to the court by forming close links first with several powerful Castilian noblemen and an influential group of Franciscan friars. When finally he gained entry to the two royal personages he attempted to persuade them to finance his proposed expedition. In doing this he linked his expedition to the gaining of great riches for their nation which could be used to pay their huge war-incurred debts and also to advance Christianity in several different ways. In 1486, his proposals were rejected with only Queen Isabella persuaded. Over the next several years he was rebuffed several times also but he was persistent using several different persuasive tactics until he received the support he needed in the form of three equipped ships and the approval of royalty.

In the voyage he faced down several minor rebellions; however, he persuaded his crews to continue on. He preached a message of hope and optimism and seized upon every bit of evidence he could (sightings of birds, whales, debris, cloud formations, rain patterns, etc.) to convince his men they were approaching their goal. He used religious services to quell fears and promised rich rewards to those who first discovered new lands. Finally a lookout on the ship *Pinta* cried out "Tierra, tierra!" In explorations around the newly discovered islands, Columbus faced many more persuasive challenges not only from the ships' crews but from the native peoples encountered. On his return to Spain with evidence of his discoveries he received great credibility and support for further voyages. However, after several voyages he was widely criticised by enemies and even spent a good deal of time in prison. Today his memory is celebrated by many on the political right but his memory is reviled from many on the political left. Ethnicity also plays a role in how he is perceived today.

—Timothy Moffett, *The Life and Times of Christopher Columbus* [1]

Anita Roddick, the founder of the Body Shop which consists of more than 1800 stores worldwide, has a rather unique problem in persuasion as compared with other business leaders. Since she and her husband view the firm's purpose as improving life world-wide through various actions, mostly their attention is focused on world issues such as child labour, rights of indigenous peoples, female discrimination, and wage inequalities. However, they often face problems persuading their employees to accept these actions and have experienced some persuasive failures. This is largely due to the traditional business focus on profits that their employees have. Despite this, she has had huge success in her efforts as a result of her remarkable persuasive abilities. First, she has a great passion for her causes which comes across in her presentations and also in her one-on-one interactions with others. As a former history teacher she is quite adept at tying her firm's activities to the long history of social responsibility activities of famous British businessmen. She also points out how these activist stands benefit the business in an economic sense by attracting both customers and superior employees. In addition, she also allows her employees to take time off to participate in charitable causes and periodically engages them at an emotional level with her overall ambitions for the company.

John DeLorean was a star executive on the world stage for many years. As a young executive in General Motors and graduate of his own company's university he was identified early as a rising star with potential for a future position in an executive role. He was very intelligent, had a nice appearance, excellent knowledge of the automobile industry, and had good ideas about automobile styling. However, the attention he received seemed to go to his head and he started to act in ways quite different than other company executives. He drove flashy cars, became a fashionable dresser with expensive taste, and dated movie actresses. He wrote a book which many felt mocked the company and he subsequently resigned. He then decided to create his own automobile company and sell an innovative flamboyant car which he participated in designing. He persuaded officials in Northern Ireland to provide a significant part of the financing to create the manufacturing plant. Unfortunately, due to various political issues in the country there were delays in building the plant which eventually stopped the project. In response to the unanticipated crisis he desperately searched for new financing from various famous celebrities. Shortly after, he was seen on the news in pictures showing his arrest for his involvement in a drug sale. In prison, he wrote a critical autobiography of his life and behaviour up to that point. He wrote about his life and his pursuit for power and wealth, a life of self-aggrandisement with little concern for his fellow human beings which ultimately brought despair and great unhappiness. In his own words:

"My life has been marred by pride and arrogance ... I have consistently rationalised my objectives and motivations as noble but in reality I did things for myself. Many of the things I did in confronting and making things difficult for my superiors was really done to attract attention to myself. Too many people had said I couldn't succeed. Pride said I had to prove them wrong. What drove me to the brink of destruction was pride, not my faith in the future, not a rational appraisal of the actions I was taking. Stripped of my business, my friends, and my power, there was no more reason to be proud. By trying to walk alone, to live a life of foolish arrogance in pursuit of selfish personal goals, I had lost everything."

—John Z. Delorean, *Delorean* [2]

Persuasiveness as a means to significant ends

Christopher Columbus' persuasive skills enabled him to make an extremely significant impact on the world. His discovery changed the world in many ways. New nations came into being and the relative power and influence of older nations were affected greatly. Millions died as a result of the voyages. The discoveries created great human migrations and offered new opportunities to millions. As a result of his successful voyages, he triggered the emergence of countless great explorers and leaders.

Similarly, the persuasive skills of Abraham Lincoln not only enabled him to achieve the Presidency of the United States but he also saved the nation in one of the most dangerous times in the country's history. He faced enormous challenges and opposition in deciding to confront the Civil War and despite suffering defeats in battle he kept the nation focused. His persuasive skills and inner nobility won over the general public, soldiers, generals, congressmen, cabinet officials, and world leaders at the time. These skills saved his nation and in turn preserved the democratic ideology. Since the United States was an experiment in democracy for the entire world, Lincoln's abilities and successes were critical for all other nations. His persuasive skills enabled him to leave an enormous legacy.

Persuasiveness is a key element in achieving many desirable goals in life. This is especially so when achievement requires the efforts of others. For example, Anita Roddick's persuasiveness developed the world for the better in many countries. Certainly, there is such a thing as self-persuasion which may start the whole process. It is really quite impossible to think of truly great deeds, admired at least by most, without a reference to this skill of persuasiveness in the creators of positive change at the level of an individual, group, organization, and nation. Of course, persuasiveness has also resulted in many undesirable ends. Although there were many benefits from the voyages of Columbus there were many bad outcomes as well. Indigenous people in the world died by the millions perhaps due to sickness imported from Europe, warfare with Europeans, and slavery emerged from the discoveries of Columbus. We have described many other harmful consequences of persuasiveness. Leadership can be toxic as well as beneficial. This is why we have tried to align persuasiveness with ethical and moral ends in this book.

Changing life roles

We have discussed the challenging and changing nature of various life roles we have always had to perform in different ways. For example, in the workplace, we now encounter knowledge-based organizational structures and systems which force us to persuade others to cooperate with us to better coordinate work activities. We have also described new organizational realities which impact the performance standard we are held accountable for achieving. One of these, as pointed out by many organizational scholars, is the demise in the importance of authority in achieving organizational and individual goals and plans. Work is no longer self-contained within a unit or organizational boundaries. Traditional autocratic authority associated with the industrial era is now less effective unless called upon in times of need. We increasingly must cooperate with others often across national boundaries to complete work projects. Even if we possess authority over others, their expertise and knowledge enables them to act independently. Moreover, our own children are now living in a new culture where obedience and conformity can no longer be taken for granted. Of course the older generations have always had a sacred duty to help the new generations adapt successfully to the strains of life's trials. Some of these developmental trials are revealed in the notes on the opera *Eugene Onegin* presented above. The torch must be passed on. This is an important role responsibility of persuasive leaders, as we indicated in Chapter 1. For these reasons and others, persuasive abilities are far more important than they were in the past.

The human search for happiness

Throughout history, over the more enlightened stages of human existence, a basic question posed by millions of human beings is what is happiness and how can it be attained? Epicurus, a Greek philosopher, who lived more than 300 years before the birth of Christ, wrote about this issue. For Epicurus, happiness involves having many true friends and being able to obtain ample opportunity to converse with them, preferably within a pleasant environment. He also expressed that happiness involves a life of freedom untainted by social pressures and the turmoil of self-sufficiency and independent of material wealth. Finally, he postulated that happiness occurs when one plans life following an intense process of self-reflection and analysis. This would ensure that one could build a life based on the realization of one's own true nature and values. This is reminiscent of Socrates famous statement, "the unexamined life is not worth living." In fact, Greek philosophers scorned the ideology that the pursuit and attainment of wealth and power would bring you happiness. Socrates and others espouse that living in accordance with your deepest basic values, which they believed involves partly living a noble life, is the key to human happiness. Plato said that the pursuit of justice and beauty would bring the greatest sense of self-satisfaction [3]. Later, intellects have mentioned the importance of living a life with a minimum amount of regrets and having left a legacy. One day, Carroll asked a fellow volunteer health counsellor, vastly experienced as a hospice volunteer, how to deal with a dying patient. She explained that based on her experience with patients there were three basic questions that a dying patient tends to have:

- Will I die alone or with people who love me?

- Will I die in pain?

- Did my life have meaning?

What is true (rather than perceived) happiness?

Given the above observations, it becomes clear that materialism, hedonism, consumerism, and other afflictions associated with modern society are not factors which contribute to true happiness. They are merely distractions born from boredom and ennui and, from our perspective, are self-created manifestations which provide a means of escapism. Just because an individual says they are happy does not mean they really are. Through servitude and achieving the love and respect of others and making a contribution however small one can attain true happiness. We propose that leaving a legacy, even in a small corner of this earth, represents a life's contribution in return for the gift of life itself. It is by concluding life with self-pride that happiness evolves. It is therefore rather clear that a life encompassing the skills of influence to elicit affection from others and that of leadership can help one attain such goals.

Expectations and happiness

Making individuals or groups happier than they might be at a certain point in time sometimes rests on following certain basic principles. Dealing with expectations is key. Much unhappiness is caused by unrealistic expectations; therefore, expectations must be formed with this fact in mind. Unhappiness is also often a failure to think about contrasts. One's success, failure, or misery can be contrasted to those who are worse off rather than to those who are better off. Parents do this frequently. Making individuals or groups aware of mitigating circumstances or factors may be helpful. Considering the unexpected difficulties or catastrophes we experienced, we did very well. Correcting understandings may be important, "I'm afraid that's not the way that works." Of course one must always consider the needs, wants, and values of individuals or groups rather than one's own in judging the appropriateness of their emotional responses to events.

Good and evil ends

When one contemplates the issue of legacy it can be useful to reflect on great people whom the world holds in great reverence and those whom it holds in utter contempt. Persuasive skills can be used for the attainment of evil ends or for noble purposes. It appears that noble political, religious, industrial, and even military leaders are greatly esteemed, admired, and even worshipped in this world. In stark contrast, it is leaders such as Hitler, Stalin, and other tyrants, despite their excellent persuasive skills, who create revulsion throughout the world from most. Also, the followers of such fundamentally evil men will or should bear terrible shame for submitting themselves to carrying out and supporting the evil intentions of such poisonous leaders for selfish purposes. In the last century, as we mentioned previously, King Leopold of Belgium, in pursuit of personal power and wealth, gained control over a vast area of Africa which became known as the Belgian Congo. He promised the native Africans, his countrymen, his fellow Europeans, and the Americans that his activities in that area would elevate and uplift the people living there. As a consequence of such a noble proposition he received widespread support for his intrusions. Despite the sincerity of his promise there was a clandestine murder of more than five million people and millions more were forced to live under unspeakable conditions for generations. The King himself died a very unhappy man. His thousands of collaborators feverishly denied their involvement in the evil wrongdoings. To collaborate in evil and subsequently deny your collusion surely should be a source of shame and guilt. Unfortunately, still to this day there are countless people in the world trying to survive in a similar situation under a different leader.

Redeeming oneself

Recently there has been an attempt to better understand the nature of human beings through the use of life narratives. This approach involves writing reflective essays about themselves (i.e., their history, characteristics, and life goals, etc). It does not seem to involve much persuasion to obtain such reports. Individuals seem to want to tell their stories. They seem to want to voice and tell others what they have been mind-wrestling about for some time. Carroll has seen a large auditorium at a healthcare convention very energized by this exercise. The analysis of such stories has brought some renewed interest on the topic of generativity which is discussed at some length in a book titled *The Redemptive Self* by Dan P. McAdams [4]. The concept of generativity was originally coined as we understand it by a well-known psychoanalyst, Erik Erikson, who explored how an individual's mental growth changes over a lifetime.

Erikson describes how in the past we have had to confront and resolve various conflicts about who we are and who we want to be [5]. For example, do I resolve the conflict between attaining power versus attaining love? He believed that a mentally healthy and emotionally mature individual will eventually strive to achieve generativity. In essence, generativity involves wanting to give something back to society. This usually involves accepting teaching, mentoring, leadership, and good citizenship roles and responsibilities. People with a high propensity towards generativity tend to try to leave the world a better place than how they found it and work for the good of posterity. Erikson saw that attaining this mindset is the prime virtue of adulthood. Generativity is most typically directed towards one's family but many direct their efforts at larger communities. There are some individuals that McAdams refers to as generativity superstars.

The generative adult according to McAdams has six general themes in their life story. The first theme is a feeling of having some early advantage or gift which gives them a feeling of being blessed. Next, those attaining high generativity as an adult mention their observation of suffering in others (e.g., Lincoln observing a slave auction in his youth, etc.). Then comes internalization at an early age of a set of religious and/or social-political values that form a fundamental perspective toward others in the world. Another theme is what McAdams calls redemption—a period of enlightenment or insight about oneself and orientation or moral strengths. Following this is a resolution between one's striving for power over others and relating to them in a more loving and/ or egalitarian way. Finally, there is a theme of carrying out more pro-social goals in the future as time and resources permit.

Naturally, these sets of themes do not occur for everyone and only some individuals become high generativity–oriented adults as a result of experiencing such themes in their life stories. This process of encountering such life stages can be for many the reasoning behind the active search for leadership roles. Such roles are often described in terms related to the characteristic of nobility, which is being exceptional or superior in a moral sense or seeking and/or attaining a moral virtue. McAdams believes that the life of Lincoln reflects this process and can be found expressed in his famous Gettysburg address. McAdams saw it in stories from the *Bible*; however, it can also be found in literature and film. In a riveting film based on a play titled *The Corn Is Green*, a former teacher goes to live in Wales and is overcome with emotion as she observes a long line of boys covered in coal dust emerge from a mine. She resolves to start a school for these children and asks them to write essays about themselves and reads them. When she encounters a poetical essay about life in the mines (. . . and the Corn is Green . . .) she realizes she has discovered a great talent who needs to be taken out of his existing world and prepared for a higher role in society. She commits herself to this task; at great sacrifice to herself she succeeds in doing so.

The ideal persuasive leader in fiction

The ideal persuasive leader has often been described in biography and fiction. Such a person was Don Walling, described in Cameron Hawley's novel *Executive Suite* (later made into a film). An interesting aspect of this story depicts persuasion as being quite often a matter of competition. In politics, for example, voters get presented with a choice between various leaders and their particular persuasive messages. In the US, during the 1980s, a senior staff member to the President recounts how various staff members would provide conflicting advice to the President. He explains that he always waited until the end of each presentation, as he could then refute the arguments of the others and also because the President did not seem to remember the earlier arguments as vividly as the last.

In Hawley's novel, a business tycoon who created and built a company suffers from a sudden heart attack on a Friday as he leaves his office and dies on the sidewalk. A thief steals his wallet as he lies on the ground and he remains unidentified for some time. The four vice presidents of the company proceed to compete for the presidency over the weekend. The most political of these, Shaw, the Vice President of Finance, appears to be winning and goes into the directors' meeting on Monday with confidence in his impending selection as president. The board consists of the vice presidents, the former president's widow, and a major outside investor. The widow asks the group to explain the type of qualifications one should have as a president. Shaw immediately replies saying it depended on an organization's most pressing needs at any given time. He further explained that, many years before, company presidents came from manufacturing since that's where the problems were at the time. Later, sales or marketing backgrounds were viewed as the most important to reflect new priorities. He then explained that there were now new priorities in the business world and financial problems were paramount; he continued to describe how he had contributed more to earnings per share with a changed accounting procedure compared with the other vice presidents' contributions. The widow then asked if her husband had been the right man for the job. Shaw replied that he certainly was for the time; however, the company now needed a different type of CEO. Walling, the Vice President of Design (a more artistic person), seeing a reproach in the widow's manner asked Shaw whether a management team that measures its accomplishment entirely in terms of returns to stockholders would be required to exercise very strong management—to which Shaw responded in the affirmative.

Walling replied: "Suppose you were to spend the next 20 years—all the rest of your life—in doing what you say needs to be done. Would you be satisfied to measure your life's work by how much you had raised the dividend ... is that what you want engraved on your tombstone when you die—the dividend record of the company?"

Shaw replied: "That's all very well, Mr Walling—to take the high-minded attitude that money isn't important—but how far do you think you'd get next month if you offered the union negotiators a sense of accomplishment instead of the ... that they are demanding."

Walling then asked Shaw if the workers would work tirelessly to increase production to raise the dividend rate. Walling said of course we have an obligation to the stockholders but a bigger obligation than raising the dividends was to keep the company alive. He went on to say, in a very animated way, "No man can work for money alone. It isn't enough. You starve his soul when you try it—and you can starve a company in the same way." Walling went on to criticize the whole company approach in dealing with its workforce and denounced the cheap line of products the company had adopted explaining that the employees hated to make such shoddy products. (In the film he dramatically picks up a table the company makes and shatters it against the wall to show how badly it is made.)

Seeing approval in the eyes of most of the others he continues, "Yes, we'll drop that line. We'll never again ask a man to do anything that will poison his pride in himself. We'll have a new line of low-priced furniture someday—a different kind of furniture— as different from anything we're making now as a modern automobile is different from an old Mills wagon. When we get it, then we'll really start to grow." He went on to talk about the advantages of growth based on this new strategy of quality and low prices.

This greatly inspired and excited those present and consequently voted Walling as the new president.

This case provides a good example of the contrast between the relative power of different persuasive appeals. The individuals involved chose an approach which they themselves could take more pride in and gave them a more noble purpose in life which would ultimately help meet the needs and desires of the company's majority. Walling's appeal illustrated persuasive noble leadership as it combined morality and positive emotions coupled with a logical strategy to accomplish a future vision for the company and its workforce. The book also describes the evolution of Walling himself as a leader and how, as a protégé of the founder, he learned much about value without being blind to his mentor's weaknesses. This highlighted things to avoid when developing his life and perspectives. Every leader is a model for future leaders, whether they provide good or bad mentorship; unfortunately, it is often easy to forget to uphold this responsibility.

When Carroll showed this part of the film to executives and several faculty members at a university a few years ago, he emphasized that it was only a movie. Nonetheless, several faculty members and executives in attendance expressed how very accurate it represented conflicts and issues observed in many organizations today. It was also mentioned that the film was a great reminder of the importance of considering the choices in the values and ends we seek in life and how the pursuit of certain values can thoroughly engage the human mind.

Search for a meaningful life

In a famous book, psychiatrist Viktor Frankl, a concentration camp survivor, remarked that in facing death his fellow internees were most concerned with whether they had had a meaningful life [6]. The importance of having a meaningful life was also cited by Seligman, the founder of the field of positive psychology, whom we previously discussed. Seligman explained that his investigations into human happiness indicated that happiness could be reduced to leading three different lives:

- a pleasant life
- an engaged life
- a meaningful life.

The development of persuasive leadership skills can be used as a tool for attaining all three of these lives. Leadership skills open up many more options for careers and rewarding activities and enable an individual to engage more effectively with critical problems and issues in the world. By engaging in such issues a resultant beneficial legacy emerges; then, one can be satisfied that their life has had at least some meaning.

Expectations and success

What is an achievement in relation to one's abilities and expectations? Expecting too much or being hopelessly unrealistic about what one can achieve given one's abilities can result in a disappointment even if there was an actual achievement. A leader or a parent can unknowingly create such disappointment by persuading others to accept unrealistic pressures or goals given their circumstances.

Avoidance of regrets/remorse

As someone once said "remorse is thinking of heaven and feeling like hell." It is, of course, typical that in the conclusion of one's life there will be some, if not many, regrets over past behaviour or choices. The authors use a painting to introduce this topic. Mascio's famous painting *The Expulsion of Adam and Eve* depicts Adam and Eve with extremely tortured expressions on their faces which are truly riveting. The painter effectively reminds us of the emotional impact that remorse has on human beings. Certainly, by living a noble life one must produce fewer regrets and persuade others to live up to their actual potential. This can be an extremely gratifying experience to a persuasive leader in any work or life situation.

What are some of the major reasons for experiencing regrets? On many occasions, an individual would regret an action because of the natural change in one's character over time. As a result, s/he is experiencing regret for the previous choices. They may now have different values, goals, and even a different self-identity. At the time, it is possible that they perhaps lacked information when a decision or behaviour occurred. During this period, they could be ignorant of their own nature until feedback from others made them more aware. Such an experience is depicted in the last scene in the novella *The Dead* by James Joyce. In this famous short story, an arrogant Irish journalist attends a holiday party at the Dublin home of two elderly aunts. He typically acts as the master of such ceremonies at this annual tradition. During the evening, he receives feedback from three people—a servant, a political activist attending the affair, and his wife—that he is not the person he appeared to be. He is not such a clever man, he is not a patriot or good citizen of his nation, and he is not a good husband. He discovers that despite many years of marriage he does not know his wife as well as he thought. His wife tells him of a sad romance or great love that she had as a young girl that he knew nothing about all his life. She falls asleep sobbing and he looks at her, himself, and his country with new eyes. The silent monologue begins as he gazes upon her form on the bed:

> "So she had had that romance in her life: a man had died for her sake.
> It hardly pained her now to think how poor a part he, her husband, had
> played in her life ... A few light taps upon the pane made him turn to the
> window. It had begun to snow again ... The time had come for him to set out
> on his journey westward. Yes the newspapers were right: snow was general all
> over Ireland. It was falling on every part of the dark central plain, on the
> treeless hills, falling softly on the Bog of Allen and further westward into the
> dark mutinous Shannon waves. It was falling, too, upon every part of the
> lonely churchyard where Michael Furey (her first love) lay buried. It lay thickly
> drifted on the crooked crosses and headstones, on the spears of the little gate,
> on the barren thorns. His soul swooned slowly as he heard the snow falling
> faintly, like the descent of the last end, upon all the living and the dead."
>
> —Last paragraph of *The Dead* by James Joyce

When Carroll asked a group of executives how many had similarly experienced remorse for the manner in which they treated their spouse at some stage in the past—all raised their hands. Of course the most significant remorse is felt when one does significant harm to others even though one had no inkling of what the consequences of a particular decision would be. Such remorse is most likely from a sensitive leader:

> "I had THE enemy pinned down on a ridge. I set up a base of fire and sent 13
> marines into the tree line in order to envelop the enemy. Thirteen marines went
> into the tree line and all 13 were killed. And gentlemen, there is not a day that
> goes by when I don't think about that."
>
> —A lieutenant-colonel quoted by Jim Webb, a US senator, in an article on
> what it takes to be a leader (*Washington Post*, May 18, 2008, p. 4)

Persuasion and performance and a changed self-identity

When individuals are persuaded to reach for a goal, engage in an action, or to perform in a certain way, the resulting performance changes a person's self-concept. Much literature documents this process. In a very famous novel, The Red Badge of Courage, a very young soldier, fighting for the Union army, is unsure of himself and lacks self-confidence [7].

This results in his being overly dependent on the wishes and advice of others. He finds himself in the midst of a horrendous battle where many of his comrades are slain. His officers, some with their backs to the enemy, are trying to persuade their troops to charge and overcome a Confederate force on the other side of a fence. They do so and succeed and are filled with joy at their success. The young soldier, on reflection of his behaviour and courage, changes his self-concept to a more independent, mature, and confident individual with a new view of what is important in life as the last paragraph in this great novel indicate:

> "He felt a quiet manhood, non assertive but of strong and sturdy blood. He knew he would no more quail before his guides wherever he should point ... He was a man. So it came to pass that as he trudged from the place of blood and wrath his soul changed ... He had rid himself of the red sickness of battle. The sultry nightmare was in the past. He had been an animal blistered and sweating in the heat and pain of war. He turned now with a lover's thirst to images of tranquil skies, fresh meadows, cool brooks—an existence of soft and peace. Over the river a golden ray of sun came through the hosts of leaden rain clouds."
>
> —Stephen Crane, The Red Badge of Courage [7]

Role of positive values

Socrates believed that living up to one's own positive values is a fundamental source of happiness in life. However, one should contemplate where these positive values come from in the first place. Positive values are learned most often from parents, family members, and various other leaders involved in our lives. Unfortunately many parents seem to pass on values that are at best shallow and at worst destructive not only to their children but to others around them. As a persuasive leader we have the potential to impact the values of others. We can here attempt to dissolve toxic values. It is equally important to reflect on our deeply held values and determine whether our behaviour mirrors such chosen values. By following such ideals, the persuasive noble leader can inspire and motivate others to conduct similar self-examinations. This, of course, is not easy to do—typically there is resistance to looking at oneself critically.

Life as a search for beauty

What is the good life? This is a question that has not only intrigued all of our previously cited philosophers and teachers but also dominated the thoughts of most of the human beings on this sweet earth for possibly thousands of years. The arts have especially attempted to focus on the two great human attributes of truth and beauty discussed by our earliest philosophers. A life as a search for beauty can be a helpful perspective, but beauty is not only the beauty of nature; it is not only the beauty illuminated in the creative works of painters, musicians, writers, poets, dramatists, dancers, and other artists—beauty can be found in human relationships as well. Indeed much of the arts is concerned with the beauty in individual human lives and in their relationships with others. Witness the popularity of certain themes in various novels, memoirs, biographies, films, and plays. We respond with joy and pleasure with the sight of parents interacting with their children in socially beneficial ways, with young lovers exploring their attractions to each other, and with examples of noble behaviours exhibited by others in all walks of life. Obviously the inherited genes of most of us predispose us to such aesthetic responses but social learning also plays a significant role in all of this. We all have a fundamental responsibility to contribute to the ever-increasing progress of the human race even if our contributions are rather small in comparison with others. These smaller contributions may be very large in the eyes of just a few or just one person. We are all leaders in one way or another. In such endeavours a search for truth and beauty is fruitful as a guide to our behaviours and choices.

SUMMARY

Considerable attention today is given to exploration of the good or satisfied life. Numerous books have been written on the subject of happiness and research shows it cannot be achieved through mindless consumerism and escapism. Making a mark on the world and having a purpose in life beyond your own self-centred preoccupations is increasingly being viewed as important. This may require a critical examination of oneself as advocated by Socrates and other early Greek philosophers. Here the suggestions are to know thyself, change thyself to a higher state of nobility—do not be false to any man, then to thine own self be true. Again, we argue that assuming a moral leadership role and developing the skills necessary to carry out that role is one way of leaving a positive legacy and avoiding a life full of regrets.

However, making a mark on many or only a few requires an examination of not only oneself but of others. It has been said by linguists who study languages scientifically that there are between 5000 and 6000 languages depending on what definitions one uses. Each of these languages can be further segmented into separate dialects by different social classes or social entities within a nation. Most human beings are happiest when they live a life that is pleasant, engaged, and meaningful. They have fewer regrets, less remorse, and a more positive mental state when their self-respect is higher for having lived a life by their deeply held values. This is especially so when such values are noble. Learning to be a more persuasive noble leader can contribute to these ends not only for oneself but for those you have influence over. Again, narcissism has been described as a major cause of many of the major social and behavioural problems we have today. The definition speaks for itself. This book hopefully describes leaders and individuals who do not suffer from an excessive degree of this disorder.

END CASES

Jane Hughes began to study braille and methods for teaching the blind in her forties after her two children left home. After an internship in England she agreed to take an assignment to Nigeria from a government agency for the very low salary of $6500 a year. She took over a school composed of 42 young blind girls in a very humid, hot, and remote location in the northern part of Africa. She ran the school very effectively for five and a half years often coping with bandits and terrible weather conditions as well as with the personal, physical, and psychological problems of her young students. After a year back in England, she volunteered to do similar work in Namibia in the south of Africa. She stayed there three and a half years until she was hurt in a jeep accident and had to return to England for medical treatment. She then followed her two children to New York City in the United States where she took a job as a counsellor to the blind living in an apartment complex built especially for the blind. She has been rated as very effective in helping and inspiring these blind adults to cope with their many difficulties. Although she has very little money she feels good about herself. In looking back on her life she feels that compared with most of her childhood friends and siblings, she has had an especially lively interesting life and has left a legacy that she can take pride in, even if nobody else is aware of it except the recipients of her activities and acts.

"The individuals I work with are all graduates of prestigious universities. Most have MBA degrees—some have masters degrees in public policy disciplines like I do. They pretty much are all concerned with making as much money as

they can and are quite indifferent to those in our nation who are poor and disadvantaged never mind the suffering of people elsewhere in the world. I am cautious with almost all of them because I don't trust them to be at all concerned with my life and my personal issues and also because I just don't relate to people so self-centered—period."

– A former student of Steve Carroll

In the play *Our Town* by Thornton Wilder, Emily a young woman who died during childbirth gets an opportunity to revisit her life for one day while she is in the after world. She chooses the day of her birthday at the age of 12 years. After observing the events of that day, she exclaims to the other departed standing with her in the afterlife, "I can't. I can't go on. It goes so fast. We don't have time to look at one another." She breaks down sobbing. "I didn't realize all that was going on and we never noticed. Take me back—up the hill—to my grave. But first; wait! One more look. Goodbye. Goodbye, world, Goodbye, Grover's corners ... Mama and Papa. Goodbye to clocks ticking ... and Mama's sunflowers and food and coffee, and new ironed dresses and hot baths ... and sleeping and waking up. Oh earth, you're too wonderful for anybody to realize you ... She looks at her guide ... and asks abruptly through her tears: "Do any human beings ever realize life while they live it? every, every minute?"

"Her (Dorothea) full nature ... spent itself in channels which had no great name on the earth. But the effect of her being on those around her was incalculably diffusive for the growing good of the world is partly dependent on unhistoric acts; and that things are not so ill with you and me as they might have been, is half owing to the number who lived faithfully a hidden life, and rest in unvisited tombs."

—George Eliot, epilogue to the great novel *Middlemarch* [8]

Exercise

1. List the various reasons why it would be beneficial to you to become an effective persuasive leader? These reasons can include your own ideas in addition to those mentioned in the chapter.

2. Make a list of all the ideas from the various arts which might be of most value to you in becoming a successful persuasive leader at work or in life.

Works cited

[1] Moffett, T. (1994) *The Life and Times of Christopher Columbus*. Parragon Book Service.

[2] DeLorean, J.Z. and Schwarz, T. (1985) *DeLorean*. Grand Rapids, MI: Zondervan.

[3] Stavropoulos, S. (2003) *The Wisdom of the Ancient Greeks*. Fall River Press.

[4] McAdams, D.P. (2006) *The Redemptive Self: Stories Americans Live by*. New York: Oxford University Press.

[5] Erikson, E. (1959) Identity and the life cycle. *Psychological Issues*, **1**, 140–141.

[6] Frankl, V.E. (1963, reprinted 1984) *Man's Search for Meaning: An Introduction to Logotherapy*. New York: Simon & Schuster.

[7] Crane, S. (1994) *The Red Badge of Courage: An Episode of the American Civil War*. Puffin Classics.

[8] Neale, C. (1989) *George Eliot, Middlemarch*. London: Penguin Books.

APPENDIX A

Another brief look at some of the relevant arts and humanities (Chapter 2)

Literature, as we know it today, began at the beginning of the 18th century. Before that, the distinction between factual and imaginative writing was not so pronounced. The fictional literature can take a variety of forms such as novels, short stories, poems, and plays. Of course literature can and does in fact illuminate the truth about human relationships and human thinking far better than factual descriptions (as in history), as many have pointed out. The mind and the emotions which are not directly observable can be explored in depth in literature. Also, literature enables us to explore and emphasize certain significant aspects of human behaviour and thinking which may be hidden and much less salient in everyday observations. The narratives of the characters described can also represent more common and far-reaching aspects of human existence than the common awareness of most human beings allows them to see.

Literature focusing on the lives and experiences of imaginative others (who may be based on actual persons) allows us to transcend the limitations in experiences imposed on us by our age, gender, culture, ethnicity, or other limiting factors. The *Mutiny on the Bounty* trilogy exposes the modern reader to the behaviour, thinking, and actions of some significant leaders (William Bligh and Fletcher Christian) in the British Navy in the last century. Even though the book is fiction, the individuals involved and their actions were based on real-life incidents. Literature can be a humanizing, vicarious experience which at both an emotional and a reasoning level can increase our understanding of others. Such exposure can facilitate our understanding of various possible audiences and provide examples of exemplary, persuasive leaders whose skills in action we can observe. Of course, one can then say that these persuasive leaders are imaginative and as such serve as unrealistic behavioural models. However, when the behaviours of such fictional leaders are compared with successful persuasive leaders in biography and also with controlled behavioural science investigations of successful persuasive leaders, validation of their leadership skills can be demonstrated.

The widespread acceptance and internalization of human stories across many different cultures over thousands of years attest to the power of stories to engage human interest and inspire behavioural change. Witness the powerful stories and parables from the *Bible* and other religious books that engage human attention and become parts of the listener's memory. It's not surprising that most persuasive leaders utilize narrative in part or entirely in their persuasive efforts whether directed to groups or to individuals. Poetry is especially engaging and instructive. As compared with fiction, poems are typically sonically interesting. Human beings, like living creatures of all kinds, are very sensitive to sound since such sound awareness is related to eliciting certain emotions related to species survival such as danger, pleasure, and security. The words themselves having musical elements excite the listener. Through the use of meter, alliteration, rhyme, and other poetical devices the ear is engaged and the message is not only heard but often becomes memorable. Steve Carroll's mother, although 97 years of age, can still recite word by word poems she learned as a child of nine years. The appeal of poetry reflects the human love of rhythm harmony, as well as surprise. Equally, speeches should be exciting and move individuals to think in different ways. The apt imagery of metaphors in poetry compels the listener to examine topics or subjects in ways that previously escaped their attention. Metaphors excite, stimulate, and foster new and creative ways of seeing. Another feature of poetry is in its economy and efficiency of word usage. Great insights and observations can be expressed vividly with very few words. Poetry expresses insights, perceptions, and observed truths in memorable ways by building on aesthetic principals. Any particular persuasive talk directed at the accomplishment of practical ends is likely to contain both poetical and prose elements.

Plays can be especially effective when observed instead of being simply read. In this way, the audience can observe the human actions and behaviours directly instead of vicariously. Good actors are especially clever in communicating the emotions behind their actions and words. Observing individuals in action attracts interest and can provide the underlying justifications for the actions that are observed. Theatre has been used in persuasive efforts for thousands of years. Morality plays sponsored by religious authorities were very popular throughout the Middle Ages. Theatre also aims at amusement as well as teaching. Many of the most popular theatrical productions throughout human history achieve the goals of providing amusement and learning at the same time. Political and ethical plays have been widely popular for hundreds of years. Again, playwrights typically have a teaching objective in addition to that of providing entertainment value and therefore serve as good models to all leaders and teachers who have the same goals in staging their daily performances. Although in the professional theatre, teaching objectives may revolve around essential truths about human existence problems and issues (e.g., Shakespeare, Ibsen, Checkov, Synge, Arthur Miller, etc.). Dramatic principles can be applied in a useful way for communicating more mundane truths to a non-paying audience.

Biography and history are especially instructive of leadership issues and have long been used in leadership education programmes. The life stories of both effective and ineffective leaders, as well as leaders considered good and evil, are quite instructive of leadership in general and of persuasive leadership in particular. While typically such writings emphasize the lives of famous and well-publicized leaders, their strengths and weaknesses, assets and liabilities, and situational success and failure factors can provide leaders at all levels in a society with lessons of value in an action sense. Certainly, the cultural predispositions of the audience may play a significant role in deciding which leaders are studied in depth; however, certain leaders have attracted attention all over the world. The first author examined a private collection of more than 3000 books on Joan of Arc. While the majority of these were written in English or French, books relating to this particular leader have been published in Chinese, Japanese, and Spanish, to name a few. World-wide interest in the lives of certain leaders is shown in the fact that more than 25,000 books have been written on Joan of Arc alone. Similarly, books on famous religious leaders (Jesus, Moses, Buddha, etc.) and political leaders (Napoleon, Lincoln, Churchill, etc.) also number in the tens of thousands.

Fine arts

Painting and sculpture have been practised by individuals since early antiquity. Obviously it is a human characteristic to describe nature and the living entities within the natural world. Such activity probably has many different functions and goals. Some art is for the purpose of communicating the special insights of the artist to the world or to certain individuals within it. It has been said by many that great art is about seeing—the skill of the artists is not in the hand but in the eye. Actually this attribute of having special insights or seeing more clearly is often associated with leadership—the ability of leaders to notice or see what escapes the observation of most others or of seeing reality more clearly than followers. This of course is one reason that individuals emerge as leaders and are accepted as leaders. Our global community or some of it is aware of the need for such insights. Some would also include photography among these arts—a newer art form, which can also present us with meaningful images. Presenting such images clearly has a teaching function.

The fine arts have many other functions as well. Much art is about reminding us of past leaders, past events, or attributes of distant or even possible future places or events. This is not only true of most religious art but also political and social art as well. Many persuasive communications, oral or written, also refer back to historical persons, events, or places. This is not only in the realm of politics but in business and other types of settings as well. One of the authors in his academic work often starts off with a description of Socrates (his favourite philosopher) trudging through the streets of Athens in his worn sandals and somewhat dirty robe. Before the annual persuasive speech of a CEO of a large Chinese company in Taiwan, one of the authors observed how the managerial audience is exposed to pictures of the many facilities they own around the world and the many quality and other prizes the company has won.

The fine arts also teach us how to make our messages vivid, engaging, and memorable. Art appeals to our inborn aesthetic sense and produces a delight when images are presented to us in very pleasing ways. Obviously, the persuasive/teacher leader must first elicit the attention and interest of the viewer. Then the message or image must be presented in such a way as to make it memorable. The principles for doing so translate well from the fine arts to the world of words—oral or written. Of course artistic images can also accompany text, as they often do, to create a greater understanding of the message and/or interest in it. The lives of artists and the process they follow in achieving their creations also provide us with many lessons involving the creative process (see Vasari, *The Lives of the Artists*). Great art is created by talented individuals who master a particular ability, who persist in their artistic quests through the many obstacles that may arise, and are dedicated to finding the truth as they understand it. They usually seek the mentorship and advice of others who have gone before them. At the same time they usually attempt to identify a signature individuality which makes them stand out from others.

Music

Musical composition teaches us the importance of creating variety and surprise in the overall pursuit of some type of ultimate balance or harmony. It teaches us the importance of being innovative while at the same time building on the past. It teaches us the importance of eliciting certain emotions in pursuit of achieving a particular end result. Musical pieces can be effective in reminding us of past events and what we may as listeners or participants have in common. Music is often used to establish preparatory emotions before a persuasive effort. A teacher may start a class with a certain piece of music. In the persuasive annual speech given by the CEO of the Taiwanese company, the company choir sings the national anthem and the company's special song before the speech begins. One company CEO uses the theme music from the film *Chariots of Fire* in his persuasive talks. Of course leaders of all types have been compared with composers and conductors who must create a harmony and whole out of many diverse elements. This involves creating a unity out of a diversity which could lead to chaos. Typically, orchestra conductors must also spend a great deal of time in improving the performance of individual musicians and also in planning musical performances. In this respect they behave like executives. Unlike the other arts the effects of music on workplace behaviours has been studied in a systematic way. The benefits arising from music have been well documented although one can think of many more research possibilities.

The performing arts

Dance involves a planned set of human movements designed to create certain aesthetic effects. In addition, dance can be effective in eliciting certain emotions as well as providing a vivid way of communicating certain messages or understandings through an engaging presentation of certain narratives. How we move and handle our bodies is important in getting others to react to us in certain ways. Also, how we move affects our own moods and emotions as well—in obvious ways. Dance has been used in various societies throughout human history to implant certain emotional states needed for particular situations such as to prepare for battle, to alleviate fear, to create optimistic illusions of control, and to express sadness or joy depending on the situation. At any rate we have seen little about variations in movement among leaders. However, the authors did view the excitement generated by the wild dance and dramatic speech of the President of Microsoft before a particular audience. Rock-and-roll music audiences are quite used to viewing rather energetic body movements synchronized with musical performances. At any rate this is certainly a neglected subject in leadership. It has not escaped the notice of the authors that movement alone has often been a factor in how an audience reacts to an actual or potential leader. Obviously leaders and teachers wishing to be more dramatic in their performances have many models to observe closely.

Film

Films have long been used in the training of leaders as well as teachers and seem to be more popular than ever for this purpose. Both authors have used films extensively in the training and education of managers and leaders. Many films describe both factual and fictional leaders in action. However, even films of real-life leaders are likely to be fictional in part. Nevertheless such films can be very effective in allowing the observer to observe all aspects of the persuasive or teaching process (often in an ideal way). By observing leaders behaving effectively in a film, one can see how choice of words, body movements, tone of voice, speaking style, dress, makeup, and situation or setting characteristics can combine together to produce certain audience effects. Films can be used to validate certain principles of persuasion-teaching, recommended by purported experts in this area, which have been used in this way by the authors. Of course films are stories and clips of films can be accompanied by a summary of the story or narrative presented in the larger work. All serious stories present a message of some type which reflects the attention of the author. As is obvious stories are remembered if they are vivid and interesting. By placing separate stories throughout a longer narrative, interest can be sustained over a long exposure time. Many historical stories are of this type obviously.

Not all art is influential and persuasive. Instead of engaging an audience and creating positive emotions, an artistic creation may not only fail to achieve its objectives of message through aesthetic pleasure it may disgust, repel, or disengage an audience. Disgust is also, of course, an aesthetic response, as some would see it. Sometimes disgust is directly induced by the material in pursuit of some social, political, or moral objective. Of course one can go too far here. Some critics have said that the power of traditional art to influence human behaviour has been negated because what they see is ugliness in not only the appearance of works of modern art but actually the creation of antithetical mindsets to those intended.

APPENDIX **B**

Happiness (Chapter 8)

Some happiness findings

Sonja Lyubomirsky, *The How of Happiness:*[1]

- Happiness is based on emotions which have a bio-chemical basis. One's genes affect the secretion of brain chemicals which affect one's mood. Darwin found that all higher animals have and express similar emotions which can be recognised by others.

- Circumstances account for 10% of experienced happiness, genes 50% and intentions or thinking 40%.

- Identical twins separated at birth and in different circumstances tend to have the same levels of happiness.

- Lottery winners are only temporarily happy. Money, beauty, material resources such as houses account for small amount of the differences in happiness among individuals.

---

[1] The authors highly recommend Lyubomirsky, S. (2008) *The How of Happiness: A Scientific Approach to Getting the Life You Want.*

- People are adaptable to bad situations. For example, patients going on dialysis revert back to the usual state of happiness after a short period of time and their overall happiness levels tend to be not much different than the rest of the population.

- A strong materialistic orientation in college is related to less happiness later in life.

- Individuals who achieve much after years of struggle are no happier than others.

- Most individuals have a gene that helps them ward off depression but some with mutations on this gene (5HTTCPR) cannot ward it off. But if such depressed people learn how to manage stress and if they have social support they can manage their depression.

- Happiness varies with age. For an individual happiness tends to be higher until age 16 then it goes down somewhat, then up again at 65, then down again at 75.

- Those who consciously pursue happiness are happier.

- Those who express a desire to have a happy marriage tend to be happier in such a relationship.

- Frequently expressing gratitude to others is associated with having more positive emotions.

- Over-thinking and being self-critical is associated with having more negative emotional states.

- A useful exercise for having more positive emotions is thinking of three good things about your life each day.

- Unrealistic expectations are associated with disappointment and less happiness. As expectations become more realistic, happiness increases.

- Church attendance and religiosity are related to being happier. Why? Probably because the notion that God loves you and will help you create positive emotions. Also church attendance gives one a sense of being a member of a cohesive community. Also, belonging to a church makes one feel they have social support when they need it. However, believing in a strong, arbitrary, and vengeful God is related to less happiness.

- Anything that creates positive internal values helps increase positive emotions.

- Meditation helps to create positive emotions.

- Those who see a meaning in their life are happier.

- Cognitive-behavioural therapy CBT) is often effective in dealing with depression, the opposite of happiness. This popular type of therapy seems to work because it attacks negative thinking, false thinking, over-thinking and other causes of depression.

- Genes impact the amount of serotonin secreted by neuro-transmitters which then impacts the amount of positive or negative emotions being experienced.

Reflections on happiness

Manfred F. R. Kets de Vries, Reflections on happiness:[2]

- Happiness overall requires someone to love, something to do, and something to hope for.

- Happiness is the ultimate goal for most people.

- Happiness is not a circumstance but a state of mind.

- Happiness is never complete or constant.

- Happiness is defined by different people in different ways.

- Happiness is often the result of a comparison with a past state one was in.

- Having a confidant seems to be necessary to feelings of happiness.

- Friendship is important to happiness but having friends requires work and determination.

- Partners help to buffer individuals against the difficulties of the world.

- Friendship requires a fair and just exchange.

- True narcissists have difficulty in establishing real friendships.

- Having work that gives us a sense of purpose is important to happiness.

- Work is not as important to happiness as having close relationships.

- It's wonderful when we can work at something we like, when work is a duty life is slavery (Gorky).

- Hope gives us a sense of destination.

---

[2] See Kets de Vries, M. (2000) The business graduation speech: Reflections on happiness. *European Management Journal*, **18**(2).

- Dreams are things we can look up to.

- Externals believe things outside of themselves determine their fate.

- Internals think they themselves are masters of their fate.

- Achieving equilibrium in life and work is related to happiness.

- Seize the day is important—don't let opportunities pass you up.

- Successful accomplishment does not guarantee happiness.

- Happiness is not outward success but internal success.

- The ability to play and manage leisure is important to happiness.

- Success is a matter of making the best out of a bad hand, not receiving a good hand.

- Ongoing learning means embracing life.

- Wisdom involves discovering how ignorant you are.

- Handling stress and being healthy are very important to happiness.

- Our physical state determines our mental state to a high degree.

- We must try to be honest with ourselves.

- We must ourselves love learning to be good teachers.

- Being authentic and wisdom are close friends.

C

Behaviours of the best and worst bosses (Chapter 12)

Best

- Encouraged me by providing positive feedback.
- Assigned me projects usually handled by higher grade employees.
- Willing to "show me the ropes" by working alongside me.
- Stood by what he said.
- Tough but fair.
- Set clear, reasonable goals and then left me alone.
- Willing to let you make mistakes and learn from the experience.
- Let me manage in the way I chose.
- Encouraged my development.
- Never played staff against each other.
- She talked to you in a way that showed she cared.
- Exhibited sincerity and displayed integrity.

- Gave you more responsibility when you could do it.

- Gave you thanks to show his appreciation.

- Supported me in tough situations.

- Allowed me to make decisions and work independently.

- Looked out for my career development by mentoring me.

- Recognized the problems and situations I had to deal with.

- Was available when I needed help.

- Made us feel valued.

- Reacted quickly to changing needs.

- Treated everyone with respect.

- He took my side or at least showed he understood.

- She demonstrated all of the leadership methods when necessary—autocratic, persuasive, motivational.

- Good teaching skills—showed you how it's done.

- Had high standards.

- Recognized that supporting subordinates was critical to getting the job done.

- Was willing to subordinate short-term goals for employee development and morale.

- Was patient, understanding, respectful of others, honest, and compassionate.

Worst

- Unwilling to accept other viewpoints—although he would listen it was like talking to a wall.

- Created work that was totally unnecessary.

- Was extremely opinionated and demeaning of others in your company.

- Was critical of higher management but lacked technical expertise himself.

- Was too bossy—his authority over you went to his head.

- Did not ever know where we should be going.

- Did not know enough about how to do the job.

- His relationship with employees was based on the premise that they were out to cheat the system and this resulted in mutual distrust.

- He was not interested in mission accomplishment and was only focused on what affected him.

- He talked down to you. He did not trust people.

- Pushed his own ideas period—micro-managed.

- Was vague and inconsistent—too "touchy-feely".

- Did not pass along important information.

- Did not allow people to work to the level of their competence.

- His micro-management interrupted my work.

- Took credit for the work of others.

- Constantly changed direction.

- His attention was directed only at individuals not the group.

- He did not trust others.

- Did not treat everyone fairly—had favourites.

- Did not support employee development.

- Could not admit he was wrong.

- He did not look out for my interests.

- He was fearful I would take his job. He didn't trust me or others.

- Saw employees only as "tools" that did not have useful inputs.

- Would not listen to suggestions.

- Nothing was ever good enough for her even when standards were met.

- Never gave you the opportunity to make even the smallest decision.

- His favourite expression was "let me check with _____".

Selected social science theories relevant to persuasive leadership

Positive psychology theories: A large number of studies over the years support the effectiveness of positive psychotherapy (PPT). It works well with depression compared with other therapies by focusing on creating positive emotions, engagement, and meaning. What interventions work here? Be more active, socialize more, obtain meaningful work, develop closer relations with loved ones, have lower more realistic expectations for yourself and others, and prioritize being happy. Other mentioned interventions include: attempt to foster increased persona psychological growth, develop more autonomy and self-acceptance, create more positive relations with others, and build environmental mastery. Some therapists target a client's troubling emotions, bad relationships, and faulty negative cognitions. Still other therapists say one should aim at achieving a meaningful life and a purpose in life. There are courses in positive psychology which have many mandatory exercises. These often include such assignments as writing out three blessings you have, paying a visit to someone who has given you a benefit, and forgiving somebody who has wronged you. Other assignments ask you to list your strengths and decide how to better use them, study several happy and engaged lives, and learn how to savour daily events such as eating.[1]

Implications: Leaders must emphasize hope and optimism in their persuasion

---

[1] See Seligman, E.P. and Csikszentmihalyi, M., Positive psychology: An introduction. *American Psychologist*, **55**(1), 5–14 for more information.

attempts and listen to their subordinates or audience to identify negative beliefs and counteract these by having others remember positive things such as past successes and favourable comparisons rather than negative ones.

Social learning theory: This is currently the most influential theory of how we learn. Albert Bandura, a Stanford University psychology professor, has demonstrated that we learn how to behave in new ways by observing others who model behaviour for us. The modelled behaviour is a guide to our own future behaviour in a similar setting or situation. Also, when we observe others like ourselves performing successfully we tend to believe we can be successful as well.

Implications: Leaders are inescapable models of behaviour. People will take their cues for behaving from many around them in the various social entities they are affiliated with. Our feelings of confidence in carrying our certain activities or reaching certain goals are determined in large part by observing others like ourselves. Thus, in persuasion, leaders must model the desired behaviour themselves and not rely on words alone. Also, it is important in persuasion to make an audience believe they are capable of attaining certain types of performances. Reminding others of past success or persuading them to think of the successes of other groups can help establish feelings of self or group efficacy for the performance being discussed.

Social exchange theory: Social change is the result of negotiated exchanges between social entities. Human relationships are formed on the basis of subjective cost–benefit calculations by those involved. If the perceived costs of a relationship are believed to be greater than the benefits, then a person will want to leave or change the relationship. Elements to be considered by the parties involved include direct rewards, expected reciprocity and future benefits, expected gains in reputation, power, or influence, as well as intrinsic rewards such as pride in oneself.

Implications: Leaders should make it worthwhile for others to want to relate to them or to follow them by making sure that there are benefits to others for doing so. Also favours granted to others will probably be reciprocated.

Social influence and comparison theories: Human actions are considered to be embedded in a complex of influences from other valued individuals. These social influences often create significant pressures to conform to the chosen commitments, decisions, and behaviours of others important to a given person. It is assumed that individuals go through a process of comparing their opinions as well as their abilities with certain other specific or idealized persons when making personal decisions. In this social influence process, certain individuals in any social entity or group can be especially influential in the persuasion of others.

Implications: Leaders can increase their persuasive powers with others by first convincing others who have influence over targeted individuals. Influence over an individual may be contradicted by influence of other persons in contact with the initial persuaded person.

Forced compliance theory: This highlights the perceived obligations individuals have to comply with as a result of a lifelong conditioning process. Some research on this theory indicates even disliked figures can be influential in changing attitudes and behaviour if a message is accepted for other reasons.

Implications: The leader can add to his persuasiveness by reminding others in subtle ways of his or her authority, power, or status.

Priming theory: This involves priming individuals or groups to react in a positive or negative way to something that is introduced. For example, descriptive words such as "warm", "cold", etc. when applied to persons can have significant positive or negative priming effects in determining reactions to such persons.

Implications: Leaders should be creative in devising what will be effective in priming particular audiences in specific ways.

Attribution theory: This indicates that people attribute causes to outside factors largely outside one's control or to "internal or dispositional" factors that make one responsible for an event. Failure is very often attributed to outside causes while success is often attributed to inside causes such as competence, intelligence, or to various moral virtues.

Implications: Leaders must be aware of the basic tendencies of human beings in confronting successes or failures.

Self-verification theory: Individuals want to be perceived or known to others in a way that corresponds to their strongly held beliefs about themselves. Proposed personal actions that are in line with such positive self-identities are therefore more likely to be accepted.

Implications: Knowing how an audience of one or many view themselves is a great aid in devising successful persuasions.

High- and low-arousal theory: These focus on how individuals can be stimulated and aroused by the presence of others and by various situational factors that they have experienced in the past. It also focuses on individual differences in the need for stimulation from one's personal and present environment.

Implications: Leaders must be aware of the need for arousal before persuasive messages as well as what might create arousal in specific audiences.

Theory of social penetration: Human relationships grow from initial superficial exchanges to closer and deeper ones as the parties involved use more self-disclosure. We tend to like those who disclose to us and like those that we disclose to.

Implications: Leaders can foster stronger emotional ties with others through humility and self-disclosure.

Threat to self-esteem theory: Reactions to receiving assistance depend on whether the recipient feels appreciated and cared for or whether s/he feels inferior and overly dependent.

Implications: Respect for others is always critical in creating good relationships. Making others excessively dependent on leaders is unwise if one is to create resilience and self-motivation and positive emotions in others.

Social impact theory: The influence of one person over another is stronger when the influencer is perceived to have high power, status, or ability, when the influencer is physically closer to the influence, and when multiple social influencers are present.

Implications: Persuasion success is due in large part to preceding events, as described above.

Need hierarchy theory: This assumes that human needs for sustenance, security or safety, companionship, and for self-esteem are activated in a certain order such that the higher order needs such as affiliation, self-esteem, and personal achievement will not come into play unless a person's basic needs are at least somewhat satisfied.

Implications: Ensuring safety and security is a prerequisite to making appeals to higher level affiliation and ego needs.

Theory of emotional intelligence: This comprises the ability to rein in emotional impulses, to read the emotional states of others, and to manage emotions effectively to improve one's relationships with others. Emotional intelligence can be modified by training and experience.

Implications: Leaders should strive to produce in others and themselves higher levels of emotional maturity.

Alienation theory: In general this refers to the feelings of estrangement of individuals from each other or from specific situations they encounter. One version of this focuses on feelings of powerlessness, meaninglessness, isolation, normlessness, and self-estrangement as a reaction to various types of work or employment relationships.

Implications: Leaders should strive to build a collective identity in others and to foster a sense in others that what one does is meaningful in some way.

Gestalt theory: This looks at any social entity such as an individual or group as a coherent whole which cannot be understood by breaking it down into its constituent parts or elements as is often done in empirical research studies. A gestalt is a coherent whole.

Implications: Leaders must not approach others on the basis of only narrow and quite specific characteristics. They must appreciate the complexity of others.

Social justice or equity theory: These refer to the distribution of outcomes such as reward and cost that result in perceptions of fairness or feelings of equity. Later versions also include a concept of procedural justice which focuses on the perceived fairness of organizational or personnel procedures which are used to pursue certain ends.

Implications: Leaders must be aware that all actions and programs impinging on others will be evaluated by them in terms of their concepts of social justice and ethics.

Cultural and social identity theories: These propose that reactions to various messages are dependent to a significant degree on past national or ethnic cultural training experienced by an individual. Such cultures differ with respect to many common assumptions of appropriate or desirable/undesirable behaviours and modes of thinking. The degree of cultural identity is a major factor, however, in predicting such human reactions to various messages.

Implications: Leaders must recognize that culture is a major determinant of reactions to attempted persuasions. They should also recognize the culturally determined expectations of those they target for persuasion so that they can consider such factors.

BIBLIOGRAPHY

Allen, T.D. and Eby, L.T. (1988) *The Blackwell Handbook of Mentoring*. Blackwell.

Anderson, C.R. and Carroll, S.J. (1980) Predicting performance and operational measures. *Proceedings of the Academy of Management Annual Convention, Detroit, MI.*

Andrews, E. (1988) *The Poetry of Seamus Heaney: All the Realms of Whisper*. London: Macmillan.

Arendt, H. (1963) *Eichmann in Jerusalem: A Report on the Banality of Evil*. New York: Viking Press.

Beardsley, J. (1997) *A Model of Christian Charity: Governor John Winthrop (on board the Arabella)*. New York: Norton.

Brehm, S.S. and Kasin, S.M. (1996) *Social Psychology*. Houghton Mifflin.

Brown, L. and Hort, L. (2008) *Nelson Mandela*. Paw Prints.

Burns, J.M. (1978) *Leadership*. New York: Harper & Row.

Cannon, L. (1991) *President Reagan: The Role of a Lifetime*. Simon & Schuster.

Carnegie, D. (1982) *How to Win Friends and Influence People*. New York: Pocket Books.

Carroll, S.J. (1969) Beauty, bias, and business. *Personnel Administration*, **32**.

Carroll, S.J. (1998) Implementing strategic plans through formalized goal setting. In: P.C. Flood, T. Dromgoole, S.J. Carroll, and L. Gorman, *Managing Strategy Implementation*. Oxford: Blackwell Publishers.

Carroll, S.J. and Gannon, M.J. (1997) *Ethical Dimensions of International Management*. Thousand Oaks, CA: Sage Publications.

Carroll, S.J. and Gillen, D.J. (1987) How useful are the classical management functions in describing managerial work? *Academy of Management Review*, **12**, 38–50.

Carroll, S.J and Nash, A.N. (1970) Some personal and situational correlates of reactions to management development. *Journal of the Academy of Management*, **13**.

Carroll, S.J. and Tosi, H.L. (1977) *Organisational Behaviour*. Chicago: St Clair Press.

Carroll, S.J., Paine, F.T., and Miner, J.B. (1977) *The Management Process: Cases and Readings*. Macmillan.

Carson, R. (1962) *Silent Spring*. Boston: Houghton Mifflin.

Chamberlain, J.L. (1915) *The Passing of the Armies: An Account of the Final Campaign of the Army of the Potomac, Based upon Personal Reminiscences of the Fifth Army Corps*. New York: G.P. Putnam's Sons.

Côté, R.N. (2004) *Strength and Honor: The Life of Dolley Madison*. Mt. Pleasant, SC: Corinthian Books.

Crane, S. (1994). *The Red Badge of Courage: An Episode of the American Civil War*. Puffin Classics.

Curtis, R.H. (1993). *Great Lives: Medicine*. New York: Charles Scribner's Sons.

DeLorean, J.Z. and Schwarz, T. (1985). *DeLorean*. Grand Rapids, MI: Zondervan.

Eden, D. (1975) Implicit leadership theory as a determinant of the factor structure underlying supervisory behavior scales. *Journal of Applied Psychology*, **60**, 736–741.

Eisenhower, D.D. (1948) *Crusade in Europe*. New York: Doubleday.

Emerson, R.W. (1836) *Nature*. University of Michigan.

Erikson, E. (1959) Identity and the life cycle. *Psychological Issues*, **1**, 140–141.

Erikson, E. (1963) *Childhood and Society*. W.W. Norton & Co.

Fasano, T. (2008) *The Dead by James Joyce*. Claremont, CA: Coyote Canyon Press.

Fausold, M. (19??) *The Presidency of Herbert Hoover*. The University Press of Kansas.

Feshbach, S. and Weiner, B. (1986) *Personality*. Lexington, MA: D.C. Health.

Feshbach, S., Weiner, B., and Bohart, A. (1995) *Personality* (Fourth Edition). Wadsworth Publishing.

Flamarion, E. (1997) *Cleopatra: The Life and Death of a Pharaoh*. London: Abrams Publishers.

Flood, P.C., Dromgoole, T., Carroll, S.J., and Gorman, L. (1998) *Managing Strategy Implementation*. Oxford: Blackwell Publishers.

Frankl, V.E. (1963, reprinted 1984) *Man's Search for Meaning: An Introduction to Logotherapy*. New York: Simon & Schuster.

Freud, S. and Brill, A.A. (1995) *The Basic Writings of Sigmund Freud (Psychopathology of Everyday Life, the Interpretation of Dreams, and Three Contributions to the Theory of Sex)*. Modern Library.

Gandhi, M. (1957) *Gandhi: An Autobiography—The Story of My Experiments with Truth*. Beacon Press.

Geneen, H. and Moscow, A. (1984) *Managing*. New York: Doubleday & Co.

Ghiselli, E.E. (1971) *Explorations in Managerial Talent*. California: Goodyear Publishing.

Gibson, W. (1956) *The Miracle Worker*. Simon & Schuster.

Gilbert, D. (2005) *Stumbling on Happiness*. Vintage Books.

Gilligan, C. (1982) *In a Different Voice*. Harvard University Press.

Gladwell, M. (2000) *The Tipping Point: How Little Things Can Make a Big Difference*. Boston: Little Brown & Co.

Golding, W. (1956) *Lord of the Flies*. Faber.

Goleman, D. (1995) *Emotional Intelligence*. Bantom Publishing.

Griffin, M. and Atkins. E.M. (1991) *Cicero on Duties*. Cambridge University Press.

Haidt, J. (2005) *The Happiness Hypothesis: Finding Modern Truth in Ancient Wisdom*. Basic Books.

Hawley, C. (1952) *Executive Suite*. Ballentine Books.

Hedges, C. (2006) *American Fascists: The Christian Right and the War on America*. New York: Free Press.

Hill, A.S. (1895) *The Principles of Rhetoric*. New York: Harper & Brothers.

Hillegass, C.K. and Skaggs, M.M. (1969) *Autobiography of Benjamin Franklin: Notes*. Lincoln, NE: Cliff Notes.

Hoar, W. (1984) *Architects of Conspiracy: An Intriguing History*. Western Islands.

Hochschild, A. (1998) *King Leopold's Ghost*. London: Macmillan.

Hume, D. (1910) *An Enquiry Concerning Human Understanding*. Harvard Classics, Vol. 37.

James, H. (2004) *The Beast in the Jungle*. Kessinger Publishing.

Jones, H. (1988) *Mutiny on the Amistad: The Saga of a Slave Revolt and Its Impact on American Abolition, Law and Diplomacy*. Oxford University Press.

Katzenstein, G.J. (1990) *Funny Business: An Outsider's Year in Japan*. Prentice Hall.

Kets de Vries, M. (2000) The business graduation speech: Reflections on happiness. *European Management Journal*, **18**(2), 302–311.

Kidder, J.T. (2000) *The Soul of a New Machine*. New York: Back Bay Books.

Kohlberg, L. (1981) *The Philosophy of Moral Development: Moral Stages and the Idea of Justice*. Harper & Row.

Lawson, H.C. (1991) *Aristotle: The Art of Rhetoric*. Penguin.

Lay, B. (1981) *Twelve O'clock High!* J. Curley Publishers.

Lee, H. (1960) *To Kill a Mockingbird*. New York: Harper Collins.

Lessing, D. (2003) *The Kreutzer Sonata/Leo Tolstoy*. New York: Random House.

Lief, M., Caldwell, H.M., and Bycel, B. (1998) *Ladies and Gentlemen of the Jury: Greatest Closing Arguments in Modern Law*. New York: Touchstone.

London, J. (1903) *The Call of the Wild*. New York: Macmillan.

Lowen, A. (1985) *Narcissism: Denial of the True Self*. New York: Collier Books.

Lutz, A. (1976) *Susan B. Anthony: Rebel, Crusader, Humanitarian*. Zenger Publishing.

Lyubomirsky, S. (2008) *The How of Happiness: A Scientific Approach to Getting the Life You Want*. New York: Penguin.

Machiavelli, N. (2004) *The Prince*. London: Penguin Books.

Maier, N.R.F. (1963) *Problem Solving Dscussions and Conferences: Leadership Methods and Skills*. New York: McGraw-Hill.

Manz, C.C. and Sims, H.P. (1980) Self-management as a substitute for leadership: A social learning theory perspective. *Academy of Management Review*, **5**(3), 351–367.

Manz, C.C. and Sims, H.P. (1987) Leading workers to lead themselves: The external leadership of self-managing work teams. *Administrative Science Quarterly*, **32**, 106–128.

Manz, C.C. and Sims, H.P. (1995) *Business without Bosses: How Self-managing Teams Are Building High-performing Companies*. John Wiley & Sons.

Marshall, G. (1994) *Oxford Dictionary of Sociology*. Oxford University Press.

Matthews, R.K. (1986) *The Radical Politics of Thomas Jefferson: A Revisionist View*. Unversity Press of Kansas.

McAdams, D.P. (2006) *The Redemptive Self: Stories Americans Live By*. New York: Oxford University Press.

McKenzie, E.C. (1980) *14,000 Quips and Quotes for Writers and Speakers*. Crown Publishing.

McNeill, W.H. (1963, reprinted 1991) *The Rise of the West: A History of the Human Community (with a Retrospective Essay)*. University of Chicago Press.

Mill, J.S. (1909). *On Liberty*. New York: Collier & Son.

Miner, J. (1965) *Studies in Management Education*. Springer Publishing.

Moffett, T. (1994) *The Life and Times of Christopher Columbus*. Parragon Books.

Montagu, A. (1986) *Touching: The Human Significance of Skin* (Third Edition). New York: Harper Perennial.

Neale, C. (1989) *George Eliot, Middlemarch*. London: Penguin Books.

Nin, A. (1948) *Under the Glass Bell*. Swallow Press.

Nordoff, C. and Hall, J.N. (1936) *The Bounty Trilogy*. Boston: Little Brown & Co.

Obama, B. (2006) *The Audacity of Hope: Thoughts on Reclaiming the American Dream*. New York: Random House.

Peters, T. and Waterman, R.H. (1982) *In Search of Excellence*. New York: Harper & Row.

Prochnow, H.V. and Prochnow, H.V. Jr. (1942) *5100 Quotes for Speakers and Writers*. Grand Rapids, MI: Baker Book House.

Quinton, A. (1999) *The Great Philosophers*. New York: Routledge.

Rand, A. (1992, reprinted 1957) *Atlas Shrugged* (35th Anniversary Edition). New York: Dutton.

Roddick, A. (2000) *Business as Unusual*. New York: Harper-Collins.

Roosevelt, T. (1913) *An Autobiography*. New York: Macmillan.

Russell, B., MacKendrick, P., and Howe, H.M. (1952) *Classics in Translation*. University of Wisconsin Press.

Sacks, M. (2008) *Musicophilia*. New York: Vintage Books.

Screech, M.A. (1991) *Montaigne, Michel De Four Essays*. Penguin.

Seligman, M.E.P. (2002) *Authentic Happiness: Using the New Positive Psychology to Realize Your Potential for Lasting Fulfillment*. New York: Simon & Schuster.

Seligman, M.E.P. and Csikszentmihalyi, M. (2000) Positive psychology: An introduction. *American Psychologist*, **55**(1), 5–14.

Seligman, M.E.P., Steen, T.A., Park, N., and Peterson, C. (2005) Positive psychology progress: Empirical validation of interventions. *American Psychologist*, July/August, 410–421.

Shaw, G.B. (1924) *Saint Joan: A Chronicle Play in 6 Scenes and an Epilogue*. London: Constable & Co.

Skaggs, M.M. (1991) *Autobiography of Benjamin Franklin*. Lincoln, NE: Cliff Notes.

Skinner, B.F. (1953) *Science and Human Behavior*. New York: Macmillan.

Sinclair, J.D. (1991) *Dante's Paradiso*. Oxford University Press.

Smith, K.G., Carroll, S.J., and Ashford, S.J. (1995) Intra- and interorganizational cooperation: Toward a research agenda. *Academy of Management Journal*, **38**, 7–23.

Solzhenitsyn, A. (1963) *One Day in the Life of Ivan Denisovich*. Harmondsworth, UK: Penguin Books.

Stavropoulos, S. (2005) *The Wisdom of the Ancient Greeks: Timeless Advice on the Senses, Society, and the Soul*. Fall River Press.

Stirling, J. and Elliot, R. (2008) *Introducing Neuropsychology* (Second Edition). Psychology Press.

Strock, J.M. (2001) *Theodore Roosevelt on Leadership*. Forum.

Strunk, W. and White, E.B. (2008) *The Elements of Style* (50th Anniversary Edition). Longman.

Thatcher, M. (1995) *The Downing Street Years*. London: Harper Collins.

Toffler, A. (1981) *The Third Wave*. Bantam Books.

Torricelli, R. and Carroll, A. (1999) *In Our Own Words*. Kodansha.

Tosi, H.L. and Carroll, S.J. (1982) *Management*. John Wiley & Sons.

Tosi, H.L., Rizzo, J.R., and Carroll, S.J. (1990) *Managing Organizational Behavior*. New York: Harper & Row.

Traven, B. (1935) *The Treasure of Sierra Madre*. Alfred A. Knopf.

Vasari, G. (1991) *The Lives of the Artists*. Oxford University Press.

White, R.D. (2006) *Kingfish: The Reign of Huey P. Long*. Random House.

Whyte, W.F. (1943) *Street Corner Society*. University of Chicago Press.

Wilder, T. (1957) *Our Town* (three-act play). Harper & Row.

Wright, W.A. (1936) *The Complete Works of William Shakespeare* (Cambridge Edition Text). Garden City Books.

Yukl, G. (1989) *Leadership in Organisations* (Second Edition). Prentice Hall.

INDEX